Inclusive love,
not exclusive attachment
is the unfoldment of heaven.

not what you desire.

Do not lose the treasure of your Self
for the pleasure of the senses.

Transform your unilateral passion
into universal adoration.

A person thinking rationally today
is a needle in a haystack.

You are more concerned about
your act of kindness
than thought of kindness.

Give your personality a lift,
you lift the whole world.

VEDANTA TREATISE

The Eternities

A. Parthasarathy

First	Edition	1978
Second	Edition	1984
Third	Edition	1989
Fourth	Edition	1992
Fifth	Edition	1995
Sixth	Edition	1997
Seventh	Edition	1999
Eighth	Edition	2000
Ninth	Edition	2001
Tenth	Edition	2002
Eleventh Revised	Edition	2004
Twelfth	Edition	2004

ISBN No: 8187111-57-7

Published by:
A. Parthasarathy
1A Landsend
Dongarsi Road
Malabar Hill
Mumbai 400 006
India
www.vedanta-edu.org

Printed by:
Arun K. Mehta
Vakil & Sons Pvt. Ltd.
Industry Manor, 2nd Floor
Appasaheb Marathe Marg
Worli
Mumbai 400 025
India

CONTENTS

PREFACE

The Vedanta Treatise presents the ancient philosophy of Vedanta. A philosophy which enunciates the eternal principles of life and living. Living is an art, a skill, a technique. Few have understood it to be so in the span of human history. Nevertheless, you need to learn and practise the technique of living. As you would for playing a musical instrument or flying an aircraft.

The world today is unaware of this process of learning. It is not taught in a school or university. Nor in a moral or religious institution. Thus people go through a mechanical way of living merely following a routine of their predecessors. They lack this fundamental knowledge of living. And become victims of stress and strain.

People everywhere have lost the pleasure in action. They try to find peace and happiness by abstaining from action. Hence everyone looks forward to weekend and vacation. Even seeks premature retirement from work. This is a human weakness. Do not fall a prey to it. If you cannot find peace and happiness in action you can never find it through abstaining.

The world presents two distinct classes of people. One class is active, productive and prosperous. The western world seems to fit into this category. But by their own admission they have lost their peace of mind. While the other class of people is relatively peaceful and happy but without much action. Since they lack action they are not productive, prosperous. Some of the eastern countries face this problem.

Thus there is action without peace on one side and peace without action on the other. One wonders if it is possible to combine dynamic action with mental peace. Vedanta provides the answer. The few who have imbibed the knowledge of Vedanta, learnt and practised the technique of living, live a dynamic life of action while enjoying perfect peace and happiness within.

Above all, the Treatise helps you evolve to greater heights in your own spiritual path. It provides you with the knowledge and guidance to reach the ultimate in human perfection. The goal of Self-realisation.

The book contains twenty-one chapters spread over three sections. The first section introduces the concept of Vedanta to help those unfamiliar with it. The second deals more with its practical application. How Vedanta can be ingrained in your lives. The final section covers the highest tenets of its philosophy culminating in the transcendental experience. It ploughs through human ignorance and delusion to discover the pristine glory of one's supreme Self.

SECTION I: INTRODUCTION TO VEDANTA

The first section introduces Vedanta to the layperson. Vedanta is a systematic knowledge which explains the meaning and purpose of your existence in the world. A knowledge that is founded on its own authority. It trains you to think for yourself. To analyse, investigate and realise the quintessence of life. Not to submit yourself to blind faith, superstitious belief or mechanical ritual. Ultimately, it leads you to spiritual Enlightenment.

The knowledge of the *unknown* can be gained only through the use of *known* factors. Therefore, to unravel the mystery of

God you need to use the world of objects and beings known to you. Start with the study of the world, the individual and the relationship between them.

How are you to relate with the world to find peace and harmony? It is not the world that bothers you as you believe it to be. But your relationship with it. You need to learn the principles of right living. Change the character of your action from selfishness to selfless service. Mend the quality of your emotion from preferential attachment to universal love. Raise your knowledge from the mundane to the supreme Self within. Thus you shall reach the culmination of human life, the ultimate state of peace and bliss, the goal of religion.

SECTION II: PRACTICAL VEDANTA

The second section covers the practical application of Vedanta in life. Explains the composition of a human being. The five layers of the human personality enveloping the inner Self. The three states of conditioned-consciousness known as waking, dream and deep-sleep. Every human being goes through the cycle of these states. None realises the pure Consciousness, the Core of one's being. Vedanta directs you to discover the Core, the supreme Self within.

Humans fall under four distinct classes depending on the development of their mind and intellect: the predominantly emotional, predominantly intellectual, balanced in both, underdeveloped in both. Accordingly the four paths of Devotion *Bhakti*, Knowledge *Gnana*, Action *Karma* and Compulsion *Hatha* are prescribed respectively for their spiritual development. Practising these disciplines the seeker evolves to the state of dispassion. Which prepares him to enter the final stage of meditation. And through meditation he reaches Self-realisation.

A Self-realised person is one with God. He revels in absolute peace and bliss. Becomes a beacon for the rest of the world to follow and steer their lives towards evolution.

SECTION III: THE ESSENCE OF VEDANTA

The third section expounds the real philosophy of life. Exposes the exact nature of the terrestrial world. Points out the transcendental Reality beyond the phenomenal world. Helps you discover that underlying Reality to be the supreme Self within.

A. Parthasarathy
1A Landsend
Dongarsi Road
Malabar Hill
Mumbai 400 006
INDIA
www.vedanta-edu.org

Section I

Introduction to Vedanta

CHAPTER I

ROLE OF VEDANTA

Science and Vedanta

Vedanta literally means culmination of knowledge. *Veda* means knowledge, *anta* means end. The knowledge of your real Self. The Self within is supreme. Presently obscured by your body, mind and intellect. You are aware of the body, mind and intellect but not your real Self. Vedanta helps you unfold your Self. Discover the true nature of your inherent Being. Your real Being is divine. The Abode of absolute peace and bliss.

Humanity is unaware of the intrinsic wealth within oneself. People seek wealth and enjoyment in the external world. They are governed universally by two motivations. To acquire wealth and to enjoy what is acquired. Thus is the life of human beings propelled by these two forces. Few realise that there can be no satiation or fulfilment through acquisition or enjoyment. Through external pursuits.

Life is defined in Sanskrit as *anubhava dhara*, stream of experiences. As long as experiences flow there is life. When the flow ceases life is extinct. An experience is therefore a unit of life. Constituted of two factors. Subject and object. The individual, you is the subject. The world, the object. When you contact the world, subject meets object, you gain an experience. And the flow of experiences is life.

One class of thinkers worked upon the object, world to provide humanity with greater peace and happiness. They were the scientists. Science has made a colossal contribution for human welfare. It has developed the world to near perfection, with press-button comforts. Nevertheless, people are not as happy as they should be. In a perfected world there seems to be only worry and anxiety, suffering and sorrow everywhere. That is a paradox. Another class of thinkers investigated the cause of the paradox. They were the ancient sages living in the Himalayan ranges. These great philosophers analysed the anatomy of an experience. And discovered that the subject, the individual was unattended, neglected to a point of fault. While the world was well taken care of by science. Consequently, the unprepared individual lived in stress and strain in a world of plenty and prosperity. The sages thus focussed their attention on the subject, the individual. And gave out the sublime philosophy of Vedanta. The knowledge designed to rehabilitate the individual to perfection.

Subjective development prepares the individual to meet the challenges of the objective world. Human beings alone are faced with the dilemma of choosing their action. They need to exercise their choice of action every moment of their life. All other creatures have a computerised, pre-set programme of action. They do not have the problem of choosing their action. A tiger cannot become a vegetarian. Nor a cow become a meat-eater. They are constrained to follow a course of action to suit their particular nature.

Vedanta equips you with the knowledge to make the right choice of action. Also provides you with the technique of action. A technique you can apply in your home, in your business, in society, everywhere. It gives you a practical way of life to satisfy your material and spiritual needs. Following that course you enjoy prosperity with peace of mind.

Vedanta, the Base of Religion

Vedanta is known as *Sanatana dharma* meaning Eternal principles. It is systematic knowledge which gives you the true insight into life. Draws you towards your innermost core. Provides you knowledge that reveals your real Self. Your Self is essentially divine, be you sinner or saint. Divinity is the core of every person. Vedanta helps you identify your divine Self. Attain your absolute state of peace and bliss. That is the goal of all religions. To discover your true nature. Unfold your real Self. Draw the Divinity out of the matter layers that veil It. Etymologically, the word *religion* means that which binds one to the origin. In Sanskrit also, the term *yoga* means to unite with the Self.

Furthermore, Vedanta excels in its scientific exposition. It expounds the truth methodically, logically. It does not rely on the authority of a preceptor. Its truth is its authority. No master or messiah can claim it. No religion has a hold on it. It belongs to one and all. Bears no distinction of caste or creed, community or country. Its universal application appeals to all lovers of truth.

Vedanta trains you to think independently. Helps you probe into the essence of the human personality. Directs you to study, reflect and realise the fundamental truth of life. Thus in the past, generations after generations put in effort to discover the real Self. Later on, some spiritual enthusiasts brought out their own abridged versions of truth. They were well-meant but feeble readings of the original truth. People began to follow their teaching blindly. They lost their independent reflection and judgement. Spiritual education was no longer liberal. The masses were led by the opinion of others. And fell a prey to authorities. In the name of religion fanatic superstitions and parasitic ideas infested humanity.

Which has plunged people in ignorance. And the world is steeped in sorrow and suffering.

The root cause of suffering is that people do not look within. Hardly investigate the truth of life. Nor exercise their own judgement. They rely on outside forces to do their thinking. And function predominantly on blind faith and mechanical ritual. This is spiritual suicide. Castes, creeds and sects are the ghosts haunting the world. The role of Vedanta is to free you from infatuation to celebrities and educate you on the Eternities.

Thus the great science of religion has been reduced to mere allegiance to personalities. The present religious systems are governed by maxims and mandates. There is a saying: Grammar is the grave of language. Try to save the grammar, keep it invariable, the language will be dead. Just so, the rigidity of preceptors and precepts saps the vitality of religion. The intelligentsia, particularly the youth the world over, detest rigidity. They do not wish to be dictated to by doctrines and dogmas. They revolt against such unnatural education.

Young men and women ought not to be pestered with *Thou shalts* and *Thou shalt nots*. Whatever is forced is never forceful. *Dos* and *don'ts* are not designed for human beings. Desire for anything increases with restriction and prohibition. Static precepts, superstitious beliefs and mechanical rituals are being thrust on people. It frustrates them. Rather, they need to be educated with the knowledge of life and living. The higher values of religion have to be presented systematically and logically to the modern intellects. The philosophy of Vedanta answers the requirements of seekers of truth. The process may take time but is sure to elevate them.

People today need to delve deep into the merits of religion. Look at Vedanta in its pristine glory. Make an independent assessment of truth without relying on authorities. The great humorist, George Bernard Shaw once remarked that the most intelligent person he had met in his life was his tailor! When asked why he thought so, he promptly answered, "Because he is the only one who takes fresh measurements every time I go to him." Take up Vedanta in the same manner. Verify the knowledge taken in with its practical application in life. Try out the philosophical truths in your day-to-day living. Thus working them out practically you become truly religious.

Instead, people the world over let themselves be hypnotised by the views and opinions of others. Even the intelligentsia have been accepting religious doctrines and dogmas passively. Some accept a religious belief just because it is the oldest. Others accept it only because it is followed by vast numbers. Still others accept it because it comes from a great personality. Few get to the merit of the teaching. Much less imbibe the spirit of religion. There is a blind following everywhere. Such an approach to religion has brought about a spiritual epidemic. It is practically destroying the human race.

If religion is to serve people it has to be judged and accepted on its own merit. Not on authorities. The study of Vedanta will reveal to you that it is founded on its own authority. It is based on reason and logic. You must, therefore, approach Vedanta as you would science or mathematics. When you study science you do not accept the statements therein on sheer authority. Just because they have been laid down by a Newton or an Einstein. A faith that is founded on authority is no faith. Take up Vedanta on its own merits. Do not allow the personality and life of a spiritual master interfere with his teaching. The life and teaching should be considered separately. Then alone will you be able to enter into the spirit of religion. Whatever knowledge Vedanta places before you examine it per se. Analyse it yourself. Apply your faculty of reason and judgement. Assimilate it. Put it into practice. Verify it in your life. Thus make it your own. Truth is your own. Nobody can claim it. You do not have to sell your liberty to any spiritual guru. The gurus drew their inspiration from their own Self. The same fountainhead of inspiration is within you. You can do the same. There is no use relying on external forces for gaining internal strength.

There is a general belief that one has to retire to the solitude of the forests for the study and practice of Vedanta. Lead the life of an ascetic. This is not true. Vedanta does not expect anyone to live a life of resignation. It is not a retirement plan but a technique of dynamic living. No doubt this knowledge of life and living had sprung originally from the deep recesses of the Himalayan ranges. The *rishis* sages had to retire to the jungles to pursue their study, reflection and experimentation. Like a scientist would require to isolate himself to master the science he pursues. But practitioners of Vedanta having acquired this knowledge are obliged to work in their own fields of activity. Translate their theoretical ideas into practical living. Besides, history reveals that even preachers of Vedanta were actually engaged in serving the world. They were not recluses but men of action working in a spirit of renunciation.

Tributes to Vedanta

Several savants and sages have paid glorious tributes to Vedanta. Some of their observations are quoted below. The glory of Vedanta is not dependent upon these observations. Vedanta stands on its own merits. Perhaps these quotations may enthuse those initiates who value authorities. The assurances may help them launch their study with greater interest.

The great philosopher, Arthur Schopenhauer has hurled abuses on other philosophies save his own. But on Vedanta he says: In the whole world there is no study so beneficial and so elevating as that of the *Upanishads* (Vedanta). It has been the solace of my life, it will be the solace of my death.

Max Müller, the renowned German Orientalist comments upon this assertion of Schopenhauer: If the words of such an independent philosopher require any endorsement, with my life-long study of all the religions in the world and all the systems of philosophy in Europe, I am ready to humbly endorse this experience of Schopenhauer. If philosophy or religion is meant to be preparation for the after-life, a happy life and happy death, I know of no better preparation for it than Vedanta.

Paul Deussen, professor in the University of Kiel (Germany) found the philosophy of Parmenides, Plato and Kant in a nutshell in Vedanta and advised the Indians: Vedanta in its unfalsified form, is the strongest support of pure morality, is the greatest consolation on the sufferings of life and death. Indians, keep to it.

The Indian sage Swami Vivekananda declares: While every other religion depended on the life of some person who was its founder, Vedanta was based upon eternal principles. It was on this that it based its claim of being the universal religion. All ideals are true and the different religious systems were but special paths for the attainment of these various ideals, which when intensified, were certain to draw out the divinity in man.

The greatest apostle of truth, Swami Rama Tirtha pronounces: Vedanta brings you a religion which is found in the streets, which is written upon the leaves, which is murmured in the brooks, which is whispered in the winds, which is throbbing in your veins and arteries, a religion which concerns your business and bosom, a religion which you have not to practise by going to a particular church, mosque or temple only, a religion which you have to practise and live in your everyday life about your hearth, in your dining-room, everywhere you will have to live that religion.

Another great philosopher Schlegel says that in comparison with the Indian thought the highest stretches of European philosophy appear like dwarfish pigmies in the presence of the grand, majestic Titan. In his work on Indian language, literature and philosophy he remarks: It cannot be denied that the early Indian possessed a knowledge of the true God, all their writings are replete with sentiments and expressions, noble, clear and severally grand, as deeply concerned and reverentially expressed as in any human language in which men have spoken of their God. And with regard specifically to the Vedanta philosophy he says: The divine origin of man is continually circulated to stimulate his efforts to return, to animate him in the struggle and incite him to consider a re-union and re-corporation with Divinity as the one primary object of every action and exertion.

Reason, the Sap of Vedanta

The faculty of reason is a human prerogative. It arises from the ability to think. All other beings lack this faculty. Reason makes a human the *chef d'oeuvre* of creation. But few care to develop the art of thinking, reasoning. People do not seem to realise that thinking is skilled work. That you need to learn and practise it. On the contrary you believe that it is a natural process like breathing or eating. That you can think clearly and accurately without putting in the necessary effort on your part. It is not so. If you are to develop the faculty of thinking, reasoning you need to devote as much time and effort to it as you would to learning any other skill.

In the world today few have developed the art of thinking. People are possessed with groundless beliefs. Propositions are accepted without question as a matter of course. Their beliefs rest upon superstition. Or someone's mere assertion. They bear no proof. Do you realise that many of your strongest beliefs had taken root in your childhood? Now as an adult you find it difficult to question their veracity. They seem to be obviously true. You feel even to question them would be absurd.

Take the example of two men professing different religious beliefs. One, a staunch Hindu. The other, a devout Christian. They were born the same day in a maternity ward forty years back. The attending nurse committed a colossal blunder. She mistakenly exchanged the newborns in their cradles. The Hindu baby was placed in the Christian mother's cradle. And the Christian in the Hindu mother's cradle. And the two children were brought up unknowingly with the opposite domestic, social and religious influences. You could imagine the natural consequence. Both have now grown up holding beliefs totally opposed to their original family and religion. And each now swears by his particular belief!

William Drummond remarks: *He who cannot reason is a fool; he who will not is a bigot; he who dare not is a slave.*

With these facts in mind look at the present-day world. One set of people is hawking spirituality with their own views. Another set is blindly accepting them. Religion has been reduced to mere parroting of ideas picked up from preachers. Neither the preacher nor the pupil can claim to have gone through any systematic study and research, reflection and absorption of the truths of . life. People are confused and confounded. In such an irrational state of affairs how can there be any spiritual edification? The world remains as poor as ever morally and spiritually. People are afflicted with worry and anxiety. They undergo mental strain. Suffer from stress. This has been a perennial problem with human beings.

The world must wake up from its slumber. You must start thinking, questioning, enquiring, reasoning with the truths of life. The philosophy of Vedanta satisfies the tests of reason and logic. It complies with the principles of sound judgement. The truths that are acceptable to your intellect you should apply in your life. Verify their authenticity. Then you begin to taste the joys of higher and chaster living. With your personal experience you would delve deeper into the essence of Vedanta. Attain peace and happiness.

Your real Self

Human beings have lost the knowledge of their real Self. Vedanta expounds your Self as supreme, whole, absolute. He who realises the Self enjoys infinite peace and bliss. Having lost the infinite state, humans feel a sense of imperfection. Feel a void within. This feeling generates thoughts to flow towards the world to fill the void. To perfect the imperfection felt within. These thought currents are called desires. Like thoughts going towards food when the stomach is empty, is the desire for food.

The desires thus generated use the body to find sensual pleasure. Use the mind to indulge in emotional joy. The intellect to seek rational satisfaction. The quest for happiness goes on perennially. Only the one who has discovered the Self within finds complete satiation, total fulfilment. His quest for happiness ceases. His pursuit of pleasure and peace through his body, mind and intellect ends. This truth has been demonstrated in the lives of Self-realised sages and saints.

Your real Self therefore remains ever in absolute peace and bliss. That is your original Being. No sooner you lose the Self you develop desires. The desires keep pressurising you to return to your original Self. To your primal nature. A simple experiment demonstrates this truth. Place a coil spring four feet high on a table. Press it down with your palm to one foot. The pressure built in pushes your palm upward. Release it to two feet. The pressure reduces. Release it to three feet. The pressure reduces further. Release it to four feet. There is no pressure at all. That is because it has reached its original state. Likewise desires incessantly pressurise a human to gain peace and pleasure. The pressure ends on realising the Self. Hence the Self is said to be your original Being.

In the diagram, line AB represents human evolution from zero to hundred per cent. Position A indicates a human being at the lowest state with no spiritual development at all. Position B, the absolute State of Self-realisation. A person evolves from position A to B by dropping his desires.

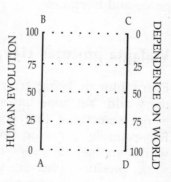

Line CD represents his dependence upon the world. Point C represents zero dependence on the world of the Self-realised person as he is totally self-sufficient. Nothing that the world offers can enhance the infinite peace and bliss he enjoys. He is like the ocean whose waters do not rise with all the rivers pouring in. He remains ever absolutely fulfilled. Whereas, point D represents total dependence upon the world of a person who has zero development. He is like a piece of wood or stone.

In the present world hardly anyone belongs to the extreme positions. The entire range of human beings falls in between A and B. As one evolves spiritually from A to B one's dependence on the world diminishes correspondingly from D to C as illustrated. Thus, the evolution of a person and his worldly needs are inversely proportional. It is a law.

The knowledge of Vedanta serves you both ways. It helps you evolve spiritually to reduce your desires. It also enhances the clarity of thought to gain success and progress in your field of activity. Thus providing you with material wellbeing. Consequently, you command material prosperity while your demands remain minimal. That puts you on a pedestal of peace and happiness.

Vedanta procures Happiness

Every human being tries to find peace and happiness in the world. Yet none has succeeded in gaining it. Happiness is not something that you draw from the external world. For example, a person finds pleasure in smoking cigarettes while another detests smoking. The cigarette being the same, produces pleasure to one and pain to another. Again, one wants to divorce his wife. Another waits anxiously to marry her. The lady being the same, produces sorrow to one and joy to the other. Hence pleasure or pain, joy or sorrow is not inherent in the objects or beings of the world. They are in you. Depending on how you relate to the world outside.

Not realising this truth people try to use their body, mind and intellect to gain pleasure and joy from the world. The enjoyments gained therefrom are transient, impermanent. They pass away. While true happiness lies within you. You will have to find it in your own Self. The German philosopher Arthur Schopenhauer puts this idea succinctly: *It is difficult to find happiness in oneself but it is impossible to find it anywhere else.*

Vedanta guides you towards your inner Self. Every human being is constituted of his supreme Self within enveloped by the material layers of the body, mind and intellect. People identify with their material components. They entertain themselves with the instant pleasures that these outer layers provide. Little do they realise that the happiness derived from them soon wears away. Hence to find enduring happiness you will have to delve deeper into your personality. Transcend the limitations of the body, mind and intellect. Get to the divine Core of your personality. And find the Abode of absolute bliss.

Vedanta provides Material Prosperity

The world abounds in material wealth. Yet you could remain in poverty. To gain prosperity you need to learn the technique of drawing the wealth from the world. Vedanta has the formula for efficiency and productivity. Three main disciplines constitute that technique:

1.   Concentration
2.   Consistency
3.   Cooperation

You need to learn and practise them to gain success and progress in your life.

The discipline of concentration is to keep your mind focussed on the present action. The natural tendency of the mind is to slip into the past or future. It hardly stays in the present. It worries about the past or becomes anxious about the future. Your mind thus dissipates your energy. You need a powerful intellect to control the mind. The knowledge of Vedanta helps you to strengthen the intellect and hold your mind in the present without allowing it to slip into the past or future. Which is concentration. Which renders your actions objective. You then become more efficient and productive in your field of activity.

The next discipline is maintaining consistency of purpose. Directing your actions towards a set goal. Your intellect chooses an ideal in life. A cause beyond your self-centred interest. Having fixed a goal, the intellect directs your actions towards it. Your actions then become consistent. Which develops power, dynamism. This is clearly seen when water flowing in one direction develops power. Similarly, wind blowing in one direction has power. So has light focussed at a point. Thus through consistency your actions are rendered more powerful, more successful.

The third discipline is to recognise and maintain the spirit of cooperative endeavour. To achieve results in any field of activity you will have to work with your colleagues as a team. You need to develop the support and cooperation of others related to your work. Work performed with such cooperation reaches heights of achievement.

Vedanta therefore presents you the knowledge for your spiritual evolution as well as your material wellbeing. With this knowledge you will command peace and comfort in your life. People are ignorant of the worth of this knowledge. They dub Vedanta as a religion of resignation and retirement.

Thus denying themselves this precious knowledge they are lost in the world. And suffer from worry and anxiety, stress and strain. Vedanta cries out to one and all: You are making a veritable hell of the world. Acquire this chaste knowledge. You will then turn the world into a heaven. And fulfil your mission in life.

Eternal Bliss within

Your real Self is the abode of eternal peace and happiness. Every human being tirelessly seeks it in the world through action, emotion and knowledge. The search for bliss goes on. None has ever found it. Only the rare one who has directed his search inward has reached that State of supreme bliss. He finds it through realisation of the Self within.

History reveals nations conquering nations. The world has been indulging in hot and cold warfare. What purpose do these conflicts serve? What do they seek? What is their ultimate goal? You would find that all external conflicts are directed only to find internal happiness. People believe that outer conquests can bring about inner peace and bliss. It is a false belief arising out of spiritual ignorance. India has passed that state of spiritual infancy long, long ago. The ancient *rishis* sages understood the hollowness of such pursuits. They had discovered that happiness dwells not in the outward charms of materiality. Real happiness abides in the core of your personality. The native home of happiness is your own Self. You discover it through Self-realisation.

External pursuit of happiness is futile. It is like trying to grasp the head of your shadow. The more you try the more it recedes. You can never succeed that way. Instead, let your hand hold your head. The shadow is caught! The source of true happiness lies within you. You need not run after shadows. Instead seek your inner Self. You will reach the fountainhead of bliss.

If this be true, then why do people still chase material objects? Why are people fascinated by the world? Can all go wrong? No. There is a reason for their external pursuit. The sense-objects of the world give them instant pleasures. They pursue the external world for these immediate joys. Think carefully. These pleasures are fleeting, not enduring. They disappear as fast as they appear. The wise do not indulge in such transient pleasures. While the ignorant are lost in them.

Here is a simple experiment. Hold a candy in one hand and a wad of currency notes in the other. Offer them to an infant to pick one of the two. The infant reaches for the candy. It knows only the immediate pleasure of the candy. Now if the same were offered to you, what would you pick? What really makes the difference? The infant is ignorant. You are equipped with knowledge. So is it with the world. People in their ignorance pick *candies* in the world. And deprive themselves of the bliss of the Self within.

This lasting happiness, this enduring bliss lies not in outward splendour and grandeur. Not in riches. But in your own Self. You must gain the knowledge of your inner Self. The living knowledge of the Reality through the spiritual laws of life. You will have to approach it as university students pursue their studies. Take up each idea. Reflect upon it. Make it your own. Apply this knowledge in your life. Thus through knowledge and application discover the primeval source of happiness within you.

CHAPTER II

WORLD AND HUMAN BEING

Mystery of the Origin

The origin of the world baffles human comprehension. Creation poses a great mystery. Whence did all creatures originate? Their ancestry perplexes scientific enquirers. Did the chicken come first or the egg? Did the tree come first or the seed? Who is your father's father's..... first father? The answer to this question seems to be held in utmost secrecy, obscurity, mystery. The best of human intellects have failed to throw light on this fundamental question. Did the cause appear first or the effect? Is there a primal cause? Can there be a causeless cause? The mystery that surrounds these questions has perturbed the human mind. To appease the disturbed mind a name was given to that causeless cause. The name was God.

God is believed to be the primal cause of everything. He is reckoned to be the origin of the world. Reputed to be the creator of the universe. Some posit a personal God with a form. Others, an impersonal God without a form. Few understand that the introduction of *God* as creator is a mere intellectual proposition. No enquirer of truth would be satisfied with such a bare postulation.

In mathematics, a problem is solved by first assuming the final answer to be x. Surely, x is not the answer to the problem. x is only a postulation. The real answer has to be derived methodically by applying the laws of mathematics. In a typical problem, the volume of a room is given as 2400 cubic feet. The length of the room as 16 feet and breadth, 15. You are asked to calculate the height of the room. The answer is derived thus:

Let the height of the room be x feet

Volume	=	length multiplied by breadth multiplied by height
2400	=	16 multiplied by 15 multiplied by x
2400	=	240 x
$\therefore x$	=	2400 / 240 = 10 feet

Similarly, *God* was initially assumed as the origin of the world. None realises that *God* is just another word for origin. That does not solve the fundamental question as to the origin of the world. Nevertheless from time immemorial humanity has passively accepted God as the originator, creator of everything. They in their innocence claim that the concept of God is clear to them. Ironically, they criticise intelligent enquirers who probe into this mystery. And condemn them as blasphemous, sacrilegious.

Thus fanatic concepts have assumed epidemic proportions. Judgement has been thrown to the winds and people have lost their reason. Mere words are being parroted by reputed preachers to innocent masses. These stories and histories of God, no doubt transmitted faithfully for generations, can never solve the mystery of the unknown. Vedanta unravels this mystery. It puts forth no theory. Nor proposition. Nor hypothesis. Its approach to the problem is scientific and experimental. It enunciates the facts of life. Proceeds logically from the known to the unknown. Reaches you wherever you are. Takes you shoulder to shoulder, step by step from ignorance to knowledge. From delusion to enlightenment. You then understand, appreciate, experiment, verify and experience the ultimate truth.

From the Known to the Unknown

The origin of the world is unknown to the masses. People wish to know the unknown origin. They enquire. They question. The ready answer provided to them is: God is the origin. God created the world... Most people accept it. They are quite satisfied. But it does not answer the question since God is equally unknown. How can one unknown convey the knowledge of another unknown factor? Knowledge of anything can be conveyed only through known factors. Any number of unknown factors cannot provide you with a grain of knowledge. Knowledge proceeds from the known to the unknown. It is the fundamental principle of education.

A simple illustration elucidates this principle. A tourist wishes to visit the local museum. He does not know its location. He enquires. You tell him that it is behind the public library. But the location of the library is unknown to him. He cannot find his way. You then tell him that the museum is next to the hospital. He still cannot locate it since he does not know where the hospital is. You may give him scores of other factual details of the location of the museum. None of them can help as long as they are unknown to him. But give him a known factor, tell him that the museum is opposite the clock tower. And he knows where the clock tower is. This known factor instantly conveys the knowledge of the unknown location of the museum.

Similarly, the mystery of the unknown can be solved in terms of what is already known to you. This principle of education has been ignored. The unknown God is described in other unknown terms. God is said to be infinite love, infinite mercy, infinite power etc. But the human intellect cannot conceive infinity. All these terms are unknown. Such unknown agents cannot solve the mystery of the unknown.

The great Persian poet-philosopher Omar Khayyam makes a satirical reference to such futile descriptions of the supreme Reality: *They talked about and about, I came out of the same door I entered.* But the mass of humanity is innocent. They struggle with these unknown terms and terminologies. Little do they realise the limitation of their efforts. The true knowledge of God remains ever in obscurity. The intelligent become conscious of their incapacity and give up their pursuit of God. The ignorant believe that they know God. In their innocence they parrot their undigested concepts to the world.

The present custodians of religion are like the blind leading the blind. They try to convey their concept of God out of their fanatic beliefs. They are like the six blind men who described an elephant in a poem by John Godfrey Saxe. These blind men wanted to know what an elephant was. They groped and felt the different parts of the animal. Arrived at different conclusions. That it was like a wall, a spear, snake, tree, fan and rope. And each declared authoritatively his own opinion of the elephant. All of them were right from their limited viewpoint yet all of them were fundamentally wrong. The poem:

The Blind Men and the Elephant

It was six men of Indostan
To learning much inclined,
Who went to see the elephant
(Though all of them were blind),
That each by observation
Might satisfy his mind.

The First approached the elephant,
And, happening to fall
Against his broad and sturdy side,
At once began to bawl:
"God bless me! but the elephant
Is nothing but a wall!"

The Second, feeling of the tusk,
Cried: "Ho! what have we here
So very round and smooth and sharp?
To me 'tis mighty clear
This wonder of an elephant
Is very like a spear!"

The Third approached the animal,
And, happening to take
The squirming trunk within his hands,
Thus boldly up and spake:
"I see," quoth he, "the elephant
Is very like a snake!"

The Fourth reached out his eager hand,
And felt about the knee:
"What most this wondrous beast is like
Is mighty plain," quoth he;
" 'Tis clear enough the elephant
Is very like a tree!"

The Fifth, who chanced to touch the ear,
Said: "E'en the blindest man
Can tell what this resembles most;
Deny the fact who can,
This marvel of an elephant
Is very like a fan!"

The Sixth no sooner had begun
About the beast to grope,
Than, seizing on the swinging tail
That fell within his scope,
"I see," quoth he, "the elephant
Is very like a rope!"

And so these men of Indostan
Disputed loud and long,
Each in his own opinion
Exceeding stiff and strong,
Though each was partly in the right,
And all were in the wrong!

So, oft in theologic wars
The disputants, I ween,
Rail on in utter ignorance
Of what each other mean,
And prate about an elephant
Not one of them has seen!

— John Godfrey Saxe

Vedanta gives no such names to God as these blind men
did to the elephant. Its approach to God is methodical.
It systematically bridges the gulf between you and God.
It provides you the philosophy to study, contemplate,
assimilate and apply it in your life. For you to evolve
spiritually. And reach the ultimate state of Self-realisation,
God-realisation.

The supreme Godhead lies within you. It is your original
nature. Your ignorance veils your supreme Self. Vedanta
gives you the knowledge to discover your Self. It is an
exercise akin to medical treatment. When a disease seizes

your body you lose your original health. You consult a doctor. The doctor prescribes medicine to eradicate the disease. When the disease is removed you regain your health. Health is your original state. The doctor cannot give you health. He can only remove ill health. So too, the Self is your original Being. Ignorance is the disease. The knowledge of Vedanta removes ignorance to restore your Self to yourself.

Vedanta only serves as a pointer indicating God. Terrestrial. knowledge however subtle cannot take you directly to the transcendental Reality. It is not possible to capture God with words, feelings or thoughts. God is infinite. Finite efforts cannot achieve the Infinite. Nevertheless, one cannot reach God without this knowledge. Knowledge can take you only to the subtlest terrestrial experience. Thereafter you will have to experience the Reality subjectively.

The moon-branch analogy aptly illustrates this truth. It is known in Sanskrit as *chandra-shakha-nyaya*. The analogy explains how the moon can be pointed out with the help of a branch of a tree. Sometimes you see the crescent moon in the bright, sunlit sky. It appears no more than an arc of a circle. In the wide expanse of the sky you find it difficult to point it out to another person. He is unable to spot it in the glare of sunlight. Besides, there is nothing else in the sky with reference to which you may point it out. The analogy gives a practical way of doing it. You first point to a particular tree in the meadow. Then to its trunk, a branch and to the tip of the branch. Let him follow the line of vision up to the tip. Thereafter, ask him to gaze at the sky far beyond the tip of the branch. The moon suddenly appears to him. The unknown moon is now known.

You will appreciate that none of these aids has anything to do with the moon. The tree, trunk, branch or tip is not the moon. The moon is far beyond them all. Yet without these pointers he could never have located the moon. These are essential aids to find it. But if he sticks to these aids and not go beyond them, he will never succeed in locating the moon. So it is with realisation of your supreme Self. Vedanta provides all the knowledge necessary to reach your Godhead. Its philosophy is meticulous. It takes you from your present state to the point of perfection, short of Self-realisation. Vedanta, or for that matter any knowledge, cannot take you beyond that point. You should not get involved in this knowledge and remain there. It is like fixing your attention on the branch and not going beyond it. Hence, be not content with mere knowledge. No doubt you need the knowledge. But make good use of it and go beyond it. Vedantic knowledge will purify your mind. Make your mind contemplative, meditative. Plunge the purified mind into the silence of meditation. You will then discover your Self within.

Therefore, to realise the unknown God you will have to proceed from the known world. Study and analyse the world. Make full use of it to explore the realm of the unknown.

Composition of the World

The world comprises four principal kingdoms: mineral, vegetable, animal and human.

The mineral kingdom consists of inert, insentient matter. Matter has no life in it. The mineral world is crude, opaque. It has no awareness. No conscious power. No capacity to express itself like the other three species. But if life is defined as energy or motion then matter also can claim to have traces of life in it. It does manifest a kind of motion. Undergoes physical and chemical changes. But its motion is insignificant.

Its changes and undulations are almost imperceptible. Hence considered practically lifeless.

The vegetable world exhibits a little awareness, consciousness. Some sort of expression, activity. Plants grow. Their branches reach different directions. Their roots dig deep into the soil. But they cannot move from place to place. Their motion is confined to one spot. Their manifestation of energy, motion is restricted, limited.

Animals are more conscious of the world than plants and minerals. They belong to a higher cadre of evolution. Their motion is not confined to a spot as with plants. Their expressions are far and wide. They are known to travel great distances when the necessity arises.

Humans are the most evolved among living beings. Their consciousness or awareness of the world is supreme. They exhibit far greater energy and motion than the routine, mechanical movements of animals. Endowed with paramount powers, they control all other beings. Even harness time, space and causation. No animal can conceive, much less achieve these feats. Above all, a human alone can surmise the existence of God.

The German philosopher Leibnitz says that life has three manifestations: Life sleeps in plants, dreams in animals and wakes in man.

The Human Species

The universe is a composite structure with an orderly system. It resembles a colossal spiral tapering to a point. The concentric layers of the universe display a similarity. The macrocosm and the microcosm appear to be alike. Differing

in magnitude. The forces operating in the cosmos are
strikingly similar to those in an atom. The four seasons of
the year appear in a miniature scale in the day. Spring as
morning, summer as noon, autumn as evening and winter
as night.

One would notice an analogous relationship existing
between the world and a human being as well. The four
kingdoms of the world — mineral, vegetable, animal and
human — appear to be faithfully reflected in humans. The
nature of some humans resembles that of matter. Others
are close to vegetation. Yet others are akin to animals. Only
a small fraction fits into the calibre of a human being.
Whereas, it is difficult to find one in a generation who has
reached supra-manhood, Godhood.

The human species may be categorised thus under five
distinct heads:
Mineral-person
Vegetable-person
Animal-person
Human-person
God-person

The classification is based mainly on the degree of their
selfishness. Mineral-persons are most self-centred. They are
not conscious of others' existence. Not concerned about the
needs and welfare of other beings. As the species develop,
drop their selfishness they become more refined, more
evolved. Culminating in the totally selfless God-person.

Those in the mineral category are stone-like. Gross and
lethargic. Like matter, they hardly manifest any energy or
activity. They are irresponsible, indifferent, heedless. And fail
to react to the world. Remaining at the physical level they
merely gratify their senses. And satisfy their personal needs

even at the cost of their family, community or country. The nature of such persons is totally selfish. Note their traits carefully. Study and understand their character. It would help you to pull yourself up when your personality slips into those demeaning qualities.

The vegetable-persons are a little less selfish. But still everything they do centres around their self-centred desires. Their interest and attention revolves around their immediate family. Spouse and children are their altar. They do not see anything beyond the periphery of their home. They merely cater to the wellbeing of their family. Lost in the domestic unit, their interest does not go beyond it. They strive hard to stretch the world to suit the pleasures of their domestic circle. The world however cannot cater to the welfare of one family. In this struggle they become mentally disturbed, unhappy.

The animal-persons are also basically selfish. Their interest has crossed the precincts of the physical body and the family. They identify more with their caste or creed, clan or clique, class or community. And would cater to the welfare of those who belong to their fold. They are sacrificial to their own section and faction. But turn bitter to those beyond the boundary of their own group. And clash with them. The angel metamorphoses into a devil. Thus different groups are at war with one another. They breed discontent and disruption in the society. The members of each group cause more pain to other groups than the pleasure they claim to give their own.

The human-persons are far less selfish than the above three categories. They have much wider interests. Some identify themselves with their nationals. Others with all humanity. Etcetera. These do not find any distinction or demarcation within their enclave. Being favourably disposed, they advance the good of those who fall within the boundary of their circle. But not so with those who transgress their boundary. The same who are benign to their own nationals turn malign to other nationals. Thus one nation is set against another. Resulting in wars after wars. The pages of history are stained with bloodshed. The good earth has turned into a veritable hell.

Similarly, those that identify with humanity are amiable and sacrificial to humans. Irrespective of colour or creed, community or country. But their bearing, their treatment towards other creatures is distinct and different. They would destroy animals or birds or fishes for the sake of their palate. Food has no taste before it reaches the tongue. Nor after it leaves the tongue. Yet, for the few seconds' pleasure they do not hesitate to slaughter millions upon millions of innocent creatures, day after day. Just because these creatures are not represented in the U.N.O. nor even in the S.P.C.A. or P.E.T.A!

The God-person is one who has shifted focus from the terrestrial world to the transcendental Reality. Who is Self-realised, God-realised. Has reached the State of absolute peace and bliss. In him selfishness is totally annihilated. His love is all-embracing, universal. Pervading everywhere. Nowhere in particular. His identification is with one and all. None in preference. He is free from all worldly division and demarcation. His individuality has merged with the unifying divinity. Rare indeed is such a person.

In the lowest category one's love is confined to one's individuality. When the human evolves to the next category he rises to the level of his family. No more. As he evolves further his love embraces enlarging circles. In the final stage of evolution, the God-person, the Self-realised soul radiates love, peace and happiness everywhere, to every being.

Life's mission is to evolve to the highest state. To discover your real Self. To return to your original nature of divinity. Be not static. Stagnation is decay, death. Follow the example of flowing rivers. Not stagnant ponds. Rivers are steadfast, tireless in striving to reach their goal, the ocean. No obstacle can stop their determined pursuit. They reduce boulders to pebbles. Track round hills and valleys. Fall from precipices. But never stop until they merge with the ocean. Thus must you pursue your supreme Self. Make your way towards Godhood. That is your birthright. Wherever you are, whatever you be, keep moving towards your ultimate goal of Self-realisation. God-realisation.

Three Conditions of the Mind

The five categories of human beings fall under three broad mental conditions:

Restless mind
Imperfect mind
Perfect mind

Restless mind

A self-centred person is concerned only with himself. He focuses his interest and attention upon his individual self. His action and perception, emotion and thought are all directed to his own welfare. He finds no interest in anyone else.

But the world is not designed to cater to a particular individual. As a result his desires remain frustrated. They cause mental agitations. His mind remains ever discontented and disturbed. This type of mind is like a cone positioned on its vertex as shown in figure 1.

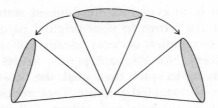

Figure 1. Restless mind

A cone on its vertex can never remain stable. So is a restless mind.

Imperfect mind

As a person moves up to the higher categories of humans his mind becomes stabler. It does not topple over all the time as would a restless mind. But when someone insults him, flings a nasty remark at him his mind becomes agitated.

The agitations may last for hours. Sometimes for days or months. A single incident can keep the mind disturbed for a long period. Even before the mind could settle down, perhaps another agency can create further mental agitation. A single disturbance can play havoc. Such a mind is termed imperfect. It acts like a cone lying on its side on a smooth surface as in figure 2.

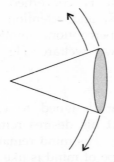

Figure 2. Imperfect mind

A cone lying on its side may normally be at rest. But when tapped on one side it starts oscillating. From one side to the other. Another tap before or after it stops, creates further oscillation. The impact from an external agency may be only for a moment. But the consequent oscillation can continue for long. Similarly, an imperfect mind goes on oscillating, swaying, agitating. Makes life miserable. You must learn to withstand external disturbances. They are an inevitable part of life. Do not allow them to agitate your mind. Destroy your peace and harmony within.

Perfect mind

A fully evolved person is free from mental agitation. His mind is tranquil, peaceful. He is the same in the best or worst of environment, situation or circumstance. Leave him in heat or cold, he is undisturbed. Give him joy or sorrow, he is unperturbed. Treat him with honour or dishonour, he is unaffected. He remains ever calm and composed. Revels in the perfect state of mind. He remains like the cone resting on its base as in figure 3.

Figure 3. Perfect mind

Oliver Wendell Holmes Sr. describes such a person in exquisite poetry:

For him in vain the envious seasons roll
Who bears eternal summer in his soul.

Vedanta would help you reach the perfect state. It provides the technique of disciplining the mind. An indisciplined mind can cause considerable damage. Even prove fatal. You must take to daily study of Vedanta. Reflect upon the truths therein. Apply them in your life. Your mental agitations gradually cease. You live a life of peace and bliss.

CHAPTER III

LIFE, ITS COURSE

Composition of Life

Life is constituted of experiences. They are of three types: physical, emotional and intellectual. The quality and quantity of experiences determine the nature of life. If your experiences are happy, your life is happy. If they are unhappy, it is unhappy. If dynamic, it is dynamic. If dull, it is dull. Therefore, to bring about a change in your life you need to change your experiences.

An experience is a unit of life. It is made up of you, the experiencing subject and the world, the experienced object. The union of the subject and object, you and world brings about an experience. It is like a chemical reaction between two chemicals.

If you wish to enrich your life you must deal with its constituents. Improve both, the world and you. Study the nature of the world you contact. Develop it to the extent possible. Also study the structure of your personality. Improve it as well. When the constituents are bettered, the experiences arising out of their union must necessarily improve. Then the law applies — as the experiences so the life. Your life takes a turn for the better.

Your life's betterment therefore necessitates a thorough study and analysis of your personality, the world and your relationship with it. Who is the individual? What is the world like? How much can you improve yourself and the world? What is the right mode of contact? Such analysis and well-determined procedures would help raise the quality of your life.

The Individual Mechanism

A human being is composed of Spirit and matter. The spiritual component is your real Self, known as *Atman* in Sanskrit. The material layers comprise the physical body, mind and intellect. The physical body is the equipment which perceives and acts. Mind is that which feels emotions. While the intellect thinks, reasons, judges. However these material equipments are inert, insentient per se. *Atman*, the supreme Self is that which lends sentiency to the equipments. You are a composite personality with *Atman* at the core and the body, mind and intellect enveloping It. *Atman*, the Self is ever at rest. The Abode of absolute peace and bliss. The wise identifies with the inner Self and merely allows his body, mind and intellect to operate. By withdrawing himself thus to his spiritual centre he becomes impersonal, detached, objective. His mind then turns peaceful. While his body remains active and dynamic. That is the key to success and progress in life.

The physical body has two sets of organs. The five organs of perception and the five organs of action. The organs of perception are the eyes, ears, nose, tongue and skin. The organs of action are the hands, feet and the organs of speech, generation and excretion.

The mind contains emotions and feelings. Love, kindness, passion, anger, hatred, envy, jealousy etc. belong to the mind.

The mind is also referred to as heart. Which is different from the anatomical heart. Beyond the realm of the mind lies the intellect. The intellect is your faculty to think, reason, judge, decide. You will have to exercise your intellect to decide on a course of action.

The mind and intellect together constitute your inner personality. Which defines your individuality. You are what you are because of your indwelling mind and intellect. The physical body is a vehicle which carries your personality from one experience to another.

You employ your body, mind and intellect to contact the world. *Atman* merely animates them. It has little to do with their activities. It serves like electricity in electrical gadgets. Electricity activates the heater to heat, cooler to cool, bulb to glow etc. But it has nothing to do with these expressions. So does the *Atman* remain a mere animating principle witnessing your physical, mental and intellectual activities.

When you contact the world three distinct transactions take place:
Receipt of sense stimuli from the world
Reaction within your personality
Response to the world

The stimuli from the world reach you through your organs of perception. Colour and form through your eyes, sound through ears, smell through nose, taste through tongue and touch through skin. Having entered therein the stimuli react with the mind and intellect. The type of reaction within will depend upon the quality of stimuli contacted and the nature of your mind and intellect reacting with them. Consequent to the reaction, you send out responses back into the world through your organs of action.

Analyse your present experience of reading this literature. Your eyes are taking in the stimuli in the form of letters and words. These stimuli reach your mind and intellect. A reaction sets in. The mind feels and the intellect judges as per their quality and texture. In some the reaction may be favourable. In that case their response will be to read further. In others the reaction may be unfavourable. And their response will be to stop reading.

Receipt, reaction and response are the three transactions constantly taking place in your life. The human mechanism resembles a manufacturing process which too comprises the three operations. Raw material is fed into the factory at one end. The material is processed by the machines. The products manufactured are despatched at the other end. To ensure the best production all three operations have to be perfected. Raw material taken in must be of good quality. Machines tuned up and operated properly. End products tested to ensure quality control. Likewise the three transactions of life have to be optimised to ensure a perfect life.

In the first transaction your sense organs are constantly perceiving sense-objects of the world. Your eyes see colour and form, ears hear sound, nose smells odour etc. Different types of stimuli reach your personality. You need to examine their quality. Avoid the inflow of impure stimuli. These are the germs which cause psychological diseases. They create mental agitations. You must examine the type of sights that your eyes see, the type of food your tongue tastes etc. Check your perceptions to ensure an inflow of pure, healthy stimuli.

In the second transaction examine the reactions that take place within you. You may regulate and receive pure stimuli. Yet they may produce impure reactions like jealousy, greed, lust etc. Depending upon the nature of your mind and intellect. There are two ways of controlling the reactions. The initial and temporary way is to become aware of them and check their effects from spreading further. But a permanent control is achieved by rehabilitating your mind and intellect through knowledge and understanding.

The third transaction of life is the responses transmitted through the organs of action. Examine the quality of actions executed by your body. If the actions are self-centred and selfish they tell upon your life. They agitate your mind. Make you unhappy. If they are unselfish they generate peace and happiness. Hence your actions have to be rendered unselfish. The knowledge of Vedanta helps you achieve that.

Wherever you are, whatever you be you must perfect the above three transactions in life. Every human being is well-equipped to set things right for his spiritual evolution. Your present nature is best suited for your development. Realise that. Make good use of your faculties to discover the peace and happiness within you.

The ignorant masses however are not aware of their inherent power to steer their way to perfection. Instead they boast over their mundane achievements or bemoan their failings in life. They suffer from either a superiority or inferiority complex. You must be careful not to develop either complex. No one is superior or inferior. Everyone has a distinct part to play in this world. So have you. Recognise your part and play it well. Thus would you progress to perfection.

The American poet-philosopher Ralph Waldo Emerson has well brought out the problem of complexes in human beings in his poem *The Mountain and The Squirrel*. The poem depicts a mountain carrying forests on its back but cannot crack a nut. Whereas a squirrel that can crack a nut cannot carry forests. Therefore none is superior or inferior in this world. All creatures serve as spokes in the wheel of life. God merely acts as the hub holding everything together. The poem:

The Mountain and the Squirrel

The mountain and the squirrel
Had a quarrel;
And the former called the latter "Little Prig."
Bun replied,
"You are doubtless very big;
But all sorts of things and weather
Must be taken in together,
To make up a year
And a sphere.
And I think it no disgrace
To occupy my place.
If I'm not so large as you,
You are not so small as I,
And not half so spry,
I'll not deny you make
A very pretty squirrel track;
Talents differ; all is well and wisely put;
If I cannot carry forests on my back,
Neither can you crack a nut."

— Ralph Waldo Emerson

Nature of the World

The world is ever in a flux of change. The year passes through spring, summer, autumn, winter. The day through morning, noon, evening, night. Energy through mechanical, electrical, sonic, magnetic. The physical body changes through childhood, youth, adulthood, old age. So do the mind and intellect change. Nothing in the world remains static. Change or perish seems to be the law of nature.

How can this ever changing world cater to individual demands? Yet you expect in vain for the world to fit into your mental pattern. And your desires remain unfulfilled. Your mind becomes agitated. You blame the world for your discontentment. You must understand the world is an admixture of pleasure and pain. Observe the play of pleasure and pain to become introvert. Use these contrasting experiences to delve deep into your inner personality. Search within and discover the seat of true peace and happiness.

The world is sometimes cruel only to be kind. Realise that. Do not abuse the plan of nature. Do not fall a prey to cynicism or pessimism in life. Instead look at the world constructively. Does not a sportsman improve his game with strong opposition? Does not trade flourish with stiff competition? Does not a government stabilise with healthy collision? Thus make good use of the apparent antagonism of nature to rise to greater heights of perfection.

A great evolutionist Dr. David Starr Jordan says, "In our discussion of social evolution we must remember that the very perfection of society must always appear as imperfection, for a highly developed society is dynamic. A static society is in a condition of arrested development. The most highly developed organism shows the greatest imperfections." Imperfection is inherent in nature. *Resist not evil* are the blessed words of Jesus Christ. Do not merely complain of evil. Instead, try to overcome it if you can. If you succeed, other imperfections will rise to the surface. Again, overpower them. It is the way to deal with the world. To keep on striving and correcting until you reach the state of absolute perfection within yourself.

Environmental conditions and situations keep changing all the time. As long as the world exists you will have to struggle with them. Meet this problem of life by adaptation and readaptation to the recurring changes.

Life evolves on the principles of heredity and adaptation. The law of heredity reigns supreme in animals. Animals owe practically all their organs and powers to the principle of heredity. They inherit virtually all of them from their species at birth itself. A human also is governed by the principle of heredity. But the predominance of the principle of adaptation or education distinguishes the human being from the animal. At the infant stage a baby is as innocent and ignorant as a pup. Perhaps more. But there is a striking difference in the later stages of their lives. The pup inherits at birth almost all it requires for its complete growth. Whereas the child can through proper adaptation and education acquire phenomenal powers. Even gain suzerainty over the world.

The evolutionists aver that the world is not on the whole a hard place to live in if one has the knack of making proper concessions. Hosts of living creatures, even plants have acquired this knack. They and their descendants are able to hold their own in the pressure of what is called struggle for existence. The ultimate solution however lies in recognising the changeless Reality in the changing phenomena. The one who realises That establishes harmony with the world.

When you do not find peace and harmony you attribute the cause of your discontent to the world. You believe the world needs correction. From time immemorial human efforts have been directed to setting right the world. But so far these efforts have met with little success. You do not realise that the solution lies in improving not the world but yourself. You can find peace and harmony just by purifying your inner personality. When you purify your mind you find the world purified. This is a law. The world is but a reflection of your mind. If your mind is good the world is good. If your mind is bad the world is bad. Therefore change the pattern of thought and feeling in your mind, the entire world changes.

Course of Life

The characteristic feature of life is energy, motion. A living being grows, moves about, executes actions. A dead creature cannot manifest any form of energy. Action therefore is the insignia of life.

The law of evolution impels all living beings to keep acting. A living creature which stops activity will perish. Evolution is marked by constant striving and struggling in life. Where there is no effort and exertion there is degradation and death.

A human being must progress. Not remain static. For example, a child playing with toys is acceptable. But an adult doing the same is detestable. Again, a young man indulging in passion is understandable. But an old man doing the same is despicable. You will have to move with time. Time marches on. If you do not keep pace you devolve. You will destroy yourself. The same is not applicable to an animal. Animals inherit a distinct nature. Their pattern of activity is set. They do not change with time or place. They lack the intelligence to do so. But a human possesses an intellect to distinguish between right and wrong, good and bad etc. And choose his way of life. Progress is spelt by right effort and exertion. Scientific discoveries and inventions are a mark of progress. A society which does not progress along with time will be ruined. This is a universal law. Many great empires which had relaxed their efforts, become lethargic, met their own destruction. History has proved this time and again.

True progress and evolution is directed towards one goal alone. The course of life leads to that supreme goal. Which is everlasting peace and bliss. Living beings seek pleasure, joy, happiness all their lifetime. Some seek through material and physical means. Others through emotions. Yet others through knowledge. For instance, a man desires wealth. Analyse his desire. What is it he really seeks? He wants wealth only to gain comforts, pleasure, happiness. So is it with emotion and knowledge. Everything you seek in the world boils down to happiness. You believe happiness resides in the world at large. You look for it everywhere. Extroverted pursuits have never succeeded in finding happiness. For, happiness lies within your own person. You must therefore direct your efforts towards your own self to find it. There is no other way.

But the problem is that the world attracts you with its instant pleasures. When your senses contact the external objects you enjoy them forthwith. You do not realise that the pleasures arising out of sense-contacts are fleeting. They diminish and gradually yield to sorrow. Conversely, you find that true happiness has a distasteful beginning. When you try to seek happiness within yourself it is bitter to start with. But with determined effort you gain more and more happiness. It is strange but true. Sorrow appears in the mask of joy and joy appears in the mask of sorrow. It is the law of nature. Consequently the ignorant masses discard happiness and court sorrow. This has been the sad history of humans. The *Bhagavad Gita* cautions you of this paradox in nature. Its eighteenth chapter states: *True happiness is like poison in the beginning but nectar in the end* – verse 37. *False happiness is like nectar in the beginning but poison in the end* – verse 38.

Goal of Life

The true course of life leads to happiness. The terminus of life is infinite happiness. You can never rest content until you reach that state of infinite bliss. Bliss lies in your inner Self. You must delve deep into your personality layers and discover the Self within. Even as you progress on the path of Self-realisation you gain commensurate freedom, peace and happiness. It is the truth. Let the world know the secret of right living. And people evolve by instilling this truth in their lives.

The real source of happiness lies within. Yet people clamour for the outward glamour of the world. Outward splendour and grandeur have no joy inherent in them. The wealth of the world cannot give you happiness. Nations the world over are chasing riches with the hope of finding happiness. And human efforts whirl around acquiring, hoarding, indulging in material wealth. What a colossal blunder!

Here is an extract from Swami Rama Tirtha's lecture delivered in the United States of America on December 13, 1902:

"There was a time when India possessed probably more riches than all Europe possesses at this time. There was a time when India had more jewels and diamonds, more pearls and rubies than all America has today. India had had her day in material prosperity. Nations after nations overran India from time to time. Greece became rich at the cost of India, Persia became rich at the cost of India, Afghanistan became rich at the cost of India and at this day England is amassing fortunes at the cost of India. India was once really the land of gold and diamonds.

We do not repent at that. We are not sorry at the present backwardness in material prosperity of India. We know that there is a law, a divine law, a law of our own nature, which is ruling affairs, which is bringing about everything. The divine hand which directs and leads our affairs we know, and knowing that, we do not pine at material backwardness.

We understand the law of nature. These things, these material objects of prosperity, all these were tried, experimented, weighed in the balance by Indians and found wanting. America is very young today; so is Europe very young. They are trying these experiments at this time. All these material things are looked upon by Indians as simply a drop of spray, nothing else. They are no factors in your happiness; they cannot make you truly happy, never, never. *Iron and gold are good for buying iron and gold; that is all.* Happiness is not of the same kind as these material objects are; it cannot be purchased. Happiness, true bliss cannot be purchased by these things."

The native home of happiness is your own Self, *Atman*. Discover your real Self. All your misery and wretchedness vanish. You gain the essence of happiness. You can never find happiness in the external objects of the world. Do not get duped by the senses. Do not search for happiness in perception, emotion and thought. Instead, find the Elysium of happiness within your own Self. Leave the quarantine of your physical body. Rise above the superstitious enclave of your mind. Release yourself from the prison-house of your intellect. Get liberated in Self-consciousness. Happy is he who gains Self-consciousness, God-consciousness.

A human being attains full stature on gaining Self-consciousness. Only when rooted in his own Self is he fully grown. But if his roots do not dig deep, if they rest in the superficial layers of his personality his growth is stunted. He will not find true fulfilment in life. Such a person is akin to bonsai. Bonsai are miniaturised trees. Some of them may be a hundred years old and yet remain a foot in height. The reason for remaining dwarfed is that their roots have been sheared periodically. Prevented from penetrating deep into the soil. The same relation, the same law holds good for you. If you do not dive deep into your

Self you remain spiritually dwarfed. You do not grow into your full stature.

Hence the knowledge of the Self becomes all-important in life. At present you do not know your Self. Your ignorance has to be dispelled. Ignorance manifests in three distinct phases:

Lack of information
Lack of understanding
Lack of experience

In the first phase of ignorance you do not know the Self. You are ignorant of your real Self. You have first to be informed about It. To get to know It you need to listen to spiritual masters or study the scriptures yourself. This is known as *shravana* which means listening. *Shravana* helps you get over the first phase of ignorance.

Having been informed of the Self, the second phase of ignorance surfaces. It is the lack of understanding. You have heard about the Self. You cannot say you do not know It. But then, you may not understand It. This phase of ignorance cannot be removed by listening or studying any more. The knowledge taken in can be understood, absorbed only through your own independent reflection. The process of reflecting, contemplating upon the knowledge received is *manana*. *Manana* means reflection.

With independent reflection you may understand the Self. But the third and last phase of ignorance lingers. The lack of experience of your Self. The ultimate experience, realisation of Self is gained through meditation, *nididhyasana*. You must maintain a constant awareness of the Self. The fixation of thought upon the Self to the exclusion of all other thought is meditation. With profound, sustained meditation you gain the experience of your Self. You become the Self. You attain the everlasting bliss of Self.

The craze the world over is meditation. People do not want to study or listen to lectures. Much less wish to reflect or contemplate. They are averse to any form of effort, exertion. They want an easy way to divinity. And look for short cuts to Godhood. This is a grave mistake. Do not fall a prey to it. You must methodically follow the procedure of *shravana*, *manana* and *nididhyasana* to get rid of your ignorance. You would then gain spiritual Enlightenment. The ultimate goal of life.

CHAPTER IV

CODE OF LIVING

Scope of Spiritual Education

The world is in a state of spiritual decadence. The custodians of religion have largely contributed to it. They have stifled the human intellect. Crammed the mind with irrational religious beliefs. And virtually denied spiritual education. It is a blunder being repeated over and over again in human history. In India, religious pundits boast of a mechanical mastery over Sanskrit language, grammar and construction. They merely memorise and recite countless verses of the language hardly understood by anyone. They learn to quote, twist and torture the old Sanskrit texts. And claim a superiority over spiritual seekers who pursue the truth with original thinking and free reasoning. These pundits are content to tickle the wild humour of their fellow-men. The mental energies of the youth are being lavished, wasted upon discussing and debating frivolities which are dubbed religious. The non-essentials of religion are highlighted by thoughtless religious leaders at the expense of its essentials. Interestingly, the followers are sincere. They blindly accept the authority of these religious heads. And have developed such bias that superstitious symbols and rituals have become centres of deep-rooted practices. Such rank ignorance prevails in the name of religion.

Education ought to promote a nation's agriculture, industry, trade etc. More so must it render the individuals' body active, heart pure and thought original. And spiritual education should instil living knowledge and culture into the people. Make them understand the truths of life through independent reflection. Imbibe the laws of living through verification in their own lives. Instead, spiritual education has come to mean a mechanical reading of ancient texts and blind reliance on authority. The spiritual gurus themselves have spent most of their time in straining these texts with their own commentaries, called *bhashyas* in Sanskrit. From layperson to scholar there is an unquestioned acceptance of these commentaries as final. As a result even intelligent men and women have lost their reason and judgement. Without independent thought and reflection the import of the scriptures becomes impossible to grasp. Thus the sublime knowledge of Vedanta has been practically obliterated by well-meant interpreters and commentators.

The supreme truth is eternal. It is that which is the same in the past, present and future. It reveals itself to a seeker directly like any scientific truth. It needs no authorities to endorse it. Just as a scientific law gains no more weight by the testimony of eminent scientists. What is needed today is not commentators' dissection of the old Sanskrit texts but a clear enunciation of the truth imbedded therein. The truth stands on its own. You need only to exercise your intellect to reflect upon it carefully until you understand it. Thereafter, verify its authenticity in your day-to-day living. Just as a student verifies the knowledge of chemistry through experiments in the laboratory. Thus you become well-established in Vedanta when you find its truths working in practical life.

Vedanta speaks of the supreme knowledge of life. You should gain that knowledge. Approach it with determination and consistency. Make good use of your present intellect to progress gradually in the path of knowledge. The way to more light is the faithful use of what you have. You may wonder how your limited intellect can gain the supreme knowledge. But it works like the headlights of your car. The lights can illumine the road only up to a few metres. But the same light can take you through hundreds of kilometres in the darkness of the night. Drive on, the light continues to illumine the entire path. You will reach your destination. Thus must you strive in the present. A little knowledge gained effaces a little ignorance. Keep moving. This process will take you to the ultimate truth.

You need to put in time and effort to learn and live the sublime truths of life. Practise them constantly. Study, reflect, verify the knowledge in your own life. The path of truth is trying, difficult in the beginning. But you must continue your practice. Cross over the initial impediments and obstacles. You will find the same path later becoming pleasant and easy to cover. Nature seems to help when you want to help yourself. Trials and tribulations, oppositions and obstacles are bound to come in your spiritual pursuit. They tease you if you are not endowed with a strong intellect. But with intellectual strength you can overcome them. These are only seeming difficulties in your pursuit of truth.

The right type of spiritual education anchors you in the supreme Reality. You ought not to let yourself be influenced by any school of thought. Not be impaired by concession or conformity to any institution. You take in the truth of life as it reveals itself to you. Not distort it with a religious bias. That marks the true way to spiritual Enlightenment.

Elements of Right Living

The knowledge of Vedanta infuses the elements of right living in your physical, mental and intellectual personalities. Your actions develop a spirit of service. Your emotions become chastened with love and other positive emotions. Your thinking is rendered clear and divine. Maintain these disciplines through daily study and reflection on the sublime truths of life. You then become attached to the higher aspects of life. Consequently detached from the lower. You live an ideal life. Evolve to the highest state of perfection.

Two broad principles govern human action. Based on the attitude of giving or taking. If the attitude of taking prevails in a society it breeds selfish demands and desires in its members. As a result they are infested with stress and strain. Let their attitude change to giving. And drop their selfishness. They enjoy harmony, peace and happiness.

The dignity of the human race is founded on the principle of giving. Victor Hugo highlights this great principle: *Life is to give, not to take.* No person has a right to claim anything as his. He ought not to desire, demand from society. Perhaps his only right in the world is to give, to serve. 'Be content to serve,' pleaded Christ. Serve the world, the entire world stands in obeisance before you. Objects and beings will be at your beck and call. You become a master, no servant. That is the law of life.

The moment you are born the good world provides you with everything you need. Oxygen to breathe, mother's milk, the right temperature within and without, pressure inside and outside and countless other things. You become totally indebted to the world. You must therefore maintain a sense of gratitude through your life. And serve the world, serve the society, serve one and all. This is the first of the elements of right living. The attitude of service maintains your spiritual wellbeing. The *Bhagavad Gita* says it is criminal to consume the resources of the world without contributing to it: *He who eats without producing is verily a thief.*

Religion educates you to acknowledge the benevolence that nature provides you. And to realise your obligation, duty, responsibility to repay. You are best when you are best at repaying. So must you perform your obligatory duties. But people take their duties as a heavy burden resting on their shoulders. Few realise that the greatest contributions of humanity can never compensate for the largesse of nature. All the material work you can offer is immaterial. Yet, everybody hurries and worries about his work. Your approach to life should be to just do what you ought to do. That is the beginning and end of your obligation. You are not to brood over or become excited about your duty and responsibility. Your real duty in life is to remain self-poised, self-pleased. Your primary service to the world, your religious duty is to keep yourself peaceful and cheerful. To be sorrowful and miserable is a social, moral, religious crime. You ought not to spread the disease of melancholy to your fellow-beings. Instead, rejuvenate their health with joy and happiness. This attitude must blend with your work.

The law of life is that you laugh and the world laughs with you. Weep and none weeps with you. Rejoice, be cheerful and people flock around you. Grieve, be miserable they leave you alone. The world shares your pleasures but not your woes.

A human being brings sorrow and misery upon himself because of his ego and selfish desires. This happens when you focus your interest and attention upon your material equipments. The demands of the body, mind and intellect are endless. They can never be satiated. As a result your mind remains disturbed, restless. You are in a hellish state. You lose the paradise in you. To regain the bliss within you need to change the focus from your ego to the divine Self. The Self in you is supreme. Ever blissful. Leave the quarantine of your body, mind and intellect. Seek the Self. Try to be aware of the Self through your life's transactions. While acting with your body, feeling with your mind or thinking with your intellect, remember you are the supreme Self. You will soon regain your Self. As you think so you become. Put this sacred law into practice.

The second element of right living is love. While the physical body engages in action, let your mind embrace the world with love. Your emotions coalesce into a mass of universal love. Love is realising your identity with the world. Your oneness with the whole. Failing which, you are lost in an island of your own. You segregate yourself from others. You suffer the sorrow of separation, isolation.

Samuel Taylor Coleridge presents this truth effectively in his poem *The Rime of the Ancient Mariner*. The poem narrates the experience of a mariner at sea. The mariner started his voyage with his heart full of love. He described the beauty of the creatures appearing in the sea. Everything turned out favourable. The ship sailed on merrily. Then came a change in the mariner's attitude. He lost love for his fellow-creatures. Even developed a bitterness, contempt for them. One day, as the ship was sailing along the shore, an albatross flew into it. The mariner drew his crossbow and shot it. Thereafter he suffered a series of calamities at sea. And was tortured with mental agony. Then came a change again in the mariner's attitude. Once again he appreciated nature and her beautiful creatures. Love seeped into his parched bosom. His heart embraced his fellow-creatures. He regained his harmony with nature. Was happy again. Everything thereafter turned favourable. He returned to the peace and happiness of land. Coleridge epitomises his great message in one verse:

> *He prayeth well who loveth well*
> *Both man and bird and beast.*
> *He prayeth best who loveth best*
> *All things both great and small.*

'Thou shalt have no other god but love' is the first law of Moses. People have violated this sacred law. Love is not a preferential attachment to beings. Love means identification with others. To feel exactly the same way as another does. Nothing more. What pleases others pleases you. What pains them pains you. Your pleasure and pain align with those of your fellow-creatures. This is true love. A feeling that emanates from a pure mind. Which keeps clear off distinction or demarcation. Wherein you see your Self reflected in all. As you see your own self in different mirrors. With pure love you rise to greater spiritual heights. But when the same emotion of love turns selfish it degrades you. You devolve. Remember therefore to rise in love, not fall in love.

The third element of right living is knowledge. As the body serves and the mind loves, the intellect must seek true knowledge. The knowledge that distinguishes the Spirit from matter. That discerns the Eternal from ephemeral. The Real from unreal. The knowledge which enables you to perceive the underlying Divinity in all beings. The changeless substratum in the changing phenomena of this world. Such knowledge is derived through independent reflection and contemplation upon the truths laid down in scriptures. It is not mere erudition and scholarship in scriptural literature. But the assimilation and absorption of the knowledge imbedded therein. The knowledge that reveals the Self within.

People have distanced themselves from the Self. Unaware of their essential Being, they are lost in ignorance. The ignorance of Self manifests as three mental temperaments.

The Three Temperaments

The mental temperament of human beings, known as *gunas* in Sanskrit, are of three types. Each has a distinct character of its own. A human is composed of all three *gunas*. They are known as:

Tamas   Inactive
Rajas   Active
Sattva   Trans-active

Tamas is the state of thoughts in inertia. A mood of lethargy, indolence, indifference. Indisposed to activity. A condition of sloth and sleep. With no intellectual conviction to pursue. Nor emotional feeling to manifest. A person steeped in *tamas* lives a dull, inactive life. With hardly any response to the world.

Rajas is the state of passionate, desirous and agitated thoughts. When a person bristles with frenzied actions. Leading to his involvement in the affairs of the world.

Sattva is the state of thoughts in equanimity, serenity, objectivity. When a person is poised, mature, contemplative. Detached from worldly involvement and excitement. Hence termed trans-active.

Sattva, *rajas* and *tamas* composed in different proportions accounts for the heterogeneous variety of human beings. Every individual possesses all three *gunas*. The proportion of these temperaments differs from person to person. Some have *sattva* predominating over *rajas* and *tamas*. They are referred to as *sattvik* persons. The predominance of *rajas* over the other two creates a *rajasik* person. And the predominance of *tamas*, a *tamasik* person.

The law of nature is such that the *sattva guna* in an individual surfaces in the early hours of the morning. Between 4 a.m. and 6 a.m. His *rajas* and *tamas* lie dormant during that period. Similarly *rajas* predominantly manifests at daytime between 6 a.m. and 6 p.m. So does *tamas* show up at night from 6 p.m.

to 4 a.m. The law holds good for everyone. From the highest *sattvik* to the lowest *tamasik* person.

The *sattvik* temperament is highest in a *sattvik* person. Less in a *rajasik* person. Least in a *tamasik* person. Regardless of the quantum, the *sattva* in a person manifests in the early hours. If the *sattvik* content is more, the pressure for its expression is maximum. That explains why a *sattvik* person wakes up early. The pressure being low in a *rajasik* person, he wakes up late. The *tamasik* has to be virtually pulled out of bed.

Besides waking a person up early, the other *sattvik* qualities are seen clearly manifest at that time. Like being calm and composed, serene and contemplative. Being averse to plunging into gross physical activity. Or indulging in sensual pleasure. Hence, early morning is said to be well suited for contemplation. And the *sattvik* time most conducive for spiritual practice. Study, reflection and meditation become effective between 4 a.m. and 6 a.m. Thus, utilising the early hours and retiring early, you can increase your *sattva*, control your *rajas* and reduce your *tamas*.

Just as *sattva* manifests early in the morning, *rajas* finds its expression during the course of the day. Whatever *rajasik* content a person has, it forces its way out after the *sattvik* time is over. Hence people are found bristling with activity during daytime. The *rajasik* person, with a large proportion of *rajas*, becomes frightfully active. The rest also are prone to be involved in some form of activity from morning till evening, commensurate with their *rajasik* content.

Tamas emerges after 6 p.m. Indulgence in intoxicants, sex, gambling etc. is conspicuous during night-time. Most pronounced in *tamasik* persons. Less in *rajasik* and virtually absent in *sattvik* persons.

Your mission in life should be to raise yourself from *tamas* to *rajas* to *sattva*. And your goal to reach *trans-sattva*. *Trans-sattva* is the state of Self-realisation, God-realisation. As you drop your *tamas* and *rajas* you attain more and more *sattva*. As you continue the spiritual pursuit your *sattva* gradually displaces all *rajas* and *tamas*. But *sattva* alone cannot exist since the human being is essentially made up of all three *gunas*. Consequently, pure *sattva* transforms itself to *trans-sattva*. You become the supreme Self. Liberated from the persecutions of the body, mind and intellect. From the balcony of the Self you watch the procession of perception, emotion and thought go by.

You must pull yourself out of these temperaments and attain the *trans-sattvik* State. You may have to initiate action where inaction prevails. It needs your personal effort. The trouble with most people is that they want others to work for them while they remain idle. They listen to many discourses. And do little thereafter. All the lectures of sages and saints are of no avail unless you are prepared to lecture to yourself. Reflect and contemplate on what you have heard or read. Thus must you learn to raise yourself by yourself.

As you move from inaction to action you slip into another difficulty. You become involved in your activities. Attached to things and beings of the world. You do not realise that you are persecuted by your own action and possession. Learn a simple law of life: Just in as much as you claim possession of anything, you remain possessed and obsessed.

You tie one end of a rope around the neck of a mule and hold the other end in your hand. And claim the mule as yours. You believe the mule has become your slave. That it is subordinate to you. The reason for your claim is that the mule cannot leave you. The mule has lost its freedom to you. It is true. But then the converse also is true. You cannot leave the mule either. You cannot leave the mule because the mule cannot leave you. You have become a slave of the mule. If you are free to leave the mule so is the mule free to leave you. By enslaving the mule you enslave yourself. So it is with the world. The moment you claim possession of the world you are possessed by the world. It is the law.

People the world over have been self-centred, selfish. And have developed a mania for possession and proprietary. Their efforts are all directed to acquisition, aggrandisement, accumulation of material wealth. The craze for mineness, the fever of possessiveness rages in their minds. This attitude has ruined the peace of mind in human society. You must therefore avoid developing a sense of mineness towards objects and beings. The feeling of possessiveness towards your possessions enslaves you. Turns your life miserable.

The feeling of mineness, possessiveness is unrelated to the quantum of wealth you possess. You could be extremely wealthy, possess a large fortune and yet maintain a dispassionate attitude towards it. A dispossessive feeling towards your possessions. You can entertain the same feeling even in penury.

The sense of dispassion, the attitude of dispossession develops as you identify with the higher values of life. And with the goal firmly set on the *trans-sattvik* State, on the supreme Self, your craving for possession and proprietary fades away. You relate to the world with dispassion. A sense of renunciation.

An attitude of renunciation towards the affairs of the world is a *sattvik* quality. It remains the same through prosperity and poverty. This idea has been well brought out in the characters of Janaka and Sudama in the scripture. Janaka was a king with an abundance of wealth. Sudama was a pauper. Regardless of their material status both were men of exceptional renunciation. Their mind was set on the supreme Self within. With little value for material wealth.

If the world today wishes to be truly civilised it must instil the spirit of service and sacrifice in the society. The spirit which would develop the attitude of dispassion towards object and being, possession and relationship. People must learn to become more impersonal. More skilled to work for the welfare of the community than their own. That would determine the dignity and prestige of a human being.

As the spirit of dispassion grows, you become more detached from the affairs of the world. The fluctuations of the world no more disturb your inner peace and happiness. You become more and more objective in life. Less and less involved in and affected by the happenings around you. You then observe the world as a witness. View your own life as an actor would upon the stage.

Theodore Tilton drives home this idea clearly in his striking poem. The poet presents the King of Persia as a picture of detachment. The king engraved a maxim on his ring: *Even This Shall Pass Away*. Rooted in the highest values of life, he revelled in the spirit of renunciation. He would not identify with the best or the worst that the world offered. The king was blessed with wealth and woman, name and fame. So did he face the pangs of disease, decay and impending death. But he had little to do with them. He maintained an attitude of perfect objectivity. Remained ever peaceful and blissful through the fluctuations of the world. The poem:

Even This Shall Pass Away

Once in Persia reigned a king,
Who upon his signet ring
Graved a maxim true and wise,
Which, if held before his eyes,
Gave him counsel at a glance
Fit for every change and chance.
Solemn words, and these are they;
"Even this shall pass away."

Trains of camels through the sand
Brought him gems from Samarcand;
Fleets of galleys through the seas
Brought him pearls to match with these;
But he counted not his gain
Treasures of the mine or main;
"What is wealth?" the king would say;
"Even this shall pass away."

'Mid the revels of his court,
At the zenith of his sport,
When the palms of all his guests
Burned with clapping at his jests,
He, amid his figs and wine,
Cried, "O loving friends of mine;
Pleasures come, but not to stay;
'Even this shall pass away.' "

Lady, fairest ever seen,
Was the bride he crowned his queen.
Pillowed on his marriage bed,
Softly to his soul he said:
"Though no bridegroom ever pressed
Fairer bosom to his breast,
Mortal flesh must come to clay —
Even this shall pass away."

Fighting on a furious field,
Once a javelin pierced his shield;
Soldiers, with a loud lament,
Bore him bleeding to his tent.
Groaning from his tortured side,
"Pain is hard to bear," he cried;
"But with patience, day by day,
Even this shall pass away."

Towering in the public square,
Twenty cubits in the air,
Rose his statue, carved in stone.
Then the king, disguised, unknown,
Stood before his sculptured name,
Musing meekly: "What is fame?
Fame is but a slow decay;
Even this shall pass away."

Struck with palsy, sore and old,
Waiting at the Gates of Gold,
Said he with his dying breath,
"Life is done, but what is Death?"
Then, in answer to the king,
Fell a sunbeam on his ring,
Showing by a heavenly ray,
"Even this shall pass away."

— Theodore Tilton

The Caste System

The much-talked-of caste system is based on the three mental
temperaments of *sattva*, *rajas* and *tamas*. The caste system
comprises the four categories of people in the world:

Brahmana Priest-class
Kshatriya Warrior-class
Vaishya Trader-class
Shudra Labour-class

A *brahmana* is one who possesses a predominantly *sattvik* nature, a little *rajas* and traces of *tamas*. A *kshatriya* has mostly *rajasik* temperament, less of *sattva* and *tamas*. A *vaishya*, still less of *sattva* and *rajas* and more of *tamas*. A *shudra* is predominantly *tamasik* in nature with a little *rajas* and traces of *sattva*. The classification of castes is applicable all over the world, not to India alone. In the distant past, India made an intelligent allocation of work, a division of labour depending upon the mental temperament of individuals. The priest-class was given the duty of preaching, being temperamentally designed for it. The warrior-class more suited for wielding weapons, was asked to protect and fight for the country. The trader-class was allocated trade, commerce, business. The labour-class, lacking the above skills, was given manual work. However, there was no law prohibiting any person from taking up the work he liked. No rigidity in the divisions. Such systems exist everywhere. It may not have been prescribed and practised as in India. There was a time when the *brahmanas*, intellectuals ruled the world. Later was an age when *kshatriyas*, chivalry reigned. These are days when *vaishyas*, business-houses control the fortunes of the world. In due course the *shudras*, labour-unions perhaps would take over everything.

The caste system was well-meant and planned for the benefit of the people. Later, the administrators misinterpreted the system. It lost its purpose. A blessing turned into a curse. The divisions developed rigidity. People stuck to their own castes. They would not cross their self-imposed walls of division. It ended in distaste and distrust in the society.

The solution to this problem lies in educating the people with knowledge of the three basic temperaments. And guiding them to the supreme Self that lies beyond the temperaments. Such education gradually breaks the walls of division and demarcation. Without it, all the scientific achievement and advancement in the world will be of no avail. And people will continue to be plagued with stress and strain, suffering and sorrow.

There is a saying: *To escape plague the only way is to live up to the law of hygiene.* So too, to escape the persecution of the terrestrial world you will have to learn and live the higher values of life. Living therefore is an art, a skill, a technique to be learnt and practised. This technique was imparted in India to the young at a very early age. By sixteen, the youth were well-educated to meet the world. They became stalwarts, prepared to face the external challenges. But by lapse of time this fundamental education to the young was lost. Now, people live the good part of life without learning the technique of living. If at all, they begin to learn it at the end of their life. Spiritual education has turned out to be a post-retirement pastime. A cart before the horse!

A burlesque illustration discloses this grave blunder in people's lives. An archer claimed to have perfected his art with 100% accuracy. That he could strike the bulls-eye every time. This drew the attention of the real champion of the country who was never able to achieve that accuracy. With humility he approached the self-proclaimed master to learn his technique. The 'master' complied, with a condition. That he maintain the secrecy of his art. And then gave out his sermon: The problem with you folks is that you prepare the target and then shoot. Whereas I shoot first and draw the target later.

So it is with human lives. People live through their life and learn the technique of living later!

CHAPTER V

EXIGENCY OF ACTION

Action is Inevitable

Action is the insignia of life. The law of life proclaims that none can remain without performing activity. Everyone is made to act helplessly according to one's own inner temperament. Yet, if you choose to remain idle you lead yourself to destruction. Nature draws your attention to this law. Observe the stagnant pool and the running brook. Where water stagnates it turns filthy, dirty. Whereas running water is clear, pure. Learn the lesson from nature. If you are to succeed in life, be prosperous and peaceful, you must adopt the principle of running waters. Follow their line of action. The river keeps moving. Overcoming all obstacles. Ever progressing. It never stops until it reaches the ocean. So must you pursue the path of action until you reach the abode of Truth. The *Bhagavad Gita* highlights the gospel of *karma* action. Emphasises the importance of fulfilling your obligatory functions in life.

The scripture warns that even to maintain your body you must be active. If any part of your body remains inactive for a period of time it loses its strength and vitality. Your body needs to be kept in constant repair. You must exercise daily. But people detest the idea of physical exercise. Instead, they choose to indulge in sensual pleasure. They do not seem to realise that even enjoyment of sensual pleasures needs proper maintenance of the physical body. The neglect of physical exercise would prove detrimental to your material and spiritual wellbeing. Hence, the first spiritual lesson Swami Vivekananda gave out to his followers was: *Go, play football!*

Vedanta insists on work, work and work. Equally so, it glorifies renunciation. There is an apparent contradiction. How can action and renunciation go together? This doubt goes when one understands the deeper import of the gospel of work. In fact, real work is founded on renunciation. Renunciation of the ego. Which is work performed without the egoistic feeling, 'I-am-the-doer. I am the sole architect of all that I do.' Real work is turned out when the body plunges into action while the mind is attuned to an ideal set for it. A true worker is one who pours out his efforts for a higher cause beyond his selfish interest. And does it without an egoistic arrogation of doership. That is the spirit of renunciation to be practised. Such work commands success and prosperity concurrently with peace and bliss. You can practise it in your home, in business, in society, everywhere. There is no need to retire to the forests for living a life of renunciation.

The greatest ideal in life is realisation of your supreme Self, *Atman*, God. Try to attune yourself to that ideal. When your mind is directed to the Self within and your body is engaged in earnest work you rise above your little self. Your ego gradually disappears. The idea of *I* and *mine* drops off. You are the greatest worker when you consider yourself no worker. You become a mere instrument of the divine Self. You then generate harmony, peace and love within and without.

The idea of working in a spirit of renunciation has confused people. Even today this concept is not understood. Much less appreciated as a way of life. People either become attached, entangled in their work or cowardly escape from it. You must realise that action is inevitable. You cannot avoid your obligatory functions. In the epic *Mahabharata* a great battle was fought between two royal forces. Arjuna was a warrior-prince leading one of the armies. He aimed at destroying unrighteousness and resurrecting righteousness in the country. The stage was set for the battle to commence. At that crucial moment Arjuna wanted to withdraw from the scene. The warrior declined to fight. He shrank from his obligatory duty. He appealed to Lord Krishna if he could leave the battle-front. It was then that the Lord gave Arjuna the sermon of the *Bhagavad Gita*. He preached the necessity of action. The art of right action. How the role of action embraces the principle of renunciation. He advised Arjuna to renounce his egoistic feeling and fight the battle impersonally for the welfare of the people.

The *Gita* pressed home the role of action in the spiritual path. Yet the Indians consider it a text more for the retired and the old. Ironically, the *Gita's* subtle principles of action are practised more beyond the shores of India. In most western countries, people have kept the nation as their altar, above their little selves. And dedicated work to the nation's prosperity and welfare. Consequently, they have become progressive, productive and prosperous.

Value of Action

Human beings must keep pace with the march of time if they are to survive in the struggle for existence. Mere acquisition of knowledge would not suffice. Knowledge comes from the past. It has to be translated currently into action. Thoughts and ideas must be transformed into deeds.

Your motto in life should be to strive, to struggle, not to succeed. Work well accomplished is the joy of life. Success or failure is immaterial. What really matters in life is your ability to adopt action to obligation. Your business lies in action alone, not in the reward accruing from it. Let not the anxiety for enjoying the fruit disturb the course of your action.

Just be in the struggle. That becomes your bounden duty. Work on for work's sake. Learn to be indifferent towards pleasure or pain, joy or sorrow, honour or dishonour that may accrue out of your action. Your life is enriched by accomplishment of right action rather than outward success or failure. Take up your work with no axe to grind. Do what you ought to do in life. Go about it in an independent spirit. Work then becomes a pleasure. Pleasure or happiness lies in the garb of work.

People do not realise the beauty and grandeur of real work. They entertain worldly motives to work. Develop desires and become attached to the objects of their desires. While trying to fulfil desires they crave for fruits of their actions. In doing so, they pitch up and pursue self-imposed duties tirelessly. And become bound by them. The result of their labour is suffering and sorrow in their lives. Instead, gain freedom and happiness. Cast off all selfish desire and worldly motive appended to your action. Render your work sacred. Surrender to the total plan of nature. *Thy will be done* should be your attitude to work. Not, *my will be done*. Your selfish desires and clingings render your business and life mundane. Work without attachment and craving is worship. That is the principle of renunciation. Why have any motive for work? Work itself is most rewarding, entertaining, blissful. Employ this simple principle of work in practical life. The wide world becomes your temple. All your activities become one divine chant. When you thus begin to work in a spirit of renunciation, the world returns your courtesy. Wealth and prosperity are at your door. That is the law.

Remember work is your creation. You impose duties upon yourself. But you are the ultimate master. Duty need not lord over you. You are your own lord. Not realising this you turn pale at the thought of duty. Become a mere machine of duty. And get into a fever of doing. Hurrying and worrying all the time. Impassioned by your responsibilities in life. Duties and responsibilities threaten you. Harass you day in and day out. You have created a frankenstein of duty. This is ridiculous. Remember your self-imposed duties and responsibilities are not indispensable. The world can take care of itself. It does not need your help. Nor does it wait for your condescension. The world will go on and on. Nevertheless, work must you perform. You ought to take to work as a prince takes to sport. Not as a drudgery or burden. Your life is one big game. Full of fun and frolic. The most laborious undertaking pursued in the right spirit is found to be all play. Intense work undertaken thus is no work at all. That should be your attitude to work.

Action performed in a spirit of detachment leads you to the state of perfection. To realisation of your supreme Self. Ironically, the scripture defines Self-realisation as the state of actionlessness. A state transcending all action. Actionlessness cannot be gained by merely renouncing actions but by acting in a spirit of renunciation. You will have to plough through action to transcend action. Use the world to transcend the world. Just as you use a thorn to remove a thorn embedded in your flesh. Hence act on in the world with your mind fixed on the Self. You are bound to reach that supreme state.

Chronology of Action

Action is a symbol of life. As long as you live you act. The type of action executed differs from individual to individual. It depends upon the inherent cause that produces it. The root of action is one's innate nature. Every human being is distinctly individualistic. His inherent tendency, innate bent, inmost nature is known as *vasanas*. *Vasanas* are the result of the past. Past actions produce present *vasanas*. And present *vasanas* produce further actions. *Vasana* is the cause and action, the effect. Again, action becomes the cause and *vasana*, the effect. This cause-effect cycle goes on like the phenomena of tree and seed, hen and egg etc.

Vasana therefore is the seed of action. The prime mover in the mechanism of action. *Vasana* is unmanifest. Action is the final manifestation of *vasana*. Each *vasana* before reaching its full expression, passes through the stages of thought and desire. In the chronology of an action, *vasana* produces thought, thought produces desire and desire produces action. The unmanifest *vasanas* in you lie dormant as your potential nature. It is the state of deep-sleep, which means dreamless sleep. When your *vasanas* manifest they first appear as thoughts in your intellect. Your intellect therefore entertains thoughts according to the nature of your present *vasanas*. In the second stage of manifestation, *vasanas* express as desires in your mind. Your desires again will be in the nature of your *vasanas* and thoughts.

Consider the example of a painter. A painter is one who has a *vasana* for painting. While he is asleep his *vasana* remains dormant without expression. When he wakes up the *vasana* expresses itself in the intellect as thought of painting. The thought manifests in the mind as desire for painting. The desire expresses in the physical body as action of painting. It follows therefore that as long as your *vasanas* exist there will be a constant flow of thoughts, desires and actions. And when your *vasanas* are exhausted, your thoughts, desires and actions become extinct. The total exhaustion of *vasanas* is the exalted state of Self-realisation. Described as the state of *vasanalessness*, thoughtlessness, desirelessness or actionlessness. People have misconstrued this state to mean abstinence from action, even as their *vasanas* remained within. Consequently, they imposed physical restraints and denied themselves material or sensual life. Little realising that *vasanas*, thoughts and desires lingered within and frustrated their lifestyle. Such practices led to suppression rather than sublimation of the personality.

The mission of human life is to eradicate *vasanas*, thoughts and desires. *Vasanas* form the mass of ignorance that veil your divine Self. You attain Self-realisation by wiping out the last trace of *vasana* in you. The knowledge of Vedanta helps you remove the mass of *vasanas* and discover your Self.

Vasana has been indicated as your inherent nature. But that would not be a proper definition. In truth, *vasana* is that which produces the inherent nature. It would be more appropriate to indicate *vasana* as being merely the primary cause or source of thought, desire and action. Your intellect can comprehend thought, desire and action. But it cannot comprehend *vasana*. Since the intellect is a product of *vasana*.

The basic material composing the human personality is *vasanas*. You are therefore a substantial form of your insubstantial *vasanas*. This idea is subtly brought out by the use of camphor in the temple. A temple has a deity in the innermost sanctum, surrounded by three enclosures. The sanctum is dark. A small oil lamp burns at the altar of the deity. The priest lights a piece of camphor from it. The camphor burns away to illumine the darkness within. The light reveals the deity to the devotee's vision.

The ritual is significant. The temple is designed to represent a human being. The deity in the sanctum stands for *Atman*, the supreme Self within you. The Self is dark, unknown. To reach the Self you must first cross the limitations of the three material layers of your personality. Symbolised by passing through the three enclosures. When you do this, reach your inner core, the preceptor is said to give you the knowledge of Self. Camphor is a solid substance. When exposed to the atmosphere it sublimates into mere fragrance. Camphor closely resembles *vasanas*. *Vasana* is a Sanskrit word derived from its root *vas* meaning scent, fragrance. *Vasanas* produce your personality traits. When your *vasanas* are good you are pleasant. When your *vasanas* are bad you are foul. *Vasanas* are insubstantial. Yet they go to make up the substantial human form. The preceptor helps you burn up your *vasanas* in the fire of knowledge. The process leads you to the goal of Self-realisation.

Renunciation in Action

Thought, desire and action emanate from *vasanas* like a video projection from a compact disc. Every being acts according to its own *vasanas*. A human alone, amongst all living beings, has the choice of action. Other living creatures are denied the freedom to act apart from their inherent nature. A tiger is ferocious. It can never be meek and mild. It must strike and kill. Whereas, a cow is docile by nature. Far from destructive. Animals thus live through a choiceless pattern of life. An animal fulfils its *vasanas* in the realm of activities into which it is born. Following its determined course, an animal neither evolves nor devolves. But a human enjoys freedom of action. He could be most sacrificial to the society. Or be extremely harmful. He could consciously exhaust his *vasanas* and rise to greater heights of perfection. Or accumulate *vasanas* and sink to lower depths of degradation. The choice to evolve or devolve is rendered possible because a human possesses the unique faculty of self-effort. Self-effort gives the freedom of action independent of *vasanas*. The present *vasanas* set the pattern of one's life. But self-effort can modify or change the pattern. This is a prerogative a human being alone enjoys.

Exercising the choice of action you must first select a field of activity conducive to your *vasanas*. From early childhood you display a distinct interest, a leaning towards a particular branch of life. It may be science or literature, philosophy or medicine, any field of activity. You would do well to choose the field of your interest. Activities which are consistent with your inherent nature are called *svadharma*. Whereas those which are alien to your nature are *paradharma*. *Svadharma* activity helps you progress, evolve in life. While *paradharma* activity is detrimental causing you to regress, devolve. People commit the fundamental mistake of choosing an alien field of activity. Because they have inherited it or is just convenient for them to do so. The scripture warns you against this error in life. It will not be in your interest to choose a field of activity alien to your nature. While choosing a field compatible to your nature would promote your material and spiritual growth.

Having chosen the appropriate field you must execute the right actions in life. This is important since you are given the choice of action. The general trend in human activity is to indulge in personal feeling. Attraction or repulsion seem to initiate your actions. You ought not to let your likes and dislikes determine your life's activities. There is a grave error in letting your emotional feelings take over your life thus. Likes and dislikes manifesting without discretion could turn out to be your worst enemy. If you feed them indiscriminately you court destruction. Your actions need proper direction. The intellect should guide your likes and dislikes in every action. Do as reason bids you. What you like to do may be opposed to what you ought to do in life.

"Perhaps," says Thomas Huxley, "the most valuable result of all education is the ability to make yourself do the thing you have to do when it ought to be done, whether you like it or not. It is the first lesson that ought to be learned and however early a person's training begins, it is probably the last lesson a person learns thoroughly." If you wish to live up to the dignity of a human being your intellectual judgement, rather than emotional impulse, should be the guiding factor in your activity. Those whose activities yield to mere emotions reduce themselves to the status of lower beings.

Satan tried to tempt Jesus Christ with all sorts of worldly attractions. To lure him away from his spiritual stance. Christ would have nothing to do with those temptations. His response to Satan turned out to be a great message to humanity: *Get thee behind me Satan, I will have none at thy hands.* Christ's mission was divine. His intellect stood by his noble mission. So must you relate to the world. Never yield to its temptations. Stand firm. Do not allow them to obstruct your mission in life. There is nothing wrong in transacting with the world. But ensure that your worldly affairs do not impair your progress in life. When they entice you away from your mission, you should take the grand stand of the Lord.

In exercising your choice of action remember that no act can be labelled virtuous or vicious per se. It would not be proper to classify certain acts as righteous and others as unrighteous. Virtue and vice is a thing of the heart. Good or bad actions have to do with the state of your mind. And not with your gross physical actions. To reform yourself therefore, it is not your body but your mind that has to be rehabilitated, reconstituted.

In a real life incident, a man pulled out an automatic in a crowded restaurant and mercilessly shot down scores of people. Another person behind him chanced to have a gun with him. He shot the killer down. Now examine their actions. The actions were the same. But one was a mass homicide. The other was an act of service to the rest exposed to death. It is the intention that makes an action virtuous or vicious.

Work is best when done impersonally. No sooner one asserts the selfish ego, work is spoilt. Thus should your mind be unattached to the work you perform. Fix your mind upon your divine Self within while you work. Be objective in what you do. Do not get mentally entangled in the affairs of the world. You must learn to live in your home, your office, society as an impersonal witness. Never get mixed up or attached to them. People believe that when they do not get attached and involved in worldly matters they cannot work, progress in life. It is an erroneous concept. The truth is the opposite. The moment you get entangled in the world your work suffers. Whereas when your ego, your little self is absent, when you are unattached and impersonal, work turns out perfect. You progress in life.

Look at the world as a witness. It becomes a source of enjoyment. Get entangled in the activities of the world. It turns into a misery. Therefore learn to perform your action detachedly. Find joy in work itself. Not in the result. The fruit of labour cannot bring you any more happiness than labour itself. Yet, the world believes the result obtained provides more joy than work. Reflect carefully. Do not give undue importance to applause or censure, success or failure. Try to understand the futility of material pursuit. Objects gained by your effort only mislead you. Be not concerned with the fruit of action. Just carry on with what you ought to do. Then alone you find true fulfilment in life.

Three Types of Action

Human activities fall broadly under three categories based upon the manner in which they are performed. They are:

Action performed with selfish desire   •
Action with unselfish desire
Action without desire

The first type of action is propelled by an individual's egocentric desire. To satisfy his selfish motive. To gain personal profit. He toils and sweats all his life for procuring more comfort and pleasure for himself. Which perhaps extends up to his family. He entertains no other ideal, goal. The purpose of life does not reach beyond his egocentric acquisition and enjoyment. This is the lowest form of existence.

As a person turns spiritual his work becomes less selfish. He visualises a high and noble ideal in life. An ideal which serves a common cause. Directed to benefit his community or country. His activity is no longer confined to mere personal pleasure or profit. As a result the desire loses its selfish stigma. The ideal for which he works embraces the welfare of the people at large. He strives and struggles for their happiness.

And as he reaches spiritual perfection he becomes free from desire. Works with a sense of detachment. Merely does what he ought to do. With no desire propelling him to act. Nor anxiety driving him to gain the fruit of action. He lives in a state of fulfilment. Revels in the bliss of his supreme Self. Enjoys self-sufficiency. None of his actions can give him any more pleasure or joy. He thus carries out his work in a spirit of renunciation. That should be your attitude towards work.

Renunciation means getting rid of the selfish ego. Banishing egocentric desires. It is work minus desire. Cast off your worldly motive to work. Exorcise the evil spirit of desire. Do not become a slave to attraction and repulsion. Be poised, objective in your work. Like and dislike, desire and anxiety pollute your work. Serve without a motive. Service is worship. The law of life is that your mind should be at rest while your body is engaged in action. Let the activities rest in your mind as objects of the world rest on the retina of your eyes. Hills and valleys, flora and fauna, things and beings lie wholly, faithfully, gently on your retina. They do not burden the eyes. Your eyes remain ever free and unaffected. Just so should your mind remain undisturbed by life's activities.

Take a look at nature. Learn your lessons from the sun, moon and stars. They work tirelessly. Impersonally. The good earth yields vegetation. The rivers flow. Flowers bloom. Give out sweet fragrance. With no ego prompting them. No personal motive. No selfish desire to fulfil. So too, let your work be free from the taint of egoism and selfishness. Try to emulate the magnificence of nature. Rise above the idea of the little self. Banish the thought of doership. Discard the selfish ego. Your work then turns out glorious. You will command prosperity and peace. But if you succumb to your ego, work suffers. You cease to be peaceful or prosperous. That is the law.

People carry the impression that work suffers when desire does not stimulate it. They are afraid that work will come to a halt if they lose their desires. This is not true. As evident from the life of a child. The child is one of the most active beings. Ever bubbling with energy. Effervescing with activity. Yet the child has no motive or desire, no plan or scheme, hope or expectation in its mind. Similarly, in your life there need be no desire for success, no expectation of reward. In fact, desire and expectation impair your activity. All you need to do is to let your intellect set a pattern of life and plunge into action. Not worry over the dead past. Nor get anxious about the unborn future. Just act in the living present. Then alone will work turn productive, successful. Few understand this law. People are steeped in conservative ignorance. Do not fall in line with the ignoramuses. Stand by this fundamental principle of action. You will be crowned with enduring peace and prosperity.

CHAPTER VI

STRENGTH OF EMOTION

Emotion and Intellection

The philosophy of Vedanta is profound. It eludes the grasp of the common person. Its true spirit has been lost. Time and again, critics raise an objection to Vedanta. They believe it inculcates callousness. That it has little regard for human relation. Destroys humane feeling. Makes one indifferent, irresponsible towards the affairs of the world. The criticism is baseless, untenable. Ironically, Vedanta engenders chaste feelings. It only changes the quality of feeling from sensual to sublime. Transforms the character of emotion from personal to impersonal, selfish to unselfish, preferential to universal. Converts the frail form of emotion into a pillar of strength. In fact, the transformation is brought about by the clarity of thought that it develops. Thus does Vedanta rehabilitate, regenerate humanity with human nature. Yet its great blessing is misconstrued and denied to the human race.

People wrongly believe that a person imbued with Vedanta is devoid of emotion. Not realising that Vedanta only cautions humanity against the onslaught of emotions. The flood of emotion can overpower you. Victimise you. Literally destroy you. William Shakespeare portrays this truth magnificently in his plays *King Lear, Othello, Macbeth* and others. You must therefore keep your emotions well under the control of your discerning intellect. Be a master, no slave of your passion.

You may entertain passion and not turn passionate. Harbour emotion and not become emotional. Have sentiment and not be sentimental. Emotionalism upsets your intellectual balance and poise. Passive subservience to emotion ruins your material and even spiritual wellbeing. Your intellect, rather than the impulse of your mind, should guide your life's activities. Do not fall a prey to your like and dislike. Nor yield to your feeling and emotion. Learn to become self-sufficient. It is the prerogative of the human race.

Oliver Goldsmith portrays an ideal human being in his poem *The Village Preacher*. The poet describes the village preacher as one whose intellect reigns over the mind's feeling and emotion. His heart is replete with chaste emotions for his fellow-beings. But never does he let his emotions disturb his intellectual poise. His head rules his heart. Goldsmith uses a striking metaphor to describe the grandeur of the preacher's personality. Compares him to a tall cliff that rises well above the level of the clouds. The clouds gather around the breast of the mountain. But do not disturb the serenity of the peak. The clouds represent the emotions of the mind. The peak, the intellect. The emotions of the preacher never unsettle his intellectual awareness. The poem concludes with this metaphor:

> To them his heart, his love, his griefs were given,
> But all his serious thoughts had rest in heaven.
> As some tall cliff that lifts its awful form,
> Swells from the vale, and midway leaves the storm,
> Though round its breast the rolling clouds are spread,
> Eternal sunshine settles on its head.

To have emotions therefore is a virtue. But it would be a grievous error to let them interfere with your intellectual awareness and judgement. That would be tantamount to spiritual weakness. Nevertheless, history reveals that humans have let their emotions overthrow discretion and judgement.

In the *Bhagavad Gita* the great warrior Arjuna was
overwhelmed by his emotions. Completely deluded, he lost
his intellect. He could not carry out his obligatory duty as a
warrior. He laid down his bow and arrow and refused to fight
a righteous war. Lord Krishna rehabilitated him with the
knowledge of right values of life. It cleared his delusion. Set
his thinking right. Arjuna rose over his weaker emotion and
fulfilled his obligation as a warrior.

Facets of Emotion

The human mind is composed of a wide variety of emotion. It
ranges from obscene to pure, gross to subtle, demonic to
divine. The quality of the emotion would depend on the
direction it takes. An emotion that merely satisfies one's
selfish, self-centred interest would be classified as impure,
ignoble. Whereas, that which extends beyond one's personal
interest to accommodate the welfare of the community at
large would be pure, noble. And when the emotion rises to
embrace the entire universe, becomes all-pervasive it is
considered divine.

Emotions become detrimental when they are concentrated in
your selfish interest. Emotion acts like medicine. Medicine
cures a disease when administered in proper dosage. The
same medicine turns harmful, even fatal when consumed in a
concentrated form. That explains why medicine bottles bear
the stamp POISON on their labels. It is meant to warn users
against concentrated dosage. So too, Vedanta cautions you
against the peril of excessive egocentric emotion. A selfish
emotion constricted to extremity could prove fatal. It is in
your interest to heed this warning and avoid the devastating
effect of emotion.

A few emotions are described below and analysed. Their
different features projected. The emotion being the same, the

difference in its quality and texture makes or mars a person. Study them carefully. Chasten your emotions. Make good use of them to mould yourself into a perfect human being.

Love

Love is being in harmony with one and all. Love means realising your identity with the world. Your oneness with beings. To regard them as you would the different parts of your physical body. Every part of the body is dear to you. You look at it, look after it as your whole being. Be it your fingers or toes, your eyes or ears. So must you feel and realise the unity with your fellow-beings. Your oneness with the entire universe. That is love. A feeling that helps you maintain a perfect harmony with the world. You then live in peace and bliss. And if you lack the feeling of oneness, consider yourself separate and distinct from the rest, you would fall out of harmony with the world. You deprive yourself of this great emotion of love. And live a life of suffering and sorrow. That is the law.

The concept of love has been totally distorted. What people call as love is far from true love. What the world understands as love is personal, preferential attachment. Attachment binds you. Makes you dependent upon the object or being of your attachment. Leads to your downfall. Little wonder people say, "You have fallen in love!" You must give up this clinging, selfish, personal attachment which passes off as love. And develop the true form of love. A perfect human being is all-love. You observe it in the child. A child is an embodiment of love. It has no motive, no desire, no personal attachment. It is not being a lover but is love itself. Everyone is drawn towards it. The whole world adores the child. You must learn to follow the example of the child. Give up your selfishness. Get rid of preferential relationship. Dissolve personal attachment. Rise above egocentric motive and desire. You thus merge with the fundamental element of love. You become the centre of attraction in the world. A magnetic personality. A true human being. Thereafter, goodness flows out of you to the rest of the world. Those who mean to serve the world would do well to develop such purity of love.

Love and attachment are opposed to each other. Attachment is perversion of love. Attachment to an object or being generates an aversion to other objects and beings. When you are preferentially fond of anybody, you distance yourself from the rest. That is a fact of life. A child has no such attachment. Its love is all-embracing. But when the child grows up into a young man, he falls in love. Now being attached to his lady love, he develops a preferential relationship with her. To that extent he turns indifferent towards others. Parents, brothers, sisters and the rest become a burden on him. He segregates himself from them. True love is lost. All that he desires, craves for is his beloved. Everyone else, everything else means nothing to him. He finds them all insipid, detestable. People call that love. In truth, it engenders hatred. So when Vedanta cries out to give up love, it means give up hatred. Inclusive love and not exclusive attachment is the unfoldment of heaven.

When you are attached to any object or being, you suffer from the sorrows thereof. Parents attached to their children are ever agitated. They are troubled with worry and anxiety through their lifetime. If you are attached to the new carpet in your home you feel miserable when someone walks in with wet feet. When you are attached to your car, a dent in its body is a pain in your heart. You must therefore transform this unilateral passion into universal adoration. Develop a unison with the world. Which is unison with God. A true spiritual master has attained that catholicity. He lives like anyone else in his home or society. But his mind is not confined to his individual unit. He meticulously carries out his obligatory duty and responsibility. Yet his mind remains ever unattached, pure and loving. Follow the footprints of such great souls. Give up your petty attachments. Harbour pure love. You then become a source of peace and bliss to humanity.

The experience of love, the expression of this feeling seems to emerge initially with your partner, your child. You perhaps did not experience it as clearly until you raised a family. Having generated this noble feeling of love, do not restrict it, confine it to the family unit. Let the rays of your affection radiate all over. Your fondness permeate every being. Your love pervade the flora and fauna, hills and valleys and fill up the entire universe. Your home therefore should be the centre and not the boundary of your affection.

Kindness

Kindness is a feeling of tenderness, gentleness. A compassionate, benevolent attitude of the mind. A noble emotion that renders the human species supreme. A fine trait that gives humans the spiritual edge. Kindness is like fragrance in a rose. An essential feature of religion. Religious practice without kindness of heart is a mockery. And yet, the much-talked-of religious stalwarts seem to ignore, much less possess the essence of spirituality. Without kindness there can be no spiritual evolution. Ella Wheeler Wilcox presents this idea succinctly:

> *So many gods, so many creeds,*
> *So many paths that wind and wind,*
> *While just the art of being kind*
> *Is all the sad world needs.*

The concept of kindness has been gravely misconstrued in India. They blunder in following the spiritual doctrine of *ahimsa*, non-injury. And refuse to inflict any form of injury. They are more concerned about their act of kindness rather than thought of kindness. Shakespeare points out this human weakness in his play *Hamlet* when he advises that one needs to be sometimes cruel only to be kind. The Hindus have followed the doctrine of *ahimsa* blindly. They have abstained from injuring anybody irrespective of the consequences accruing therefrom. Even if that led to their own destruction later. This fanatic approach to life has rendered the Hindu race passive and vulnerable. A weakness that turned out to be a diabolic weapon in the hands of the oppressors and invaders. Which was made use of to destroy the Indian tradition, culture and religion.

The epic *Mahabharata* highlights this grave error and offers corrective measures. Wherein the great hero Arjuna was overwhelmed by a flood of emotion. He refused to injure and destroy his kith and kin arrayed in the opposing forces. He would not fight. And sought Krishna's advice. Krishna recharged Arjuna with a higher vision to fight for a noble cause. To revive righteousness in the state. For which the war, injury and destruction was inevitable. Arjuna corrected his vision. He rose, fought and brought about enduring peace and happiness to the people.

Pity

Pity is a feeling of sympathy for the sufferings of others. An impulse of sorrow for their misfortune. An immature emotion. A human weakness. Some people spend their life trying to please others. Consider it cruel to break another's heart. They yield to weak pity. And torture themselves catering to others' feelings. You cannot live your life thus merely feeding others' emotions. Your character lies in upholding your intellectual conviction through your life's journey. And not letting yourself be victimised by weaker emotion.

This weakness stems from ignorance of the general plan of nature. The world is meticulously programmed by the

principle of cause and effect. Every effect has a cause and
cause, an effect. You reap what you sow. You get what you
deserve, not what you desire. It is the law of action, the law of
karma. When a pitiable scene confronts you, let your intellect
assess it. And control your surface emotion. Do not let your
emotion cloud your intellectual judgement. Thus must you
act with discretion. Your action then befits what the situation
demands.

Charity

A charitable disposition enriches life. You are rich by what
you give. The only right you can claim in this world is to
give. You may give wealth or service, feeling or knowledge.
The spirit of giving provides you with the happiness you
seek in the world. Nevertheless, you blunder in seeking
happiness through asking, taking. Prayer and worship has
been reduced to licensed beggary. People all over the world
pray for success or progress, wealth or health, property
or progeny. Their list of desires and demands is endless.
They do not realise the futility of such prayer. No sooner
the spirit of asking, taking enters you it destroys whatever
little peace and happiness you possess. You are unaware
that your Self is supreme. The kingdom of heaven lies
within you. You are a monarch, no beggar. You need not
ask for anything. You have everything. You have only to
realise that. You then develop the spirit of charity; to share,
to give.

There is a story of a sage who lived in total contentment,
peace and bliss. Two gestures summed up his life: *He gave, he
forgave*. He was a picture of selflessness. With no like or
dislike. No desire or expectation. Lord Shiva and consort
Parvati, pleased with the sage's devotion, descended upon
earth to bless him. The good man was then mending his torn
clothes. He prostrated to the divine visitors. Shiva offered

him a boon. To ask for anything he needed. The sage spoke with all devotion, "My Lord, you have provided me with everything. There is nothing I lack that I may ask thee." Ironically, he had no possession and was living on alms! Upon Parvati's insistence Shiva pressed him to choose a boon. The sage felt helpless. His eyes then fell upon the clothes he was stitching. He brightened up and asked, "My request is that the thread should follow the needle!"

This is an example of the lives of enlightened souls. The scriptures have many such episodes. Which display their total helplessness when it comes to asking, receiving. They live a life of absolute fulfilment. Desiring nothing. Expecting nothing. Try to emulate their outstanding stature. Realise that nothing in the world can provide you with peace and happiness. And learn the art of giving. Take the position of a giver. You become a personification of joy and happiness. Practise this in the marketplace, in the street, at work, at home, everywhere. Be you governor or governed, employer or employee, husband or wife, parent or child, you should occupy the position of a bestower, never a petitioner. Think and act in the best interest of the other person. Live life with the attitude of *après vous*, after you. You then become the nucleus of happiness. That is the law. Follow this law and the complexion of the world changes. There is then purity, beauty and joy in life.

Charity does not mean indiscriminate dispensation of wealth. The world comprises two types of people. The vast majority is far from being charitable. The rest indulge in unintelligent charity. Indiscriminate charity has resulted in a lot of misery. It has bred respectable beggars in society. True charity emanates from proper judgement of the intellect. Not something that oozes out of a weak emotion of the mind. In its purest form, charity has the distinction of benefitting the donee as well. Not just the donor.

Victor Hugo in his novel *Les Miserables* highlights the benefaction that charity brings to a donee. In the exceptional charity of a priest to a convict. The convict escaped from prison. Sought shelter for a night. The priest obliged. And gave him supper and a bed to sleep. The convict silently accepted the good man's hospitality. In the middle of the night he decamped with the silver plates of the house. The next morning he was brought in by the police who had caught him. The priest feigned surprise. And embarrassed the policeman, "Why did you harass him? I gifted the plates to him last night." The policeman apologised and left. The convict was astounded. To crown it all, the priest picked up two solid silver candlestick stands from his desk and gave them to the convict with these resounding words of wisdom: *Remember, life is to give, not to take.* The convict took them and departed. Thence, he was transformed into a divine person. He became a symbol of service and sacrifice. Such would be the outcome of true charity.

Likewise, the donor is blessed with the effect of charity. Sacrifice is a synonym for success. So is charity for prosperity. As Swami Rama Tirtha proclaims: *The way to gain anything is to lose it.* The more you run after wealth, the more it recedes. The more you crave for it, the more it eludes you. Leave it alone, it follows you. Work dispassionately, the reward of work courts you.

The phenomenon of colours illustrates this law of life. Light is constituted of seven vibgyoric colours. When an object is bathed in light the seven colours impinge upon it. When the object absorbs, takes in all seven, it appears black. In effect, it loses all the colours. Whereas, when the object does not take in any colour, gives away the seven colours it appears white. When an object appears blue, it has actually given away blue and taken in the other six. It appears in the colour it parts with. An object gains the colour it gives away! Learn this lesson from nature. You gain what you give away, what you sacrifice. Not what you take, aggrandise. Develop the spirit of dispassion, renunciation. You turn pure, divine. Whereas, you aggrandise, amass wealth you turn impure, demonic. That is the law. Oliver Goldsmith puts forward this idea succinctly: *Where wealth accumulates, men decay.*

Effects of Manifestation

A feeling directed to a high ideal is noble. Your attitude to serve and sacrifice is indeed commendable. They are fine emotions which embellish your personality. Nevertheless, Vedanta cautions you against the adverse effects of manifesting them indiscriminately. However chaste an emotion be, it would be unwise to express it without intellectual direction. An unintelligent manifestation of even a good emotion may bring about a negative result. For example, you may love all creatures alike. Appreciate and admire their individual beauty and grandeur. Yet you cannot express your feelings for them in the same way. You may pick up a kitten and caress it but would not do that to a serpent.

You may love your spouse dearly. But you cannot afford to express your emotion indiscriminately at all times. If you do so it would cause nausea to the other. The relationship may end in bitterness, perhaps a separation. A parable explains the effect of unwise expression of emotion. A serpent lived in the outskirts of a village. It was a menace to the villagers. It attacked and poisoned many of them. One day a sage passed that way. The serpent charged out of its hideout. It was about to strike. The sage stood unperturbed. The assailant recognised the divine person. And begged his pardon. The good man advised it not to be hateful and cruel. And create so much disharmony. The serpent repented its aggression and vowed to live peacefully.

Days later, the sage returned the same way. And found the creature lacerated with wounds. He enquired as to the cause of its pathetic state. The serpent replied ungrudgingly, "Sir, I merely followed your wise counsel. Expressed my love to one and all. The villagers pelted me with stones and brought me to this condition." The wise man rejoined, "I am sorry I had not conveyed my message properly. I did ask you to live in harmony with others. But not to express your love indiscriminately. Without a feeling of hatred you should have hissed and driven them away."

So it is with life. You must learn to manifest your inner feelings with discretion. With caution. Your intellect must ever be alert to direct your emotions into proper channels. That is intelligent living.

Root of Emotion

An emotion springs from a flow of thoughts. Your thoughts flow towards the world constantly. The thought-flow arises from a sense of unfulfilment, incompleteness, imperfection felt within you. This notion of a lacuna, void is caused by the ignorance of your Self. Your real Self within is supreme, absolute. The rare one realises the Self. Attains the state of absolute fulfilment. But humanity everywhere is ignorant of the Self. Hence, every human feels a void within. The void causes thoughts to run into the world for fulfilment. Just as they run towards food when the stomach is empty. Thus your thoughts constantly reach out into the world for fulfilling a sense of unfulfilment, completing an incompleteness, perfecting an imperfection felt within. The stream of thoughts flowing from you to the objects of the world is known as desire, *kama*. Desire therefore is caused by ignorance of your supreme Self. The Enlightened, who has gained the Knowledge-of-Self, alone is free from desire. Until you reach the state of Self-realisation you would entertain desires. And desires go through several modifications.

Desire is thought-flow. When one continues to feed it the flow thickens. The thicker stream of thoughts develops into greed, avarice known as *lobha*. If however the flow is interrupted, intercepted by an object or being, the thoughts get deflected. The deflected thought-current is called anger, *krodha*. Consider for example, Tom loves Elizabeth. Tom's thoughts run towards Elizabeth. Another suitor, John also loves her. John's courting intercepts Tom's thought-flow. Tom develops anger towards John. Anger therefore is a modification of desire. There can be no anger unless there is an underlying desire. Hence to overcome anger you need to locate the desire and eliminate it.

To control and reduce your desires you must examine your thought-flow. When a thought alights on an object or being, let your intellect observe it at the very beginning. Scrutinise it. Accept or reject it with discretion. If you follow this procedure there can be no indiscriminate thought-flow. No desire formation. Your intellect therefore must be well-developed and alert to avoid such indiscriminate flow of thoughts. If however the intellect is weak, you would develop desire, greed. And since the world cannot always cater to your desires, you become angry at the obstacles you face. As desire, greed and anger well up you would get into delusion, *moha*. Your emotions mounting up to this stage develop into arrogance, *mada* at those below your level of achievement and envy, *matsarya* at those above your level. And when you manage to maintain a level of success in your achievement in the world you entertain fear, *bhaya*. You are afraid of losing what you have gained. Thus a host of emotions invades your personality. They lead you to grief, misery. Perhaps to your ultimate destruction if left unattended. While desire remains the cause of this confusion and chaos.

Desires, besides developing into their modifications, also multiply in numbers like bacteria. They plague the mind with agitation and sorrow. All through life the human mind moves from one desire to another trying to find fulfilment. No sooner a desire is satisfied many others spring forth. Thus you become bound, burdened with innumerable desires. You will have therefore to use the intellect constantly to check, control them. You achieve this by pitching up an ideal in life. An ideal is a cause, a goal beyond your self-centred, selfish interest in the world. If your motive is merely to cater to the welfare of yourself and your immediate family, you breed more desires. But when you entertain an ideal in life, your desire is directed to the higher. Then the desires for the lower wane. Thus raise the ideal gradually as illustrated. From oneself to family to community to humanity to all beings, to the world at large.

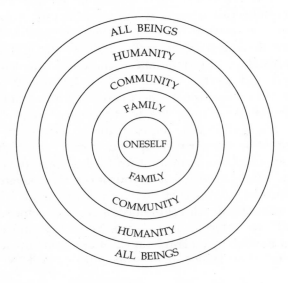

As the quality of the desire becomes subtler the quantity of desires diminishes. The ultimate mission of life is to realise the Self. When all desires dissolve into the supreme Self.

The unrelenting law of nature is that you get what you deserve, not what you desire. Practise this law in life. Deserve, never desire. Rise above desire, the objects of the world seek you. Whereas, you start desiring, craving for anything the objects of your desire elude you. The *Holy Bible* states: *Seek, and it shall be given to you; knock, and it shall be opened unto you.* That is the law. It is a great message to humanity. Seek the kingdom of God, seek the Self within, everything seeks you.

S. Baring-Gould drives home this message in his beautiful poem *The Olive Tree.* Two hermits planted saplings to grow olives. They needed olive oil for their prayer. One of them took charge of the plant. Prayed to God for rain, for sunshine and for frost. God granted them all. Yet his plant eventually perished. While the other hermit left the plant to God's care. Asked for nothing. It grew well and yielded abundant olives.

So is it with life. Everything in this vast universe works meticulously by some mysterious power. The human intellect cannot conceive it. How the infinite beings and things orchestrate into the melody of existence. One ought not to disturb this harmony by one's personal egocentric preferences. If you choose to assert your ego, then that unknown power seems to hand over the reins of control to you. You then lose its grace. Whereas, you surrender your ego to that unknown scheme of nature, you would receive its sovereignty. The poem:

The Olive Tree

Said an ancient hermit bending
Half in prayer upon his knee,
'Oil I need for midnight watching,
I desire an olive tree.'

Then he took a tender sapling,
Planted it before his cave,
Spread his trembling hands above it,
As his benison he gave.

But he thought, the rain it needeth,
That the root may drink and swell;
'God! I pray Thee send Thy showers!'
So a gentle shower fell.

'Lord! I ask for beams of summer
Cherishing this little child.'
Then the dripping clouds divided,
And the sun looked down and smiled.

'Send it frost to brace its tissues,
O my God!' the hermit cried.
Then the plant was bright and hoary,
But at evensong it died.

Went the hermit to a brother
Sitting in his rocky cell:
'Thou an olive tree possessest;
How is this, my brother tell?'

'I have planted one and prayed,
Now for sunshine, now for rain;
God hath granted each petition,
Yet my olive tree hath slain!'

Said the other, 'I entrusted
To its God my little tree;
He who made knew what it needed
Better than a man like me.

Laid I on Him no conditions,
Fixed no ways and means; so I
Wonder not my olive thriveth,
Whilst thy olive tree did die.'

— Sabine Baring-Gould

The philosopher of America, Henry David Thoreau enjoins:
> *Whate'er we leave to God, God does*
> *And blesses us;*
> *The work we choose sh'd be our own,*
> *God leaves alone.*

Desire veils the Self

Your Self within is supreme. It is divine. You are the supreme Self. The divinity in you is presently obscured by desires. Cast away, eradicate all your desires. You regain divinity.

Human being minus desire equals God.

In the process of eliminating desires you must ensure they do not reappear in another form. Desires cling to you. You may feel sure of having erased a desire. But it finds its way back in some other layer of your personality. Thus you may have got rid of your passion for material wealth only to slip into a passion for name or fame in the world. You drop a hundred copper coins to pick up a silver coin. That will not bring you any nearer to Godhood. You unveil your Divinity only when you have clean dropped all your desires. Banished your selfish ego. You cannot do it in halves. You must give up the last grain of desire. There is no other way to it. That is the price you pay for regaining your Divinity.

CHAPTER VII

LIGHT OF WISDOM

Veil of Ignorance

There is but one Reality. The supreme God. The omnipotent, omniscient, omnipresent *Brahman*. Beyond the sphere of time, space and causation. Though all-pervading, God is located in the Self within. Just as a government spread all over the country is located in its capital. The philosophy of Vedanta gradually instils the knowledge of the Self. By which you transcend the limitation of your body, mind, intellect and merge with your supreme Self. You regain your infinite Being.

Ignorance of the one Reality projects the pluralistic phenomena of the world. Just as the ignorance of a rope lying in the dark projects an illusory snake. It is the Reality, *Brahman* alone that appears to you as the universe. The creation of the universe therefore is brought about by the ignorance of your intrinsic, primal nature. With the dawn of knowledge of your true Self the entire world folds back. You merge with the supreme, all-pervading Reality.

The ignorance of Self keeps you in darkness all through your life. Groping in the self-created deluded world you get the knocks and shocks of life. Imagine yourself moving about in a room plunged in darkness. You would strike against niches and notches, fittings and furniture. And injure yourself.

So too, you grope in ignorance in the world and suffer the pangs of sorrow and misery. The solution to this problem is to bring light into the room. The light of wisdom into your bosom. Gain the knowledge of your supreme Self. It is ignorance that converts the kingdom of heaven into a veritable hell. You may use your body to enjoy sensual pleasures, your mind to indulge with emotional joys, your intellect to entertain with knowledge. They may give you some temporary satisfaction. No more. These material equipments cannot provide you with enduring peace and happiness. The knowledge of Self alone can reach you to that eternal Abode of bliss.

The ignorance of Self generates endless desires. The desires develop into several modifications like greed, lust, delusion, arrogance, envy, hatred, anger at the gross level. Or into aim, ambition, aspiration at the subtler level. All these passions hold you a hostage to the world. You are thereafter bound in the terrestrial realm of desire and ambition. The way out of your bondage and consequent suffering is to dispel the darkness of ignorance. The knowledge of your Self provides the light of wisdom which discharges your desires and worldly clingings. This light glows eternally within you. Light you are. You need not seek or pray for light. You gain the light through study, reflection, contemplation upon the truths of life laid down in Vedanta. Approach them freely, independently. With no bias. Let your intellect examine, analyse and accept the truths on their own merit. The process of learning will gradually unveil the Self within. The knowledge of Self thus dispels ignorance. Resurrects your divine Being.

Knowledge and ignorance differ in degree, not in kind. The higher rung of the ladder is knowledge while the lower is ignorance. They are relative terms like light and darkness. Light and darkness are also different in degree, not in kind.

The electric light is bright compared to the dullness of candlelight. The same electric light becomes dull apropos the brilliance of sunlight. Light and darkness, knowledge and ignorance therefore are like the positive and negative terms used in mathematics. Along the x-axis or y-axis a point is said to be positive with reference to its negative side. The same point becomes negative with reference to its positive side. Similarly, the knowledge you possess is considered as knowledge only with reference to the lower level of knowledge. The same would be viewed as ignorance with reference to the higher level of knowledge. Therefore, all knowledge acquired in the world falls in the realm of ignorance *vis-à-vis* the absolute knowledge of the Self. Thus, when you attain the state of Self-realisation your ignorance is completely wiped out. You become totally free from desire, suffering and sorrow. You attain the abode of everlasting bliss. Hence, the Reality discovered in your supreme Self is said to be absolute existence, knowledge, bliss.

The infinite state of existence-knowledge-bliss is your essential Being. Your intrinsic nature. Your Self, *Atman*. Which you constantly refer to as 'I': I am a child, I am a boy, I am a man, I am an old man. I perceive, I feel, I think. I am the person-in-the-waking-state, I am the person-in-the-dream, I am the person-in-sleep. The 'I' never leaves you. The Self has been with you forever. You can never lose It. Nevertheless, you believe you have lost your Self. You feel bound by the limitation of your body, mind and intellect. And persecuted by the ever changing world. This is an erroneous belief. The truth remains that you are eternally free. Never bound. Never harassed by the world. All the bondage and harassment you go through are as imaginary as that of your dream. You may dream that you are suffering from penury and starvation. But it is all your imagination. Brought about by the ignorance of your waking state.

Similarly, the suffering and sorrow of this waking world that you complain of is just another projection of your mind. A result of your ignorance of the Self. Your Self is absolute, immaculate, ever blissful. You are ignorant of your supreme Being. You have hypnotised yourself to believe you are the body, mind and intellect. And taken upon yourself their limitations and ordeals. Imposed a self-inflicted suffering and sorrow. This is ridiculous, absurd. You must put in all effort to dehypnotise yourself by asserting your real Self. The body, mind and intellect are mere vestures enveloping your supreme Being. They are your possessions. They belong to you. You are the immaculate Self. You must assert and regain your essential nature. Become your supreme Self, ever free, ever blissful.

The *Atman*, your divine Self is the core of your person. It vitalises your body to act and perceive, your mind to feel and your intellect to reflect, contemplate. The Self is the Abode of everlasting peace and bliss. Yet you are unaware of It. And stay disturbed, sorrowful. You behave like the lady who lamented the loss of her precious necklace. The lady was in great distress. She searched every nook and cranny of her house. Exhausted with her search she sat down in a corner weeping bitterly. Her husband found her in that pathetic state. He enquired as to the cause of her misery. She declared her terrible loss. Her husband was calm and composed. He looked at her rather confused and asked, "What then is around your neck?" The lady glanced at it and felt abashed. She found her necklace which was never lost! This, in short, is the plight of mankind.

Life's mission is to discover one's Self. To gain the knowledge of Self. You need to strive and struggle for it all by yourself. You may take the guidance of savants and saints but must put in your individual effort. You cannot delegate this responsibility. None other than you can redeem yourself.

You are your saviour. The oft-quoted pronouncement of the *Gita*: *You must raise yourself by yourself.* Therefore must you work for the Self, be devoted to the Self, contemplate upon the Self all through life. Spiritual practice is a full-time awareness of the Reality. Not a part-time ritual.

A human being alone has the potential to realise his divine Self. No other creature is blessed with such faculty. Hence, one ought to utilise this proprietary power. Human development is measured by spiritual edification. And spiritual unfoldment marks the progress of true civilisation. Material wealth, emotional wellbeing or secular knowledge have little to do with it. These are no indication of progress in human beings. The so-called advanced nations of the world are far from advanced in the true sense of the term. The much-talked-of developed countries lack fundamental human development. The present-day civilisation has gone off the rails. Modern civilised ones without self-development are but intelligent savages living in spiritual slums.

The world has been deprived of the essence of civilisation. Civilisation has come to mean mere material aggrandisement, emotional excitement and intellectual entrancement. People are enslaved by the glamour of wealth and possession. Even princes and presidents have confined themselves in material compartments with the stench of artificiality and conventionality. Others have succumbed to superficial emotions only to render their minds restless and nervous. Some are lost in the labyrinth of secular knowledges. Humanity gropes in darkness. The world is caught up in false pomp and show of progress and advancement. Neither the government nor the governed are aware of this stern reality. The salvation of nations and individuals lies in realising these falsities and awakening to the reality of the true Self.

How to Gain Wisdom

The world today is afflicted with binding principles and precepts. People are forced to abide by artificial rules of conduct. Mechanical adherence to external rules and regulations cannot change their inner nature. Even threats and punitive actions will not mend matters. Instead that would suppress their minds, frustrate them. Religious dogmas and doctrines thrust upon the masses cannot bring about spiritual development. The way to go about it is to instil the knowledge of the inner Self. That would eradicate sorrow and misery and ensure enduring peace and happiness. The process takes a while. One cannot gain it overnight. Even building the physical body takes time. Developing positive emotions involves more time and effort. While intellectual education takes years, from kindergarten to graduation. Thus, spiritual edification requires far more time, effort, endurance. That explains why people are disinclined to pursue spiritual knowledge. They do not want to set aside time for learning the deeper import of life, the higher values of living. They are averse to effort and exertion. Unwilling to strive and struggle for the truth. And would rather choose the easy way out by following the herd blindly. But that does not help them. Consequently the mass of humanity remains unspiritual. And are harassed by the trials and tribulations of the world.

A child touches a hot plate and screams. It has no knowledge of fire and heat. Educate the child. Acquaint it with the knowledge of fire. It will never get close to it again. So does humanity need the knowledge of life. The fundamental principles of living. The spiritual laws that govern humans and their relation with the world. Spiritual knowledge would remove the stress and strain of life. Lead humanity towards peace and bliss.

An essential prerequisite for acquiring knowledge is awareness of one's ignorance. You must become conscious of your ignorance concerning the spiritual aspect of life. Without being conscious of your limitation you have little chance of learning. But people the world over believe they have the knowledge already. Josh Billings drives home this truth: *The trouble with most folks is not so much their ignorance, as their **knowing** so many things which **ain't so***. It is futile to try and instil knowledge into a person who firmly believes he knows it all. Therefore, if you wish to acquire knowledge you must keep the shutters of learning wide open. Recognise your areas of ignorance. Be ever ready to receive more and more knowledge. Your pursuit of knowledge ends only with the discovery of the Self.

Acquisition of knowledge is not mere cramming of information from external sources. Presently, a person is reputed to be learned when he is acquainted with the thoughts and ideas of others. Equipped with the knowledge contained in textbooks and teachers. Few realise that true education springs from oneself. The word *educate* etymologically means to draw out. Knowledge has to be drawn out of you. Not pushed in. Luminaries like William Shakespeare or Herbert Spencer derived their wisdom from within themselves. You need to study their works to graduate from university. But neither Shakespeare nor Spencer was a graduate. Someone asked Spencer if he was a voracious reader. He instantly quipped, "No sir, if I were as big a reader as others, I would have been as big an ignoramus as others." Thus men of wisdom have been original, independent thinkers. The knowledge laid down by them is no doubt great. But it does not become yours until you contemplate upon it, assimilate, absorb it.

The basic concept of education has been lost. Education has come to mean mere acceptance of past thoughts and ideas. An unquestioning obeisance to authority. More so with regard to religious doctrines and dogmas. Religion has been reduced to fanatic beliefs, fiendish superstitions and mechanical rituals. These parasitic practices have led humanity to extreme fundamentalism. And the religious fundamentalists are destroying the world. Religious texts were no doubt products of revelations of realised souls. But people have blindly accepted them. Without spending thought and reflection upon them. Few have an understanding of the subject. The blind are leading the blind. This has crippled the modern society. Preceptors and precepts of the past are taken more on trust rather than knowledge and understanding. A child grows into a particular faith even before it becomes an adult. And adults too have lost their power of reasoning. There is hardly any study, reflection or research on the truths governing life. The world faces a total stagnation in the field of religion. The soul of religion has been slain and people are hugging on to its carcass.

Great spiritual masters of the past gave out certain aspects of the truth. But no individual master could possibly cover the whole truth. Just as one scientist, however great, cannot present the entire subject of science. Science is the amalgam of the knowledges contributed by numerous scientists. So it is with Vedanta. Vedanta is the ultimate philosophy laid down by several savants and sages who were realised souls. Later on, individual masters brought in several religions only to preserve and present the supreme truth. Like the husk does to the grain. But people all over have gathered the husk and discarded the grain. There is hardly any reasoning left in the world. To locate a person thinking rationally today is finding a needle in a haystack.

People need to go beyond the husk and get to the grain. Approach the truths of life with reason and judgement. The sages gained the knowledge through their own effort.

Through reflection, contemplation and meditation. They do not claim any supernatural power descending upon them. They made it clear that it is the prerogative of every human being to discover his supreme Self. The power that they possessed resides in you as well. If they had derived spiritual energy from the original source within themselves, so can you. It is the birthright of a human. You must educate yourself with the original truths of life. Study them carefully. Analyse them logically. Experiment with them in your life. Accept those that prove themselves. Then knowledge sinks into you. Becomes your own. Makes you spiritually wise. Thereafter, those truths manifest in your thought, word and deed. You lead a spiritual life.

Lord Buddha has cautioned humanity over 2,500 years ago on the important role of reason in human life:

> *Do not believe what you have heard.*
>
> *Do not believe in tradition because it is handed down many generations.*
>
> *Do not believe in anything that has been spoken of many times.*
>
> *Do not believe because the written statements come from some old sage.*
>
> *Do not believe in conjecture.*
>
> *Do not believe in authority or teachers or elders.*
>
> *But after careful observation and analysis, when it agrees with reason and it will benefit one and all, then accept it and live by it.*

So must spiritual knowledge be taken in regulated doses. If not, the knowledge passes through you without producing the desired effect. You could be well-versed in scriptural literature and not turn spiritual. All the sacred information that you gather may not bring about a transformation in your personality. Spiritual books read or discourses heard could make you a scholar at best. You may even author spiritual books. Give religious discourses. And yet remain far from being spiritual. Spiritual growth is measured by the stability of mind. An unstable mind perturbed in the fluctuations of the external world lacks the elements of spirituality. Such a mind is like milk, watery and easily flowing. Whereas a stable mind resembles yoghurt, thick and does not run. The process of preparing yoghurt out of milk is strikingly similar to making a person spiritual.

It has been an age-old tradition among the Indians to make yoghurt in their homes. To prepare yoghurt, milk is first heated to boiling point and left to cool to lukewarm temperature. A small portion of yoghurt leftover for the purpose is then mixed with the milk. The mixture is left overnight. By next morning the thin, running milk is converted into thick, formed yoghurt. In a similar process, a seeker initially goes through the challenges of life. Later, he chooses a relatively peaceful place for spiritual practice. Not the heat of the marketplace nor the cool heights of the mountain. That is indicated by bringing the milk to lukewarm temperature. The little yoghurt of yesterday represents a measured daily dose of Vedanta knowledge left behind by the sages. That is added and stirred. The spiritual truths taken in have to be reflected upon. The overnight period that the yoghurt takes to set indicates that the seeker needs a length of time for the knowledge to seep in. Adopting this procedure the individual emerges with a sound, stable mind. The stability of mind marks his spiritual evolution.

Religious practitioners have not been following the prescribed procedures for spiritual development. They merely run through volumes of scriptural literature. And they do so alongside their material and sensual indulgences. Give no time nor put in any effort to think, contemplate upon the matter therein. Consequently they do not assimilate, absorb the knowledge taken in. All the accumulated knowledge becomes a burden rather than a blessing. No more useful to them than gold on a mule's back is to the mule!

Whereas with the proper intake of spiritual knowledge, you rise from a physical, sensual person to emotional to intellectual to spiritual. People the world over have been denied spiritual education. As a result they are steeped in ignorance. And preoccupied with accumulating material wealth and indulging in their senses. Not realising that wealth and senses can provide only a false sense of peace and pleasure. As a person acquires spiritual knowledge he rises from the physical to the emotional level. He is no more victimised by material and sensual demands. His physical pleasures are shadowed by the joys of the mind. Thus continuing to acquire more knowledge he develops intellectual clarity and awareness. Which provides him satisfaction and solace superior to joys of the mind or pleasures of the body. The culmination of knowledge reaches the seeker to the supreme Self, the Abode of absolute peace and bliss. The ultimate spiritual experience is like blazing sunlight before all other lights.

The ignorance of Self-knowledge makes the life of a person rough and rugged. The trial and tribulation of the world produce worry and anxiety. He remains in a state of stress. But as he chooses to gain more and more knowledge he frees himself gradually from mundane persecution. Thus pursuing the Self he reaches the state of Enlightenment. The entire experience is like rising up in a balloon. On the ground one feels the ruggedness of the surface. Rising even a little above the surface, the humps and bumps are gone. Gathering more height, even hills and valleys make no difference. And at the highest point everything is smooth and graceful. So does the Enlightened feel absolute peace and bliss in the zenith of spirituality.

Those who remain in ignorance complain of iniquity and injustice prevailing in the world. That wickedness is rampant everywhere. The innocent are being deceived and harassed by the vicious. People wonder why the dishonest prosper while the honest suffer. This has been the general grievance everywhere. Few have attempted to analyse and investigate the cause for it. The layperson meekly resigns it to fate. Without realising that there is a reason for this paradox in life. The good suffering at the hands of the bad. A careful scrutiny will show that it arises from the distinctions in the nature of their inner personalities. The ones with a weaker constitution suffer. The solution lies in fortifying the weak. One needs to study the inner constitution. Reflect over it. And strengthen the intellect. Having developed a strong intellect one becomes equipped to deal with the treacherous practices in the world.

The Aggressive and the Passive

The nature of human beings falls under two broad classifications. The aggressive and the passive. The aggressive are those who use their intellect in life's activities. While the passive operate from the level of their mind. Again, each of these can be classified as good or bad. Thus there are the aggressive good and aggressive bad persons. Likewise, the passive good and passive bad. As illustrated below.

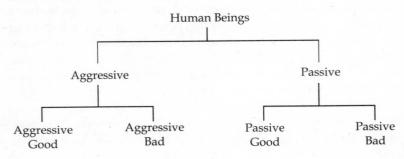

The terms aggressive and passive have a special connotation derived by the use or non-use of the intellect. The mind and intellect are the two equipments which propel human activity. The body cannot act on its own. Actions proceed from either the mind or the intellect. A person is considered passive when he acts from his mind without the guidance of the intellect. Whereas, he who uses his intellect to direct his mind and body to act is classified as aggressive.

A passive person functioning from the mental level lives by his feeling rather than reason and judgement. He does not think, discriminate with his intellect. Nor scrutinise, analyse his actions. Much less question their merit or demerit. He lives a routine, mechanical pattern of life. . Follows blindly the life of his family, predecessors. Environment, situation and circumstance shape his individuality rather than his individuality shaping them. By and large he lives an unintelligent, dogged life of passive acceptance of whatever has gone before him. He lacks the intellect, initiative to use his human resources to rise above the external influences and steer himself to a meaningful, purposeful life.

Such passivity may lean towards good or bad. A passively bad person leads a wrongful, immoral life without really intending to do so. He does not wilfully, guilefully plan or scheme activities to meet his private ends. He does not mean to be bad. He continues to live a wrong way of life usually inherited from his past. His intellect does not consciously examine the nature of his activity and its repercussion. He is caught up in a mode of living which happens to be bad.

So it is with the passively good person. He is involved in a way of life which happens to be good, moral without even realising it to be so. He merely leads his life based on good impulses. He does not plan and execute a virtuous way of

117

living. His intellect has not gone through the process of analysing and determining a right course of life. He carries on unmindful of the repercussion of his action. Such indiscriminate action, however good, may at times prove detrimental to himself and his society.

The aggressive nature is the opposite of the passive. An aggressively bad person viciously plans and schemes, manipulates and manoeuvres immoral, corrupt ways of life for pursuing his selfish motives. He observes no scruples. Breaks custom and tradition, rule and regulation all for his self-centred, personal aggrandisement. The aggressive constantly employ their intellect in programming their life. Whereas, the passive never do so. Consequently, the aggressive are more powerful. The aggressive bad dominate over the passive good and bad. And freely exploit them to serve their personal interests.

The fourth cadre is the aggressively good person. Rare indeed is one in this category. The aggressive good is inherently virtuous, divine. He uses his intellect to plan and programme his course of life for the benefit of one and all. Never functions impulsively. His reason and judgement steers every activity. Directed to the wellbeing of the community. He studies facts, foresees consequences and works towards the best interest of the people. A single aggressively good person can bring about peace and harmony in the community.

The proportion of the passive far exceeds the aggressive everywhere. The reason being that human beings hardly use their intellect. They live at the level of their mind and its emotions, feelings, likes and dislikes. And suffer the consequences. They do not care to exert, strive for bettering themselves. The passive are rising in numbers. Among the aggressive, the good are indeed very rare. So the aggressive bad exploit the weakness of the passive good and bad. The passive become victims of the vicious practices of the aggressive bad. This explains why the honest suffer while the dishonest prosper. It is the intellect scoring over the mind. A law of human nature. The passive do not realise their weakness. Make no attempt to strengthen their intellect. They choose to remain in their mental and emotional frame. Get overpowered by those who operate from the level of the intellect. And complain of the world being corrupt. To solve this problem they must shed their complacency and develop their intellect. Until they fortify themselves they may need to seek intellectual guidance from others to combat the viciousness of the aggressive bad. Thus must the passive turn into aggressive good to be able to confront and conquer the aggressive bad elements in the society. There is no other way to it.

The epic *Mahabharata* presents a picture of the passive and aggressive natures of human beings. The royal cousins, Pandavas and Kauravas, in the epic represent these two categories. The Pandava princes were distinct in their passive goodness. And the Kauravas in their aggressive badness. Consequently, the Pandavas suffered untold humiliation at the hands of the Kaurava prince, Duryodhana. He was a clear specimen of aggressive badness. He schemed and planned the destruction of his passively good cousins.

The Pandavas sought the guidance of Lord Krishna. Krishna was a personification of aggressive goodness. He employed his intellect effectively to destroy the vicious plans of Duryodhana and the rest. The aggressive good prevailed over the aggressive bad. Krishna relieved the suffering of the Pandavas. And resurrected righteousness in the country.

Joy of Learning

The knowledge of Vedanta confers aggressive goodness on you. A knowledge that develops a powerful intellect. Which clearly distinguishes virtue from vice. Provides you the guidelines to destroy evil and protect the good. Thereafter, you will not be victimised by anyone nor would you victimise others. You would mean and do good to the society. Become a beacon of knowledge and virtue for the rest of the world to follow.

People carry the general impression that Vedanta is abstract, terse, inaccessible. Not meant for the common people. And that only those who are brilliant should attempt to approach it. This is not true. The misconception arose because the subject matter of Vedanta has to be learnt and practised like any technique, skill or art. And the process of learning takes a while for the learner to relish it. The initial period of learning is trying. It puts off even some sincere seekers. Ironically, it is a knowledge which is most fascinating. The study of Vedanta in the early hours of the morning becomes most inspiring. An enchanting experience day after day.

The knowledge of Vedanta is best grasped between 4 a.m. and 6 a.m. If impractical you may choose a time as close to it as possible. The knowledge has to be taken in regulated doses. Approach it as you would any scientific knowledge. Study and reflect daily upon the truths therein. Do not proceed further until you have absorbed the portion already covered. Thus through systematic study and reflection you gain the light of wisdom. A light that will guide you towards spiritual Enlightenment.

CHAPTER VIII

CULMINATION OF HUMAN LIFE

The Role of Religion

The word *religion* is derived from two Latin terms *re* and *ligare*. *Re* means back, again. *Ligare* means to bind, join. Religion is meant to unite one back to one's origin, the supreme Self. Every human being is born with inherent desires which separate him from the Self. The Self within is the Abode of absolute knowledge, peace and bliss. So are you born divorced from the Self. Having lost the Core of your personality, you have meandered into Its enveloping sheaths of the body, mind and intellect. You are now caught up in the maze of perception, emotion and thought. Religion, divested of its dogmatic outgrowths, essentially relieves you from the persecutions of your material equipments and reveals your spiritual Self. It is a mysterious process by which your mind-intellect traces back and loses itself in the inscrutable source, *Atman*, the supreme Self, the soul of all religion. Religion therefore is used to regain your lost identity with your Self. Attain the ultimate spiritual Enlightenment.

This state of Being lies within you. Your Self, *Atman*, *Brahman* is supreme. You will have to transcend the limitation of your body, mind and intellect to reach your Self. The sense organs of the body cannot perceive It. Nor the emotions of the mind feel It. Nor the thoughts of the intellect conceive It. Your Self is the subject, not the object of experience. Hence you cannot contact the Self with your material equipments. You can only become the Self by pursuing the spiritual path. Like the dreamer becoming the waker. The dreamer also cannot perceive, feel or conceive the waker with the dream body, mind and intellect. The dreamer can only transform himself into the waker. The role of religion is to bring about the transformation from the waking state to Self-realisation. That is the goal of human existence. You then become all-knowing, all-blissful.

Your body, mind and intellect transact pleasure, love and knowledge. But they cannot provide you with ultimate satisfaction, contentment, fulfilment in life. The more the pleasures your body indulges in, the more you seek. Likewise the more love your mind is involved in, the more you want. So does your intellect crave for more and more knowledge. There is no end to sensual gratification, emotional contentment or intellectual satisfaction. Hence, all the happiness derived from material equipments is limited, wanting. You can never find satiation through these avenues. For attaining the absolute happiness you will have to go beyond the precincts of your body, mind and intellect. And reach the Self within. Therein lies the absolute happiness that you seek in vain in the external world.

However, the mass of humanity perceive the pleasure and joy in the objects and beings of the world. People actually experience it. Hence they go after them. But these objects and beings present only a false glamour of pleasure and joy. They inherently lack it. This truth is never accepted as people claim their experience to be just the contrary. Even those who profess to know the truth are not well-established in it. They understand it academically. Not really, to live by it. Hence, it becomes virtually impossible to convince people of the absurdity of worldly pursuit while they firmly believe in and continue to draw their share of happiness from it.

This strange phenomenon of deriving happiness from where it does not exist is well portrayed in the reflection of light. The sun above is one while the reflections of the sun are innumerable in the countless reflecting media in the universe. There is light in the sun alone. The reflections have no light inherent in them. You appreciate this when you get close and examine them carefully. So it is with the objects and beings of the world. They do not contain any pleasure or joy. It is the bliss of the Self that is reflected in them. What you enjoy is the reflected bliss. You will realise this when your intellect gets closer and examines them. That the bliss is within you. Not in the external world.

Nevertheless, people devote all their time and energy to worldly acquisition and enjoyment. They spend their lifetime in acquiring material wealth and trying to find enjoyment in what they have acquired. So are the ignoramuses lost in the world seeking the bliss of the Self in Its reflected images. Succumbing to peer pressure, you follow the same pattern of life. Your worldly pursuits sooner or later lead you to despair. You remain confused and confounded. You need not lie low in this state of despair. Wake up to the realities of life. Get wiser with the eternal truths. Use your intellect to examine the objects and beings that seem to have pleasure and joy. Study them carefully. Understand their hollowness. And look for the real source of happiness within you. Seek the supreme Self. The Abode of eternal peace and bliss.

William Cowper portrays the mad pursuits of the human race in his magnificent poem *The Pineapple and the Bee*. The poem draws the parallel of human desires with those of a bee. A bee tries in vain to go through the glass frame to consume the pineapples arrayed therein in triplerow. After wasting half the day it takes its flight another way.

The poet compares the futile attempts of the bee to a man who desires the companionship of a woman passing by in a chariot. He complains of the chariot glass that separates them. In another comparison the poet describes a maid's desires for the jewellery behind a showglass. Both man and woman consume half their lifetime pursuing endless desires for peace and pleasure. They crave for possession and enjoyment of worldly things and beings at the physical, mental and intellectual levels. That is subtly indicated by the triplerow of pineapples. Some linger with vain hopes without doing anything about it. While others break barriers and meet with serious consequences. None realises that the solution lies in looking within.

The poet concludes brilliantly that the wise who have imbibed the truths of life can find bliss in the worst of environment and circumstance. The poem:

The Pineapple and the Bee

The pineapples in triple row,
Were basking hot and all in blow,
A bee of most discerning taste
Perceiv'd the fragrance as he pass'd,
On eager wing the spoiler came,
And search'd for crannies in the frame,
Urg'd his attempt on ev'ry side,
To ev'ry pane his trunk applied,
But still in vain, the frame was tight
And only pervious to the light.
Thus having wasted half the day,
He trimmed his flight another way.

Methinks, I said, in thee I find
The sin and madness of mankind;
To joys forbidden man aspires,
Consumes his soul with vain desires;
Folly the spring of his pursuit,
And disappointment all the fruit.
While Cynthio ogles as she passes
The nymph between two chariot glasses,
She is the pineapple, and he
The silly unsuccessful bee.
The maid who views with pensive air
The show-glass fraught with glitt'ring ware,
Sees watches, bracelets, rings, and lockets,
But sighs at thought of empty pockets,
Like thine her appetite is keen,
But ah the cruel glass between!
Our dear delights are often such,
Expos'd to view but not to touch;
The sight our foolish heart inflames,
We long for pineapples in frames,
With hopeless wish one looks and lingers,
One breaks the glass and cuts his fingers,
But they whom truth and wisdom lead,
Can gather honey from a weed.

— William Cowper

A human being is composed of Spirit and matter. His material components are his body, mind and intellect. His spiritual core is the supreme Self, *Atman*. The Self remains ever the same, eternal, changeless. Whereas, the material equipments are in a flux of change. The body changes. So do its perceptions. The mind changes along with its emotions. The intellect and its thoughts change too. These equipments make perennial demands from the world which itself is constantly changing. Since both sides are

125

in motion, their contact must necessarily cause friction, frustration. How then can there be any stability, harmony in their interaction? Any peace and happiness in the world?

Thus it is your body, mind and intellect that do not meet their demands and suffer. That is no reason for *you* to suffer. Yet you do because of your identification with these equipments. Identification with an object or being is a result of constant thought and feeling flowing towards it. *As you think so you become* is a law of life. Thus when you constantly think of, feel for the body you identify with it, you become one with it. You believe you are the body. Thereafter, whatever happens to your body happens to you. So when your body is warm, you say 'I am warm'. And when your body is cold, you say 'I am cold'. Similarly, you identify with the mind and become one with it. And when your mind is happy, you say 'I am happy'. When it is unhappy you say 'I am unhappy'. Again, identifying with the intellect you say 'I am brilliant, I am dull', when your intellect is brilliant or dull.

The body is bound to be affected by the heat or cold of the world outside. So is the mind affected by joy or sorrow. The intellect by honour or dishonour. But your Self within is immaculate. It remains ever unaffected by the attraction or repulsion of the changing world. If the world is compared to a magnet, the material equipments would be metal pieces and the Self, a wooden piece. The magnet attracts metal pieces. Metal sticks to the magnet. But the magnet does not attract the wooden piece. Wood does not stick to the magnet. If however, the metal and wooden pieces are bound together, the magnet would attract the combination. The combination sticks to it. Nevertheless, the wooden piece in the combination is free. It appears to be influenced, affected by the magnet because of its identification, bondage with the metal piece.

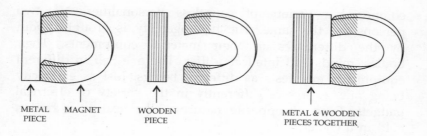

METAL   MAGNET   WOODEN   METAL & WOODEN
PIECE   PIECE   PIECES TOGETHER

Your real Self is supreme. Unaffected by the world. You are the Self. The body, mind and intellect are mere vestures. You do not realise that. And become bound to them. Due to your attachment to these material components you suffer the persecutions of the external world.

The way to get out of your self-inflicted ordeal in life is to shift your focus of attention from the material layers of the personality to the inner Core, Self, *Atman*. You have hypnotised yourself to become the body, mind and intellect. Now, reverse the process. Dehypnotise yourself by asserting your real Self. Understand you are the Self. Reflect upon It. Try to remember It in all your transactions of life. Assert your Self while you perceive or act with your body. While you feel with your mind. Think with your intellect. Never lose sight of the Self. Thus, gradually you will gain identification with your real Self. Become the Self. Regain your infinite Being. Reach the Abode of absolute peace and bliss.

Consummation of Life

The Self is one in all living beings. There is no difference between a saint and a sinner as far as the Self is concerned. The Self in the saint is the Self in the sinner. Yet their personalities are of opposite natures. In fact humanity comprises a variety of countless personalities. No two persons are the same. The heterogeneity is brought about by the differences in their material equipments. Their bodies, minds and intellects differ. The one Self in different equipments manifests as different beings. Just as electricity being one, expresses differently in the variety of electrical gadgets. Even of opposite natures. Like heat in a heater, cold in a cooler.

Your focus of attention is ever upon your body, mind and intellect, your perception and action, emotion and thought. Thereby you experience heterogeneity, diversity in the world. That causes friction, frustration. People become adversaries to combat with. Your mind remains agitated. To find harmony therefore you shift your focus of attention to the Self, the spiritual Core of beings. You will recognise a homogeneity everywhere. Your mind turns peaceful and happy.

In the past, palaces in India had rooms with mirrors all over in their inner walls. The decorated king was wont to look at himself before his appearance in public. He would view his reflections to ensure that his decoration was proper. Once, the palace dog entered the mirror-room. It saw so many 'dogs' all around. Bewildered and terrified, it barked at them. Scampered about. Pounced on them. So did those 'dogs'. Thus jumping, barking and biting, the poor animal collapsed on the floor. This has been the sad plight of human beings. In your ignorance you see the beings of the world as different, opposed to you. You develop animosity, bitterness, hatred towards the world. And suffer mental strain and stress. You must therefore learn to recognise your own Self reflected everywhere. As the king saw himself in his reflections. The Self that enlivens your material equipments is the same that enlivens all other beings. Thus do you develop an attitude of friendship, harmony and love towards the world at large. A feeling of oneness with all beings.

The sun above is all-light. But on earth people experience day and night. Likewise the *Atman*, the supreme Self is all-blissful. Yet you go through the cycle of joy and sorrow. The source of these diverse experiences is your inner Self. You have lost sight of your Self. Your attention and interest is upon the world. You experience the day of pleasure and the night of pain. You must regain your identity with the Self. Your unity with God, the supreme Reality. Utilise your equipments and the world to transcend them all and reach your original Being. The Abode of absolute peace and bliss. Into that state of Being all physical pleasure, emotional joy and intellectual rapture dissolve. That is the culmination of human life.

People the world over do not realise their real worth. The absolute state of Being that lies within them. The infinite happiness of the Self. They have discarded the nectar of divinity within. And are trying to find peace and happiness in the world. All the pleasure and joy derived from the world would not be worth a drop in the ocean of bliss within your own Self. It is a blunder you commit in courting outward objects and beings. Judas Iscariot sold Christ for thirty pieces of silver. So have you sold your Christ within for the shadows of pleasure and joy in the world. You ought to be wiser than that. Your own Self has it all. Seek within. In the Vedic text *Kenopanishad* the guru deplores this grave blunder of humanity. He cries out: He who does not realise the Self here in his lifetime suffers immeasurable loss.

A prince went to a hermitage to pay his respects to a sage. He prostrated before the holy man. The sage promptly rose and prostrated to the prince. The prince was bewildered.

He recoiled and pleaded, "O Master, how could you do such a thing?" The sage asked in turn, "Why did you prostrate to me?" "Because you are a man of renunciation," rejoined the prince, "you have given up this world which we are all running after. You have attained Godhood." The sage softly enquired, "Which do you consider superior of the two — world or God?" "God, of course," the prince replied. "Then, do you realise," continued the sage, "I have only renounced the world but you have renounced God! Who has demonstrated greater renunciation?"

The prince woke up to the reality of life. And soon realised the absurdity of worldly pursuits. So should you. Get to the real source of peace and happiness within you. Realise the divinity of your Self. The entire world pales into insignificance. You will reach the state of Enlightenment. William Cowper extols this state in his poem *The Solitude of Alexander Selkirk*:

> *I am monarch of all I survey;*
> *My right there is none to dispute.*

Personality Chart

The state of Self-realisation lies beyond the three mental temperaments known as *gunas*. Every human is constituted of the three *gunas* classified as *sattva, rajas* and *tamas. Tamas* is the state of an inactive mind. Steeped in inertia, indolence, indifference. The lowest of the three qualities. *Rajas* is that of vacillating emotion and passionate activity. And s*attva,* the highest quality of mind. Poised, serene and equanimous. Above worldly passion and excitement.

These temperaments, *gunas* combined in different proportions account for the variety of individuals in the world. The role of a human in his lifetime is to gradually rise from *tamas* to *rajas* to *sattva* and reach *trans-sattva*. Wherein lies the supreme Self. The ultimate spiritual Enlightenment. To develop the personality and attain the transcendental experience you need to study and analyse these *gunas* thoroughly. Ascertain the nature of the *gunas* inherent in you. And how they manifest in the different facets of your personality. You will then realise what is well and what needs attention, correction.

For this purpose, the *Bhagavad Gita* has classified action and renunciation under the three *gunas*. Furthermore, action itself has been dissected into its constituents as knowledge, actor, intellect, steadfastness and their three gradations defined. Lastly happiness, the underlying purpose of action, has also been classified under the three categories. Thus the grades of *sattva*, *rajas* and *tamas* have been projected on all these facets of a human being. An analysis which enables you to define the exact nature of your personality. It holds a mirror to your inner quality and character. Your nature clearly defined, you can administer corrective measures where there are faults. And rise gradually to the *trans-sattvik* state.

Knowledge *Gnanam*

Sattvik knowledge is that knowledge which recognises the core of all beings as the Self, *Atman*, *Brahman*. The supreme Reality that pervades the pluralistic phenomena of the world. The infinite substratum upon which the world is projected. It is the knowledge of the underlying unity in the diversity of things and beings. A knowledge that finds you the harmony and peace you seek in life.

Rajasik knowledge is that knowledge by which you see manifold beings and not the unifying Self within. You look at them severally. Notice distinctions and divisions. And see the pluralistic phenomena of the world. A diversity instead of the one underlying Reality. It is the opposite of *sattvik* knowledge.

Tamasik knowledge is that by which you cling obstinately to a part as if it were the whole. With no truth backing it. No reason supporting. Which carries dogmatic, fanatic beliefs. Like averring one's religion alone can save the world, none else. And not recognising the truth that lies beyond one's limited vision.

Action *Karma*

Sattvik action is based on one's obligatory duty and responsibility. And not action that merely follows personal like and dislike. It does not spring from attachment to action. Nor is it action undertaken with a craving for fruit accruing therefrom. When you do what you ought to do in the world without a selfish attachment or anxiety for the result, then the action is *sattvik*.

Rajasik action is desire-ridden. Coupled with a longing for its fruit. Undertaken with the egoistic feeling, "I do it all." Causing strain and stress to the doer. It is contrary to *sattvik* action which flows freely, effortlessly.

Tamasik action arises out of confusion, delusion. Action with no regard to one's ability, capacity to perform it. With no concern about its consequence. Heedless and irresponsible of the loss or injury accruing to another or oneself. Such actions ruin one's strength and vitality. Offend human dignity and prestige.

Actor *Karta*

Sattvik actor is not egoistic. Does not have the I-am-the-doer attitude. And is free from attachment. With no preferential relationship binding him to the world. Besides, a *sattvik* actor possesses steadfastness, *dhriti* and enthusiasm, *utsaha*. He is energetic, cheerful and joyful in what he does. And does it with consistency of purpose until the work is done. All along his course of activity he remains disinterested in the result thereof. Success or failure means nothing to him. He maintains a balance of mind through the fluctuations of life's experiences.

Rajasik actor is ever impassioned. His desires are insatiable. He craves for the fruits of his actions. He develops greed for acquisition, possession and enjoyment. And when he meets with opposition in the pursuit of his desires he is hurtful to those opposing them. He would also adopt unscrupulous ways and means to gain his personal ends. He is constantly buffeted by the joys and sorrows that arise from his selfish behaviour. Consequently, his mind remains agitated with worry and anxiety, stress and strain in life.

Tamasik actor has no ideal in life. As a result, he lacks steadfastness in pursuing any course of action. Bereft of culture and refinement, he is vulgar in thought, word and deed. He is stubborn. Obstinately attached to his way of life. Deceptive and misleading. Malicious in dealing with others. Lethargic and indifferent towards his obligatory duty and responsibility. Remains ever despondent and depressed in life. And procrastinates, puts off actions without completing them.

Intellect *Buddhi*

Sattvik intellect is that which clearly distinguishes between the paths of action and renunciation. Chooses that field of activity which is most suitable to one's inherent nature. And rejects what is not. Having chosen the right field it further decides what ought to be done and what ought not to be done therein. And does one's obligatory duties and responsibilities in life. The *sattvik* intellect directs you to fulfil them. And avoid involvement in activity outside this sphere. A human being alone faces the problem of choosing his course of action in life. No creature save the human has this dilemma. All others follow distinct patterns of life according to their individual nature. Ordered, as it were, to live through it without a choice. Whereas, the human being has been given the freedom of choice. William Shakespeare in his play *Hamlet* highlights the dilemma of choice in his oft-quoted words: *To be, or not to be; that is the question.* The *sattvik* intellect has the clarity to choose one's course of life.

The *sattvik* intellect also understands what is to be feared and what ought not to be feared. Certain facets of the world are dreadful. They are detrimental, even fatal. Other facets are beneficial, valuable. Most people in the world court what is fearful and repel what is not. They would freely indulge in the deadly senses. But dread to take to the path of knowledge and renunciation. So has Alexander Pope observed: *Fools rush in where angels fear to tread.* The *sattvik* intellect chooses the right path.

Another serious problem that a human faces is his self-inflicted bondage. He has lost the freedom of the Self. *Sattvik* intellect draws the distinction between bondage and liberation. It exposes the human weakness in attaching oneself to one's body, mind and intellect. In being enslaved by their action and perception, emotion and thought. It provides one the clarity to recognise the glory and grace of the Self within. The Self alone is the seat of true liberation free from the persecutions of the world. Thus freed from bondage the *sattvik* intellect directs a seeker to spiritual Enlightenment.

Rajasik intellect gives the wrong understanding of righteousness and unrighteousness. An erroneous concept of virtue and vice. It wrongly interprets the ethical and unethical values of life. Knows not the obligatory duties and responsibilities in life and errs in the performance of actions.

Tamasik intellect is shrouded in ignorance. Which regards the unrighteous as righteous. Understands vice as virtue. Wrong as right. Views everything perverted. It leads you on towards destruction.

Steadfastness *Dhriti*

Sattvik steadfastness is the unswerving consistency one maintains in the pursuit of the supreme goal of Self-realisation. The firmness in restraining the activities of the body, mind and intellect to steer clear off worldly entanglement and channelising all efforts to attain spiritual Enlightenment.

Rajasik steadfastness is that with which you cling on to duties and responsibilities you have imposed upon yourself. These are your creation. They need not lord over you. Not realising this you turn pale at the thought of duty and responsibility. And get into a fever of doing. That is *rajasik*.

Also, every human being is constantly driven by two motivations in life. To acquire wealth and to enjoy what he has acquired. For this purpose he develops attachment to his work and anxiety for the fruit thereof. The consistency with which he works in this manner is again *rajasik*.

Tamasik steadfastness is the consistency with which a person foolishly keeps imagining, fearing, grieving and despairing. And maintains an arrogant attitude in life.

135

Happiness *Sukham*

Sattvik happiness, arising from the clarity of intellect, is that which feels detestable in the beginning and ends up blissful. The happiness derived from the pursuit of the supreme Self within. Which entails physical restraint, emotional detachment and intellectual understanding of spiritual knowledge. These practices demand effort and discipline. The practitioners find them stiff, even painful at times. Hence the pursuit is said to be detestable in the beginning. However with continued practice they become pleasant, enjoyable. And turn wholly blissful in the end.

Rajasik happiness is the opposite of the *sattvik*. It arises from the senses contacting the objects. Feels pleasant in the beginning and turns painful towards the end. Sensual pleasure is enjoyable only to start with. But the joy diminishes with continued contact. And ends up with pain and sorrow.

Tamasik happiness springs from ignorance of the supreme Self. A happiness delusive of the Self from beginning to end. Arising from sleep, indolence or heedlessness. When you are ignorant of a malady you remain blissfully unaware. It does not agitate you mentally. So also is the pleasure or joy derived from indolence, lethargy, indifference, heedlessness. That type of negative happiness is *tamasik*.

Renunciation *Tyaga*

Sattvik renunciation is relinquishment of attachment and fruit while performing obligations in life. The practice of *sattvik* renunciation is functioning objectively in the world merely fulfilling obligatory duties and responsibilities. With no preferential attachment to action performed. And no expectation of enjoyment of fruit thereof. It is therefore not renunciation of action as such. Ironically, *sattvik* renunciation is defined as performance of action that ought to be done without appendages burdening it.

Rajasik renunciation is giving up action that is painful, out of fear of bodily strain or suffering. In such cases, one would take up the action when the element of pain or fear of suffering is removed. That is no renunciation. Consequently, it is deprived of the fruit of true renunciation.

Tamasik renunciation is relinquishment of one's obligatory duties out of delusion. A human being has to perform two types of duties. One is his regular, routine duties. As the member of a family, society, nation etc. The other is occasional, special duties. But in ignorance, he is confused as to his duty and responsibility and discards what ought to be done. That is *tamasik* renunciation.

Prepare your Chart

The above classification of different facets of action and renunciation provides the material for assessing your personality. Take up each one of them. Study it carefully. Try to match it with your nature. Thus comparing each one of them with your nature you may draw your personality chart. And estimate the quality of knowledge you possess. *Sattvik, rajasik* or *tamasik*. The quality of action you execute. The type of actor you are. Etcetera. All of them examined together present a clear picture of your personality. The areas where *sattva* prevails, where *rajas* flourishes and where *tamas* lingers. This should be of considerable help to locate the areas of your strength and weakness. And administer corrective measures for the development of your personality.

Human beings fall between zero and hundred per cent development. Zero per cent would be like an inert object. One hundred per cent would be a Self-realised soul. Hence, the entire range of people fall between the two extremities. It becomes rather difficult, if not impossible, to clearly define one's personality. The personality chart would therefore serve as a yardstick to measure your spiritual status and programme your evolution.

Section II

Practical Vedanta

CHAPTER IX

THE HUMAN COMPOSITION

Basic Constitution

The mission of every human being is to discover the supreme Self. To realise the eternal Being within you. It requires a study of your constitution. An analysis of its constituents. And how each of them reacts with the external world. Thus through self-study and a programmed application you reach the innermost core of your personality. You realise your divine Self.

A human being is constituted of the divine Self, *Atman* and the body, mind and intellect. The Self is the Spirit. The body-mind-intellect is matter. Matter is inert, insentient. But in contact with the Self it becomes a living being. A phenomenon akin to an electric bulb glowing. The bulb has no light in itself. Nor does electricity. But when the bulb is in contact with electricity there is a brilliant expression of light. So also your matter equipments have no life in themselves. Nor does the Self. But when the equipments are in contact with the Self there is a scintillating expression of life.

The physical body houses the organs of perception and action. The organs of perception take in stimuli from the external world. The stimuli are colour and form for the eyes, sound for ears, smell for nose, taste for tongue and touch for skin. The mind and intellect react with the stimuli. The organs of action send out responses back into the world. If the mind alone reacts with the stimuli, without consulting the intellect, the responses would be impulsive, eccentric, hysterical, leading to insanity. But when the mind consults, takes the guidance of the intellect, the responses would then be objective, discreet, mature.

Whatever be the activities of the body, mind and intellect the Self is the Life-Principle enlivening them all. That is said to be *Atman*, God. The supreme power which vitalises your body to act and perceive, your mind to feel and your intellect to think. Without the presence of the Self, these equipments remain inert as a mass of matter.

However, the sceptic questions the authenticity of the existence of the supreme power. He refuses to accept anything beyond the perceptible, terrestrial world because of inadequacy of thinking material required for conceiving the Transcendental. And dismisses the concept of a transcendental Being as a fanatic belief of a person without reason backing it. Ironically, there are many aspects of the world that the sceptics themselves believe, accept without reason. The most rational, even scientists would find it difficult to live in the world without assumptions and beliefs. In truth it would be practically impossible to go by reason, proof at every turn of life. How do you know that you are the son of your parents? When you go for a meal to a restaurant how do you know the food is not contaminated? When you hire a cab how do you know the driver is sane? There are numerous other questions that remain unanswered in your mind. You perhaps would *prima facie* dismiss these thoughts as absurd, ridiculous. Yet you go through these experiences by mere assumptions, beliefs.

However, these beliefs and assumptions are not totally baseless. They are supported by several corroboratory evidences which stand to reason. Hence they are not blind beliefs. Likewise, the introduction of the supreme Self as the transcendental power, the Godhead vitalising the material equipments into living beings is not a groundless belief. A careful analysis of life's experiences would provide you enough reason to substantiate the belief.

You refer to your equipments as *my* body, *my* mind and *my* intellect. The use of the possessive pronoun *my* indicates that there are two factors, the possessor and the possessed. The possessor is you. And the possessed, the body-mind-intellect. The equipments are therefore your possessions. They belong to you. If this be so, then who are you? Take away the body, mind and intellect from your personality, there seems nothing left. Yet you feel a subject integrating them and claiming these objects as its possessions. That unknown subject has been designated as *Atman*, the Self within.

Furthermore, observe the functioning of your equipments. You notice your physical body constantly changing. So do you find your mind vacillating with a variety of emotions and feelings. And your intellect growing, at times deteriorating, in effect changing. You recognise these changes taking place in your personality. Such recognition is not possible without there being a changeless entity. It is a law of science that a change is noticeable only with reference to a changeless factor. Just as the movement of a train is noticeable only with reference to the immovable objects outside. Whereas the movement of an aircraft is not noticeable as there is nothing in a cloudless sky to relate to. Therefore, the recognition of the changes in the equipments and their functions posits the existence of an unchanging aspect in you. That unchanging Being is said to be the supreme Self.

Yet another corroboratory evidence of an eternal Being is the persistent existence of the 'I' in everyone's life. You use the pronoun 'I' liberally without realising its existence, its significance. The 'I' runs through your entire lifespan. You claim: I am rich or poor, I am a boy or girl, I am young or old. You also say: I am well or ill, I am happy or unhappy, I am brilliant or dull. The same 'I' runs through the equipments and their experiences: I perceive sense-objects, I feel emotions, I conceive thoughts. Furthermore it traverses the realms of the waking, dream and deep-sleep. In the waking state you claim: I am an athlete (waker). In the dream state: I am an invalid (dreamer). And in the deep-sleep: I am nothing (sleeper). These experiences are diverse, heterogeneous. But there is a homogenous entity holding them together. The 'I' pervading the three states of consciousness. Percolating every physical, emotional and intellectual experience. That should provide enough evidence for any rational human being to investigate its presence and purpose in his life.

In a puppet-show the artist is not seen by the audience. From his unseen position he manipulates a number of wires to activate the puppets. The audience is thrilled at their movement and gesture. Children look upon the inert bodies as free agents. Consider them to be independent actors. They are not grown up to visualise the wires and the artist behind the show. But others with a limited insight spot the wires yet fail to recognise the artist behind it. They are quite complacent to believe that the wires are the cause of the show. But the intelligentsia go beyond the wires, understand and appreciate the work of the artist behind it all.

Likewise, ignoramuses look at the world with wonderment. Consider beings as free agents. Have no clue of anything beyond the external, manifested world. They give all importance to the physical body and its actions. The more intelligent recognise the inner strings of the mind and intellect playing upon the otherwise inert bodies. But those with spiritual insight see the supreme unmanifest power as the primal cause of the manifest world of beings. Perceive the divine conductor of the orchestra of life. While the ignorant, out of sheer intellectual fatigue, dismiss the existence of the transcendental Being. You would be wise to study the human composition thoroughly. Go through the process of self-analysis. Practise the appropriate spiritual discipline. Develop deeper philosophic insight and pursue the evolutionary path until you discover the supreme Self. Attain spiritual Enlightenment.

Composite Personality

The supreme Self, *Atman* is the core of your personality. The *Atman* enlivens the body to perceive and act. Enlivens the mind to feel. The intellect to think, contemplate. However the type of perception and action, feeling and thought emanating from the body, mind and intellect will all depend upon one's inherent nature, *vasanas*. If the *vasanas*, basic nature is good the expressions will be good. If bad, the expressions will be bad. Similarly, brilliant or dull, evolutionary or devolutionary according to the *vasanas*. As the *vasana* so the thought, feeling, perception and action.

The chart below gives a complete picture of a human being with his built-in anatomical, physiological, psychological and philosophical structures.

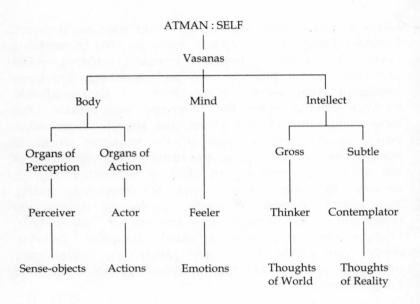

The *Atman* functioning through the organs of perception becomes the perceiver. And perceives the sense-objects of the world. Colour and form through the eyes, sound through ears, smell through nose, taste through tongue and touch through skin. The perceiver is therefore the combined seer-hearer-smeller-taster-toucher. That makes one part of the physical personality. The other part is the actor. Created by the *Atman* functioning through the organs of action. The actor executes actions. The perceiver and actor together form the physical personality.

Again, the *Atman* functioning through the mind creates the feeler. And feels emotions like joy and sorrow, love and hate, affection, passion, anger etc. The feeler constitutes the emotional personality.

The third equipment in a human is the intellect. The intellect is of two types. The gross and the subtle. They play distinct roles in life. The gross intellect is that which operates within the periphery of the terrestrial world. It is the discriminating faculty with which one distinguishes between the pairs of opposites therein. The world is constituted of innumerable pairs such as heat and cold, joy and sorrow, right and wrong etc. The gross intellect makes this distinction, also deals with profound themes of science and technology. All this would still be classified as gross by virtue of its field of operation being terrestrial. The *Atman* expresses through the gross intellect as the thinker. The intellectual personality conceiving thoughts pertaining to the world.

Distinct from the gross is the subtle intellect which distinguishes the Transcendental from the terrestrial. Which conceives the possibility of the eternal Reality beyond the ephemeral world. Discerns Spirit from matter. The *Atman* expresses through the subtle intellect as the contemplator. The spiritual personality conceiving the Self distinct from the material equipments and their manifestation.

Hence a human is a hyphenated perceiver-actor-feeler-thinker-contemplator. A synthesis of his physical, emotional, intellectual and spiritual personalities. As per the chart below.

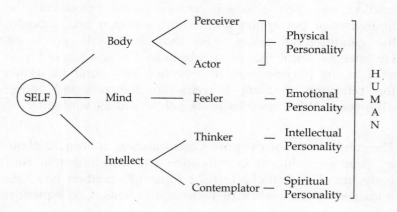

The *Atman* is said to be a homogenous mass of pure Consciousness. The same in all beings. Immaculate. Unconditioned. Yet It appears conditioned by the material equipments. Functioning through the body, mind and intellect It becomes the conditioned-consciousness, the human being. Nevertheless, the immaculate *Atman* is omniscient, omnipotent, omnipresent. Like the sun above whose rays are all-powerful, all-pervading. The sun above is singular. Untainted, unconditioned. But its reflections are manifold in the numerous reflecting media. It appears tainted, conditioned by the properties of the media. The sun seen through a blue mirror appears blue. Through a dirty mirror, dirty. Through a broken mirror, broken. Similarly the supreme Self that you are, appears tainted, restrained by the limitations of the equipments through which It functions. And becomes the limited, restricted human being.

The *Atman*, the pure Consciousness functioning thus through the body becomes conscious *of* perception and action. Through the mind becomes conscious *of* emotion. And through the intellect becomes conscious *of* thought. The pure Consciousness becomes conditioned by the equipments. When a spiritual seeker rises above his body, mind and intellect and their objects of consciousness, transcends the limitation of perception and action, emotion and thought, the conditioning ceases. The individuality is no more. He merges with the pure, absolute Consciousness. It is akin to the phenomenon of reflection and sunlight. When the reflecting medium is removed the reflected image disappears. What remains is the all-pervading sunlight.

The conditioning of the pure Consciousness is brought about by your unintelligent identification and attachment to your body, mind and intellect. Your focus of attention has long remained in the realms of these equipments. Consequently, you are held a hostage of your perception and action, emotion and thought. You can free yourself from this bondage and regain your supreme Self through the three spiritual disciplines.

Karma Yoga Path of Action for the body.
Bhakti Yoga Path of Devotion for the mind.
Gnana Yoga Path of Knowledge for the intellect.

These spiritual practices are programmed to reach you to the goal of Self-realisation. The state of pure Consciousness. The Abode of absolute peace and bliss. The disciplines enable you to control and direct your equipments to tread the spiritual path. Use your intellect to guide the mind, senses and body to the ultimate destination. If the intellect is not alert, the mind goes out of control, the senses run amok and the body perishes.

This idea is portrayed in the picture of the chariot and horses in the epic *Mahabharata*. With Krishna as the charioteer and Arjuna seated behind. When the charioteer holds the reins firmly, the horses are under control. The chariot heads to its destination. If the charioteer is not alert the reins slacken. The horses go out of control. The passenger fails to reach his destination. In the metaphor, the charioteer represents the intellect, the reins the mind, the horses the senses, the passenger the individual. When the intellect maintains a perfect control over the mind and senses the individual reaches the ultimate goal.

Personality Layers

The human being is composed of five material layers with the Self, *Atman* at the core. The diagram below represents this structural division.

ॐ *Atman* and the five sheaths

The mystic symbol ॐ, pronounced aum, at the centre is *Atman*. The five circles, the five layers of matter are known as *pancha koshas*. The outermost circle is the food sheath *annamaya kosha*. Within it is the vital-air sheath *pranamaya kosha*. Next, the mental sheath *manomaya kosha* and intellectual sheath *vignanamaya kosha*. The innermost is the bliss sheath *anandamaya kosha*.

Food Sheath

The food sheath is the physical body constituted of the five organs of perception and five organs of action. Termed so since it is caused by food consumed, maintained by food and finally ends up as food for other creatures.

Vital-air Sheath

This sheath is made up of the five physiological functions known as *pranas*. It is named vital-air since it is related to the air you breathe. The *pranas* are the following five faculties.

Prana Perception: The five senses of seeing, hearing, smelling, tasting and touching.

Apana Excretion: That which throws out, discharges faeces, urine, sperm, sputum, perspiration etc.

Samana Digestion: Digests food consumed.

Vyana Circulation: Distributes digested food to different parts of the body.

Udana Thought-absorption: Takes in fresh knowledge.

These faculties are sharp when one is young. As one grows older they gradually lose their power and vitality. And at old age people can hardly see, hear. Their capacity to digest food or absorb new thoughts and ideas becomes very weak.

Vital-air sheath is subtler, it controls the food sheath. When the *pranas* are in good shape and function properly the physical body remains hale and healthy. As they slacken, become inefficient the body becomes adversely affected.

Mental Sheath

The mental sheath comprises the mind. It controls the vital-air and food sheaths. When the mind is calm and composed the physiological functions are efficient and the body remains healthy. When the mind is disturbed, agitated both the vital-air and food sheaths are affected.

The mind is made up of impulses, feelings, emotions and other passions. It is replete with likes and dislikes. The mind desires to obtain what one does not possess and becomes attached to what one possesses. It can turn turbulent like the wind. A strong wind can uproot trees, wreck ships and aircrafts. So does a turbulent mind cause terrorism, genocide.

The mind has another weakness. It has a natural tendency to slip into the past or future. If left unattended, it would constantly worry over the past or become anxious of the future. It hardly remains in the present. This causes stress and strain to practically every adult. Whereas, little children have no stress since they are free from worry or anxiety.

Intellectual Sheath

This sheath comprises the intellect, the faculty to think, reason, contemplate. The intellect judges and decides the mental and physical activity. Controls the mental, vital-air and food sheaths.

The senses in the physical body tend to indulge in the sense-objects of the world. The mind is attracted to instant pleasures. The intellect controls, regulates the mind, *pranas* and senses. One needs a powerful intellect to practise this discipline. And intellectual strength is gained through study and reflection upon the truths of life laid down in Vedanta.

A powerful intellect must be distinguished from intelligence. The two are distinct and different. Intelligence is gained through knowledge drawn from external sources. You may be well-informed in one or more subjects through educational institutions, textbooks and teachers. You are then knowledgeable in that particular field. No more. That does not strengthen your intellect. Thus you may be well-versed in one or more subjects, yet fall a prey to mental and sensual attractions. You could find a brilliant scientist being infatuated to a woman or addicted to alcohol. When the intellect is weak, the demands of the mind and senses usurp the personality. The mind overpowers the intellect. The person then is inflicted with stress and sorrow.

The mind's nature is also to slip into the past or future. That ruins one's concentration. For concentration your mind must back your action. When your intellect keeps the mind focussed on the present action, without allowing it to slip into the past or future, then you are concentrating. You need a strong intellect to do that. Hence, people with mere intelligence and no intellectual strength find it difficult to concentrate. And become less productive in their field of activity.

Bliss Sheath

The bliss sheath consists of *vasanas*, the inherent, innate material that one is made up of. It is the seed, the subtlest form of the human personality. When you remain in bliss sheath you are in deep-sleep, dreamless sleep. In that state your *vasanas* are unmanifest. They manifest as thoughts and desires in the dream and further into actions in the waking state. Since the dream and waking states contain thoughts and desires you experience mental agitation, less or more. The moment you enter the portals of sleep all agitation ceases. You experience peace and bliss. Hence the state of deep-sleep is known as bliss sheath. But this bliss is relative, not the absolute bliss of Self-realisation.

Gross, Subtle and Causal Bodies

A human being may further be divided into three constituent bodies. Known as gross, subtle and causal bodies. These are formed from the five sheaths enumerated above. The food sheath and the gross part of the vital-air sheath together constitute the gross body. Whereas, the subtle part of the vital-air sheath together with the mental and intellectual sheaths form the subtle body. And the bliss sheath is the causal body.

The causal body contains *vasanas* in the unmanifest form. The subtle body contains thought, desire, feeling and emotion. While the gross body extends to perception and action. The *vasanas* of an individual manifest through the gross, subtle and causal bodies respectively as the waker, dreamer and deep-sleeper.

Waker, Dreamer and Deep-sleeper

Every human being passes through the waking, dream and deep-sleep states. The pure Consciousness is the substratum of them all. When the Consciousness functions through the gross body It takes the form of the waker, *vishva* in Sanskrit. The waker experiences the waking world. When the Consciousness functions through the subtle body It becomes the dreamer, *taijasa*. The dreamer experiences the dream-world. And functioning through the causal body the Consciousness turns into the deep-sleeper, *pragna*. The deep-sleeper enjoys sound sleep free from thought, desire and action. Thus the one Consciousness identifying with the three bodies manifests as the microcosm, the waker-dreamer-deepsleeper *vishva-taijasa-pragna*.

You go through the waking, dream and deep-sleep all your life. But at any time you assume only one of the three personalities. You are either a waker or a dreamer or a deep-sleeper. When you take up the position of a waker, the waker goes through the experiences of the waking world.

The waker treats the waking world as real. And rejects the dream-world as unreal, a mere illusion. Again, when you take up the position of a dreamer, the dreamer treats the dream-world as real. To the dreamer, the waking world and all that goes with it do not exist. So both the waker and the dreamer experience a relative reality as long as each is confined to his respective realm of experience. But the moment he crosses the boundary of his world, its reality is lost. Yet, both the waker and the dreamer emphatically assert that his world is absolutely real!

Janaka was a king imbued with spiritual wisdom. One night he dreamt he was a beggar. He woke up from the shocking dream and summoned his counsellors. To them he posed his famous question, "Am I king Janaka who dreamt that I was a beggar? Or am I the beggar now dreaming that I am a king?" The counsellors were confused and did not know what the king meant. So they brought in the sage, Ashtavakra to answer the question. The sage gave these pearls of wisdom to the king, "You are neither king Janaka nor the beggar. You are the supreme Self, *Atman*. In the waking state now, the Self has assumed the form of the king. A while ago, in the dream the Self had become the beggar. At another time, It would take the form of the deep-sleeper. You are not the waker, dreamer or deep-sleeper. You are the Self."

So it is with everyone. You are the supreme Self, *Atman*, God. You are pure Consciousness. The supreme Consciousness, passing through the gross, subtle and causal bodies, assumes the forms of the limited waker, dreamer and deep-sleeper. Just as colourless water appears green, blue or yellow when seen through those coloured glasses. So do you see your Self limited through these bodies. What a blunder you make of yourself to believe you are the waker, dreamer or deep-sleeper. Never do you recognise your Self in Its pristine glory. The Self that lies unconditioned beyond the three bodies. To discover your real Self you must transcend the limitation of your material equipments. Drop your identification and attachment with them through spiritual practices. You then attain your supreme Being. The state of God-Consciousness known as *Turiya*. *Turiya* in Sanskrit means fourth. You reach the fourth State, the Transcendental beyond the three mundane states.

The Consciousness is the substratum of the microcosm and the macrocosm as well. When the Consciousness functions through the aggregate of all gross bodies, It expresses as *virat* cosmic-waker. The same functioning through the aggregate of all subtle bodies expresses as *hiranyagarbha* cosmic-dreamer. And through the aggregate of all causal bodies as *eshwara* cosmic-deep-sleeper. The combination of these cosmic expressions is the macrocosm. The microcosm and macrocosm together form the world as illustrated below.

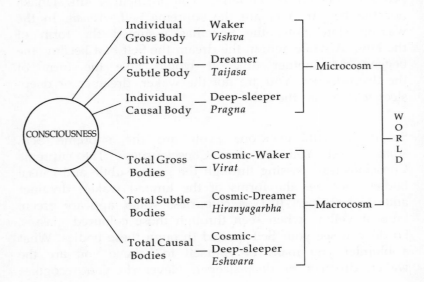

If the microcosm is likened to a drop of water, the macrocosm would be the ocean. Both the drop and ocean are water. He who understands water in the drop, understands water in the ocean, water everywhere. Likewise, he who realises the Self within, realises the Self in one and all, the all-pervading Being. Discovers the Consciousness around which the microcosm and macrocosm revolve. Attains spiritual Enlightenment.

CHAPTER X

SELF-ANALYSIS

Enquiry into Yourself

Your Self is pure Consciousness. You are the supreme Reality. Spiritual pursuit culminates in the Self. You discover your Self by turning introvert. Through enquiry into yourself. You must gradually wade through your body, mind and intellect, your gross, subtle and causal bodies to reach the divine Core of your personality. To gain the bliss of Self-realisation. But the human tendency is to be extrovert. Instead of seeking the Self within, people pursue the external world for pleasure, joy and knowledge. They get involved in mundane affairs. And the mind becomes restless, agitated. The intellect loses its clarity to enquire into the essence of life.

The divine law of life is that you shall be pure. Free from mental agitation and suffering. Your true Self is ever peaceful and blissful. But when you stay away from the Self and run after the world, you will be inflicted with pain and suffering. Sow the wind you reap the whirlwind. The law is unrelenting.

Therefore, try to diagnose the cause of agitation and grief. Get to the root of your problems. Go deeper into the inner layers of your personality. You may want to consult the scripture. Take guidance from a preceptor. With all that, you must get on to your own reflection and contemplation. You will then find out there is but one fundamental source for all sorrow, one cause for evil and misery in the world. That is, the ignorance of the Self. People everywhere have lost the identity of the Self. Instead, they have identified themselves with the body, mind and intellect. Become attached to material equipments and their endless demands. And run after the world to appease them. Not realising that the physical, emotional and intellectual appetites are insatiable. The unfulfilled desires remain to produce mental agitation and sorrow. Hence must you leave your infatuation to the body, mind and intellect. Realise you are the kernel, not the shell. Turn introvert and gain the knowledge of Self. You then liberate yourself from all agitation and attain enduring peace and bliss.

Your Self is the theme of all religions. Preceptors and preachings cannot help you find It unless you enquire into yourself. External sources of knowledge can only set you thinking. But you must make good use of the scriptural knowledge by engaging your intellect to reflect independently upon the truths therein. Do not sell your liberty of reflection to spiritual personalities regardless of their merit. You must seek the truth yourself. The Godhead lies within you. Remove the veil of ignorance and revel in the supreme bliss that lies within. Not realising your inherent wealth you try in vain to find peace and joy in the external world. So the American philosopher Ralph Waldo Emerson rightly quipped: *Every man is a divinity in disguise, a god playing the fool.*

Religious books and discourses on their own cannot bring about spiritual development in you. The knowledge contained in the scripture can make you a well-informed person. But for spiritual transformation you need to put in considerable effort in reflection and contemplation upon the knowledge received. Lectures from masters will be of no avail unless you are prepared to lecture to yourself. Lord Krishna pronounces this truth in his oft-quoted words: *You must raise yourself by yourself.*

Your Self is Supreme Reality

The problem facing humanity today is that none wants to look within oneself. People are enchanted by the fascinations of the external world. They do not find the need to go introvert. Vedanta cautions them that there is no peace and happiness in the sense-objects or beings or anything that the world can offer. They claim that their personal experience belies this statement. And dismiss the caution as baseless.

The intelligentsia argue their sense organs enjoy the sense-objects. That their eyes gain pleasure from sight, ears gain from sound, nose from smell, tongue from taste and skin from touch. So does the mind contact and experience the joy of emotion. And the intellect revel in acquiring knowledge in the world. Their argument seems tenable. They are convinced that they perceive the pleasure and joy in the world and personally experience it. Nevertheless Vedanta maintains that there is no pleasure or peace in the world. It bids you examine your conviction closely. You will then find the truth of its statement.

The error in the conviction of the intelligentsia is akin to professing that the moon has light in it. On a moonlit night you see the light emerging from the moon. The full moon, a 384,400 kilometres away, shedding its brilliant light over the earth. You use it to find your way. You enjoy the moonlight. By virtue of your experience, you aver there is light in the moon. And yet you will appreciate the moon has no light in it! It has only arid land and dust. You would know that when you approach it, when you reach it. The light that you see from afar is reflected light. The moon merely reflects the light of the sun.

Similarly, the world has no happiness inherent in it. The pleasure and joy you seem to get out of the world is a reflection of the bliss of your Self. The Self in you is all-blissful. This supreme bliss is reflected the world over in every object and being, in every perception, emotion and thought. You see pseudo-bliss and run after it. When you get close and actually encounter it, you become disillusioned. No wonder the wealthy confess that there is no peace and happiness in wealth. The powerful with all the power also find themselves duped and disappointed. So it is with any worldly acquisition and enjoyment. Therefore, the way to ride over the monotony and misery of the world, to find everlasting peace and happiness is to pursue and reach the source. Discover the Self within you. The nucleus of true happiness.

A prince approached a sage reverentially to learn all about God. A conversation ensued.

Prince : Venerable master, who is God? Where is He? How can I reach Him?

Sage : May I know who you are?

Prince : My name is Gajapati.

Sage : I appreciate that is your name. But tell me who you are.

Prince : I am a prince.

Sage : Is that not your status?

Prince : Yes, it is. I guess I am just a human being.

Sage : You say you are a human, not a bird or beast. But that is the species to which you belong. You have not yet told me who you are.

The prince then realised that he was going round in circles. And did not really know who he was. So with all humility he spoke again.

Prince :   Am I then this body, mind and intellect which define my person?

Sage :   Nay, not so. They are your material equipments. They too belong to you.

The answer left the prince bewildered. And he submitted himself to the master.

Prince :   Sir, I now reckon I do not know myself. Kindly let me know who am I. And how does that relate to my enquiry of God?

Sage :   Dear prince, you are the supreme Self. The divine Core of your person. The body, mind and intellect are mere vestures enveloping your Self. The Self is known as *Atman* in Sanskrit, God in English. You will have to find the Self within through introspection. Through study, reflection and meditation.

Vedanta helps reveal the supreme Self in you. You then realise your infinite Being. That which keeps you performing countless deeds. You move every muscle in the body. You cause each hair to grow. You eat, you produce the digestive juices in the stomach. You digest the food taken in. You distribute the digested food in every part of the body. You evacuate the waste. You operate the nerves. You feel emotions. You think various thoughts. These go on and on all your life.

God is therefore the primal source of all activity. The supreme Self which assumes the three forms of the waker, dreamer and deep-sleeper. The infinite power that operates in your personality is the same that operates everywhere. That enlivens the entire animal and plant world as well. The self-same power that causes the sun to shine, earth to revolve, rivers to flow. That supreme power is known as *Atman* in the microcosm and *Brahman* in the macrocosm. *Atman* and *Brahman* are one and the same Reality that is the omnipotent, omniscient, omnipresent God. Your divine Self.

Drift in Religion

Religion is meant to impart the knowledge of God. Knowledge of the supreme Self within you. The homogenous Being that resides in every living creature. In the world today there is hardly any spiritual education. Religion has been reduced to mere maxim and mandate. Free thinking has been stifled, strangled. And people have lost their reason, their independent judgement. The natural growth in spirituality has been stunted by forced doctrine and dogma. The well-meaning custodians of religion have turned the masses into spiritual pygmies.

There is a heartless, unnatural practice in plant culture known as bonsai. Bonsai are miniaturised trees. Three hundred year-old cedars and pines have been kept dwarfed as onion plants. This is done by cutting their inner rootlets. When the roots are not allowed to strike deep into the soil the trees cannot shoot high into the air. Likewise, when you do not penetrate deep into the core of your personality you remain spiritually dwarfed. This is the present trend in religion.

People all over the world allow themselves to be influenced by views and opinions of others. They accept religious teachings blindly. Few get to the merit of religion. If religion is to purify and bring about human evolution it has to be enquired into, judged and accepted on its own merit, not on authority. Your approach to religion should be to get to the depth of knowledge therein. Examine it per se. Judge it on its own merit. Do not accept anything because it was laid down by sages and saints. If you adopt their declarations mechanically you flout the fundamental principles of religion. You miss the spirit of religion. You would do well to take up religion as you would science or mathematics. Study its subject matter carefully. Reflect upon it over and over again. Understand it thoroughly. Apply the knowledge gained in your practical life. The knowledge thus tested becomes your own.

Religion today is far from reaching its objective. There is an inversion of a natural order. The Self is being made a slave to the ghosts of old books. Well-meaning preceptors have wasted their time torturing old texts to squeeze out the truth which was a matter of their personal experience. Others try to force their own meaning from those lifeless words. There are religious practitioners who swear by *bhashyas* commentaries which are more complicated than the original texts. They place the study of language and texts higher than the truths therein. And merely stuff the mind with authorities and quotations. Consequently, their intellects have stopped functioning. The well-meant efforts have retarded rather than advanced human progress towards God-realisation.

Therefore you must approach religion with your head and heart. Be free to think. Use reason to arrive at your own conclusion. But the unfortunate trend these days is to boost up the image of a personality. And thoughtless people rely on his authority. Take matters too much on trust. They depend on outside forces to do their thinking. Thus let themselves be hypnotised by others' views and opinions. This is spiritual suicide. The bane of all religion.

The Enlightened souls attained the supreme state by their own efforts. So must you. You may take guidance from spiritual masters but not enslave yourself. The religious leaders in the world have virtually destroyed the growth of spirituality especially among the youth. By forcing their own religious beliefs indiscriminately upon the masses. And insisting they observe obsolete codes of conduct. Do not let yourself be influenced by their imperative commandments. Rise above such unnatural influence. Strive hard on your own to get to the spirit of religion. And gain the sane knowledge of the living present rather than burying yourself in the dead past.

The Problem of Introversion

The attractions of the world are tantalising. Human beings ignorant of their inner wealth are drawn towards them. Hence the human tendency is to be extrovert. You are unaware of your infinite power within. And seek power in the external world. So are you ignorant of your infinite joy within. And seek joy in the world outside. Likewise, ignoring the infinite knowledge of your Self, you seek knowledge externally. The kingdom of heaven lies within you. Yet you pursue the world for precious trifles. The paradox arises from the problem of turning introvert. Rare indeed is the one who looks within oneself. Unless you look within, you will not recognise the inherent desires that veil the Self. Much less realise the infinite nature of your Self.

The extroverted nature makes it difficult for you to investigate your weaknesses and take corrective measures. Instead you find faults in others. You are able to do this with ease. But your own imperfections even if they be several times magnified remain obscure. This grave flaw in human beings is well brought out by John Gay in his poem *The Turkey and the Ant*. The poet describes a turkey in a barn tired

of eating grain. It decided to leave the barn and seek a
variety of food. The young ones followed the mother bird.
They soon reached a hill full of black ants. The turkey
started devouring them. And bid her young ones eat
freely. For a breakfast they consumed numberless ants. The
turkey was quite unaware of the massacre it was committing.
Ironically, it cursed man for gluttony in consuming turkey
for Christmas. A sin that seemed nothing compared to
its devastating consumption for a breakfast. The poem
highlights this problem of recognising one's own faults.
The poem:

The Turkey and the Ant

In other men we faults can spy,
And blame the mote that dims their eye,
Each little speck and blemish find,
To our own stronger errors blind.

   A Turkey, tir'd of common food,
Forsook the barn and sought the wood,
Behind her ran her infant train,
Collecting here and there a grain.
   Draw near, my birds, the mother cries,
This hill delicious fare supplies;
Behold, the busy negro race,
See, millions blacken all the place!
Fear not. Like me with freedom eat;
An ant is most delightful meat.
How blest, how envy'd were our life,
Could we but 'scape the poult'rer's knife!
But man, curst man on turkey preys,
And *Christmas* shortens all our days;
Sometimes with oysters we combine,
Sometimes assist the sav'ry chine.
From the low peasant to the lord,

The turkey smoaks on ev'ry board.
Sure men for gluttony are curst,
Of the sev'n deadly sins the worst.
    An Ant, who climb'd beyond her reach,
Thus answer'd from the neighb'ring beech.
Ere you remark another's sin,
Bid thy own conscience look within.
Control thy more voracious bill,
Nor for a breakfast nations kill.

— John Gay

You should therefore refrain from finding flaws in others. Criticising others' failings. Behind every flaw you recognise in another, perhaps you have the same more pronounced in you. Do not consume your life merely detecting the blemishes in the outside world. "Judge not others," cautioned Lord Jesus. The energy you waste in judging others could as well serve to improve yourself. Moreover, by blaming the vice in others you miss their virtues. You become involved in negativities and lose the positive side of life. Do not give up the rose for its thorns. You would soon realise the wisdom in the resounding words of Edward Wallis Hoch:

> *There is so much good in the worst of us,*
> *And so much bad in the best of us,*
> *That it hardly behooves any of us*
> *To talk about the rest of us.*

Every human being needs therefore to concentrate his efforts in investigating his own personality. Instead of prying into the lives of others. You have no right to do so. Your business is your life. If others make mistakes they will have to pay for them. Let them settle their accounts with the Almighty. You seem to be more concerned with the affairs of others than your own. You need to look within. Set your personality right. Just take care of yourself, the world will take care of itself.

It is a social crime to expect others to behave in the pattern of your like and dislike. You cannot order the lives of people to follow your whim and fancy. The primary lesson you learn in life is that all beings act according to their inherent nature, *vasanas*. Beings follow their own structure of life. But there is one fundamental difference between the structures of humans and other beings. All creatures, save humans, inherit the common nature, the collective *vasanas* of their species. Thus tigers are all ferocious and destructive. Cows are all meek and mild. Each species possesses a collective nature, a distinct set of *vasanas*. The creatures of a species do not differ from one another. Whereas human beings do not possess a common nature, collective *vasanas*. They have different traits and characteristics. No two humans are of the same kind. Every human possesses a distinct, different nature, individualistic *vasanas*.

Everyone understands clearly the natures of all species except that of humans. Consequently, people are able to conduct themselves perfectly with each species. You know exactly how to relate to a tiger and a cow. A cobra and a kitten. A scorpion and a grasshopper. But you fail miserably in your conduct with humans. That is because you do not assess human beings individually. You do not realise that each one's nature is distinct, different from others. Your understanding, behaviour and conduct with humans is alarmingly immature. You commit a colossal blunder when you expect a human to behave different from his particular nature, *vasanas*. You do not seem to understand that each one helplessly expresses one's own temperament, nature. And when they do and conflict with your expectation you grumble, you complain. And even express your disappointment overtly. All that causes you the stress and strain of life. You suffer.

You understand the nature of all other beings and conduct yourself rightly. You must apply the same principle to humans as well. Recognise their individual natures and let them live their own lives. You then find peace and harmony with humans. Remember: *All grumbling is tantamount to, "Oh! Why is the lily not an oak?"*

Extending this concept further you must assess not only human beings but the entire world as well. Your assessment of beings barring humans is perfect. While that of humans needs individual attention. You must assess separately those whom you associate with. Further, you must assess your environment, your government, the climate you live in etc. If you do not make an assessment or make a wrong assessment, then your expectations in life become unreasonable. Unreasonable expectations cause you disappointments, stress. And when you make a thorough assessment of everything you meet in life there will be no disappointments, no stress. Your life becomes peaceful and happy.

An interesting incident took place in a classroom in India. It should educate you on the importance of assessing the world. It was an extremely hot and humid day in Chennai. The boys were fussing and fuming over the heat. Their teacher walked in and noticed the fuss. He quietly walked out the other door. And gestured to the boys to come out into the open quadrangle. The boys stood under the blazing sun wondering why he had brought them out. He suddenly threw up his arms and articulated, "Isn't this a beautiful summer?" The boys thought he was crazy. He then brought them back to the classroom and spoke these words of wisdom, "Remember, the beauty of the summer is its heat. The beauty of the winter is its biting cold. The beauty of the monsoon is that it must pour and pour. But the problem is that people want the summer to be cool. Winter to be warm. Monsoon to be dry."

Apply this great principle in your life. You will then realise, "The beauty of my wife is her temper!" Viewing everything thus, all your problems are bound to disappear. The world turns out to be pleasant after all.

Practical Exercises

Spiritual practice is subjective. You must go introvert and discover the Self within you. You may seek guidance from a spiritual master. But take up his preaching on its own merits. Do not allow the life and personality of a guru to interfere with his teaching. His life and teaching must be treated separately. Do not mix them up. To live an ideal life is one thing and to be able to explain the way to live that life is quite another. Everybody tries to reason but few know the science of reasoning. People commit the grave blunder of mixing the personality of a teacher with his teaching. They transfer the personal charm, oft got without merit, to his teaching and become enslaved by him.

The pursuit of Enlightenment does not envisage your enslavement to personalities. And a blind following of their deeds and dogmas. You can attain the supreme state by delving deep into your personality layers and recognising the divine Core within. But the order of the day is that self-anointed preachers thrust their beliefs on ignorant people and bring about spiritual pauperism. When religious teaching is thus forced upon people they, particularly the youth, reject it and take the opposite direction. Thus, none realises that the truth lies within oneself and fails to pursue it subjectively.

Two men were travelling in a cabin in a railway train. One was a wealthy merchant. The other, a thief. The merchant was carrying a lot of money with him. Wads of currency notes.

170

The thief knew it. In fact he had booked his berth in the same compartment only to steal the money. The thief waited for the merchant to retire. To his surprise the merchant openly removed the notes out of his bag and started counting them. The embarrassed thief left the compartment to go to the washroom. After he returned the merchant went out. Took his own time to wash and change. Meanwhile the thief got busy and searched everywhere for the money. He could not find it! He knew for certain that the merchant did not carry it with him. How could it have disappeared? He could not sleep the whole night. While the merchant slept peacefully. The next morning they greeted each other. The thief could not contain himself any longer. He confessed his malicious intention to the merchant. And in admiration for his ingenuity enquired, "Sir, where did you keep that money?" The merchant smiled and reached for the packet under the thief's pillow! This is the story of the human race. Everyone searches for bliss all over except where it is, within oneself.

So the need is to go within. Rehabilitate the inner personality. The human mechanism faces constant challenges in the world. The trial and tribulation, worry and anxiety, stress and strain of life. You need to pull out of this onslaught for an hour or so every day to regenerate your mind and intellect. Like a ship needs dry-docking. A ship sailing in the high seas becomes corroded. It needs periodic overhaul. So do your equipments require constant attention and correction to reach the final destination of life. For sixty to ninety minutes every morning you must study scriptural literature. Reflect upon it. Contemplate on the truths therein. Be consistent in your application. You will find your intellect getting clearer. Free from doubt and indecision. Your mind becoming purer. Free from agitation and sorrow. Follow this practice daily. You cannot afford to neglect it. Does not your room need cleaning every day? Does not your body require to be bathed? So do your mind and intellect need constant rehabilitation.

Scriptural study and reflection no doubt strengthens the intellect to prevent the mind from straying into likes and dislikes. Your mind keeps doing what it likes to do and avoiding what it dislikes. To live at the mercy of likes and dislikes is not healthy living. It would turn out detrimental to you. Your intellect must therefore control your activities. But the problem is that the intellect is not always available when the action is executed. After the action is completed you realise you have acted impulsively. There are many activities performed by you which you yourself condemn as wrong. Have you not regretted at times your own actions? Then why do you do things which you realise later as wrongful? That is because your intellect was not available to you at that time. You have acted mechanically, impulsively. Therefore, the intellect has to be alert and available at the time of executing an action. This can be achieved by the practice of introspection.

Introspection is a process of self-observation. To be practised every night before you retire. It involves the recollection of your experiences during the day. Try and remember every experience you have gone through in a sequence from the time of rising to the moment of introspecting. In your initial attempts you may not remember the details of what you have done. But with repeated practice you will recollect each and every activity. This exercise should not take you more than five to six minutes. While doing so, do not analyse or criticise your actions. You are only to be aware of them. Any form of involvement in the merit or demerit of the action would break the trend of introspection. Moreover, it may develop cynicism and frustration. When you remember an action over and over again you become aware of it. And constant recollection of daily actions would render your intellect alert.

The exercise of introspection is akin to wall-practice in the game of tennis. That means practising strokes against a wall. A line is drawn on the wall at the same height as the regular net in a tennis court. The player plays his shots against the wall to gain proficiency in the game. A practice which helps him later in tournaments. Likewise, introspection helps you become aware of your life's activities. And your intellect becomes available before the action to guide it in the proper direction.

Thus spiritual study and reflection help you develop a strong intellect and a pure mind. While introspection enables your intellect to be alert. Together they render your actions more objective, meaningful, purposeful. You get nearer and nearer the core of your personality. With such stability and objectivity delve deeper into your personality. What you are looking for in life is bliss and bliss and bliss. Nothing less. You search for it in vain in the outside world through your body, mind and intellect. All bliss lies within you. Look for it here. You will find it. You will be absolutely fulfilled. Enlightened.

CHAPTER XI

THE STATES OF CONSCIOUSNESS

Waking, Dream and Deep-sleep

Life is a continuous cycle of three states of consciousness. The waking, dream and deep-sleep. Every human being goes through these states. At one time you are awake. You take the form of the waker. The waker experiences the waking world. The waking world consists of things and beings, emotions and thoughts appearing in the waking state of consciousness. The waking world exists only for the waker. And not for the dreamer or deep-sleeper. The entire waking world disappears no sooner than you leave the waking state of consciousness.

When you leave the waking state you enter the dream or deep-sleep. In the dream state you take the form of the dreamer. The dreamer experiences the dream-world. The dream-world consists of things and beings, emotions and thoughts appearing in the dream state. The dream-world is totally different from the waking world. It exists only for the dreamer and not for the waker or deep-sleeper. The dream-world too disappears no sooner than you leave the dream state of consciousness.

In the deep-sleep state of consciousness you take the form of the deep-sleeper. The deep-sleeper experiences sleep without dream. A blankness, nothingness. That experience exists only for the deep-sleeper and not for the waker or dreamer. It also disappears when you leave the deep-sleep state of consciousness.

Your life revolves around the above three states of consciousness. The personalities of the waker, dreamer and deep-sleeper and their distinct worlds. These are conditioned states. The pure Consciousness conditioned by the causal body becomes the deep-sleeper. Likewise, the Consciousness conditioned by the subtle and gross bodies becomes the dreamer and waker respectively. Hence the waker, dreamer and deep-sleeper are conditioned-consciousness. You know yourself only as a waker, dreamer or deep-sleeper. But you know not you are the unconditioned Consciousness, the substratum of the three experiences. And that your real Self is the unconditioned Consciousness and not these conditioned personalities that you believe yourself to be.

The causal body consists of *vasanas*, the seed which causes the individual personality. Hence called so. The causal body manifests first as the subtle body. The subtle body comprises thought, emotion, desire. It further manifests as the gross body which perceives and acts. The structure and behaviour of the gross body will depend on the nature of the subtle body, which in turn will depend upon the quality of the causal body. If the causal body is likened to a seed, the subtle body would be the sapling and gross body the tree.

In deep-sleep you are unconscious of everything. The deep-sleeper knows nothing. The waking and dream worlds do not exist for him. He is steeped in ignorance. People dismiss that state as emptiness, nothingness. Few have cared to study it thoroughly. Psychiatrists, even some philosophers, have paid little attention to this vital state of life. Vedanta bids you examine the deep-sleep state closely. The nothingness is your seed body. Out of this seed emerges the dreamer and waker and their respective worlds. This nothingness is the cause of the particular individual emerging out of it. A philosopher goes to sleep and wakes up as philosopher. A mathematician sleeps and wakes up as mathematician. So does a musician as musician. Thus if everyone wakes up as oneself, there has to be a continuity of the person during the period of sleep. If a musician goes to sleep and wakes up as musician, then his personality must necessarily exist in sleep in its unmanifest form. So does your individuality exist in the seed form while you are asleep. Thus out of your seed, a seeming nothing, arises your personality. And out of countless seeds, a vast nothingness, spring forth countless individuals. In fact the whole world arises from that seeming void, emptiness, nothingness. Hence the *Bible* states: God created the world out of nothing.

The philosophy of the West is drawn primarily from the waking state. It takes little notice of the experience of the dream state and practically ignores the deep-sleep state. The western philosophers base their investigations and discoveries on the experience gained in the waking state. They try to solve the mystery of the universe using that alone. The data they work with then is inadequate. With improper data one cannot draw proper conclusions. Vedanta takes up all the data. The gross, subtle and causal bodies, the three states of consciousness and the three worlds of the waking, dream and deep-sleep. It deals with all the necessary material available to reach the absolute Reality, the state of pure Consciousness.

The Consciousness in Its absolute state is homogenous. One and one alone. That is unknown to you. It assumes three known forms. The waking, dream and deep-sleep states. It functions through the gross, subtle and causal bodies to forge the waker, dreamer and deep-sleeper. They are distinct and different from one another. The consciousness of the waking state thus becomes the waker. The waker pronounces the waking world to be substantial, real, set in order by its laws and regulations. The waker disregards the other two states. Negates the dreamer and the dream-world as insubstantial, a mere illusion. An athlete of the waking state may dream as an invalid, a cripple. He dismisses his dream experience as insignificant, meaningless. His verdict of the waking state is clear, emphatic to him.

Likewise the consciousness of the dream state, the dreamer swears by the dream-world. The dreamer is equally emphatic, assertive that the dream-world is substantial, real, set in its own laws. A dreamer may be an Olympic runner in the dream, though in the waking state he could be bedridden with a terminal disease! The dreamer also dismisses the waking state as insignificant, meaningless. His verdict of the dream state is clear, emphatic to him.

Again, the consciousness of the sleeping state, the deep-sleeper experiences nothingness. And is blissfully ignorant of the waking and dream states. All that is gained or lost in these two states is of no significance, no value to the deep-sleeper. He is steeped in ignorance.

Now the question arises as to what is real. The waking or the dream or the deep-sleep state? Reality is defined as that which existed in the past, which exists in the present and will exist in the future. That which persists eternally is said to be real. Conversely, that which exists for a period of time and not before or after that period is considered unreal, false. Apply this definition to the above three states. Then none of them stands the test of reality. The waker and the waking world exist as long as the waking state of consciousness lasts. No sooner than you leave the waking state, to enter either the dream or deep-sleep, the waker and the waking world disappear. They exist only during the waking period, not before or after. The waker and the waking world are of no significance, no value to the dreamer and the deep-sleeper. The waking state does not exist for them. They dismiss it as meaningless, with no pith or substance in it. Hence the waker and waking world cannot be real. It is false.

Apply the same test to the dream and deep-sleep states. The dreamer and the dream-world, the deep-sleeper and his world, both fail the test of reality. Each of them exists only during the period of its state of consciousness, not before and after. Hence the waker, dreamer and deep-sleeper and their three worlds are said to be false. But the Consciousness exists in the waking, dream and deep-sleep states and beyond as well. That is your supreme Self appearing through the media of the gross, subtle and causal bodies. When all the three bodies drop off, the Consciousness remains in Its immaculate state. The Consciousness exists in all periods of time. Stands the test of reality. And that is your Self within. You discover It in the Core of your personality.

The waker goes through the waking state of consciousness as a particular person and declares, "I am that person." Likewise the dreamer goes through the dream state of consciousness as a different person and declares, "I am this person." So does the deep-sleeper claim his experience of sleep. The 'I' pervades the waking state. The same 'I' persists in the dream state. And does so in the deep-sleep state. The 'I' is the common factor in the three states of consciousness. The substratum of all experiences. It is your supreme Self. The pure Consciousness. The absolute Reality.

The Fourth State

In the waking, dream and deep-sleep states of consciousness you become the waker, dreamer and deep-sleeper. All through your life as a waker, dreamer and deep-sleeper, you refer to yourself in the first person singular pronoun 'I'. But you know that the waker, dreamer and deep-sleeper are distinct and different from one another. Hence these three unequal factors cannot be I. I is not the waker or dreamer or deep-sleeper. I is apart from them. The Self that holds the three personalities together. The pure Consciousness. The fourth State, known as *Turiya*. *Turiya* means fourth. *Turiya* is the state of Reality. The supreme State of peace and bliss. Those who have reached that state in different periods of history have declared that to be the absolute State of fulfilment.

The fourth state is proclaimed as the real state. Your original Self. You are unaware of your real Self. The nature of your Self is infinite peace and bliss. You have lost your original nature. You try to regain peace and bliss from the world. There is a constant pressure on you to gain more and more. You do not stop this pursuit until you reach your original state. Only a few rare souls who have reached the state of Self-realisation have ended the pursuit of happiness. They do not find the need to pursue it any more. Absolutely fulfilled, they revel in the bliss of their own Self. The pressure to gain more happiness ends when one reaches one's original state of infinite Bliss.

The pressure that a human being experiences to reach his original nature is akin to that an object goes through to regain its original state. A coil spring compressed exerts pressure until it reaches its full length. A sponge squeezed exerts pressure until it regains its original form. So it is with human beings.

Every human being feels an inherent pressure, compulsion to seek more and more pleasure, joy and happiness through the body, mind and intellect. There seems no end to your physical, emotional and intellectual demands. Your pursuit never ends. You do not rest content until you reach your original Being. Your supreme Self. Only when you realise your Self within, would you be free from the internal pressure. Revelling in the absolute bliss of your original state there is no need to seek further peace or happiness. This is evidenced by all those who have attained the fourth state of Self-realisation.

The fourth state is pure Consciousness. The Self-realised one merges with that infinite Consciousness like a river merging with the ocean. That State is an experience beyond the reach of your body, mind and intellect. It is not an object of experience. It is the Subject of all experiences. You cannot contact It physically. Nor feel It emotionally. Nor conceive It intellectually. You can only become that eternal Being like a dreamer becomes the waker. Shedding the conditioning of the waker, dreamer and deep-sleeper you regain your unconditioned, supreme Self. You achieve this by effacing ignorance through the process of attaining knowledge of the Self.

There are four means to gain knowledge:

Pratyaksha	:	Direct perception
Anumana	:	Inference
Upama	:	Comparison
Agama	:	Tradition

Pratyaksha: One way of gaining knowledge is by perception through your sense organs. Your eyes see colour and form of an object and you know the nature of that object. Your ears hear sound, nose smells, tongue tastes and skin feels the touch. The organs of perception are used to gain the knowledge of the world. But these senses cannot know the Self, *Atman* within. You cannot gain the knowledge of Self by direct perception.

Anumana: Another method of gaining knowledge is through inference. Just as you see smoke and infer there is fire. Though you may not actually see the fire. You could employ this method to get to know the Self. You learn from knowledge and experience that an extroverted, indulgent life leads one to mental agitation and sorrow. Conversely, introverted pursuit of truth brings inner peace and joy. The more introvert, objective you are the more peaceful, joyful you become. The pleasures of the physical body may be enjoyable but they have a limitation. They become insignificant before emotional feelings. The emotion of joy that the mind derives is subtler, superior to physical indulgence. One could give up a physical pleasure for an emotional joy. Far superior and subtler than emotional feeling is intellectual satisfaction. To gain the ecstasy of intellectual wisdom one would readily sacrifice one's emotional joy or physical pleasure. Thus, your happiness increases as you delve deeper into your personality. Stretch this principle further to the innermost core of your personality, the Self within. You infer the bliss of the Self to be supreme.

Upama: A third means of gaining knowledge is comparison. An unknown object is made known by comparing it to something known to you. The supreme Self within is not known to you. The fourth state of Self-realisation is unknown. One has no idea of that state until one reaches it. Howeyer, by drawing a comparison of the fourth and waking states with the waking and dream states one could possibly envision the nature of that transcendental experience. The *shastra* scripture declares that the entire pluralistic phenomena of the world you experience merges into the one Reality upon Self-realisation. All the consciousness of perception, emotion and thought retire to the one pure Consciousness. This goes beyond human comprehension. How can this solid, substantial world disappear into nothingness?

The means of comparison helps clear this mystery. The transformation of a waker into the Self-realised person is akin to the transformation of a dreamer into the waker. The waker views the objects and beings and all his experiences in the waking world as distinct, innumerable. So does the dreamer view the dream objects and beings and all his experiences in the dream-world as distinct, innumerable. The dreamer's experience of the pluralistic phenomena of the dream continues as long as the dream lasts. The moment the dreamer wakes up, becomes the waker, the entire dream-world folds back into the one waker's mind. The waker instantly realises that the one mind had diversified into the pluralistic phenomena of the dream. One ray of the mind became the dreamer. Another ray, the dreamer's wife. A third, the dreamer's child. Thus rays and rays of the mind had projected the dream sun, moon, stars, the flora and fauna and the rest of the dream-world. The dreamer's intellect can never conceive, much less accept that the countless things, beings and experiences are all but the one mind of the waker. Only the waker realises that.

Similarly, as long as the waking state lasts the waker experiences countless things and beings, emotions and thoughts. The waker's intellect can never conceive, accept the pluralistic phenomena of the waking world are all nothing but the one supreme Reality, *Brahman*. Only when the waker realises his supreme Self, moves up from the waking to the fourth state of Self-realisation, the waker and his world merges into that one Reality. Thereafter the Reality *Brahman* alone exists. The Enlightened then realises that the entire pluralistic world of the waking state is but the one Reality alone.

Agama: The fourth means of attaining knowledge is through tradition. Tradition is based on time-honoured preaching and practice. The ancient sages have tried to expound their ultimate experience of the Self. But could not effectively communicate because of the limitations of the body, mind and intellect to receive it. The fourth plane of God-consciousness cannot be captured by the waker's perception, emotion and thought in the waking state of consciousness. Much less through the states of dream and deep-sleep. Nothing from the terrestrial world can describe the transcendental Being. The sages understood the difficulty of the mortals to conceive the immortal Self. Hence they explained the waking, dream and deep-sleep states of consciousness exhaustively. They analysed these states with chaste logic and reason. And projected the possibility of the transcendental Reality. Following their methodic presentation of facts and figures one develops a faith in the Reality. Not a blind faith. But one that is born of conviction. Such faith is further reinforced by unequivocal declaration of Self-realised Souls. Rabindranath Tagore, the Indian poet-philosopher describes this faith as *a bird that feels the light and sings while the dawn is still dark*. The Vedantic tradition helps you feel the light of Consciousness even as you remain in the darkness of ignorance.

Assurance of Vedanta

Vedanta assures the Self is within the reach of every human being. That you can gain the fourth State of absolute peace and bliss. Attain it by merging with the Self. That is your mission in life. If you do not achieve it, your life is spent in vain. You suffer the greatest loss. None seems to realise this. Nor even aware of the purpose of human existence. The trend everywhere is to crave for material possession and sensual enjoyment. People are enchanted by the attractions of the external world. And live a superficial life. With no concern for the underlying Reality within them. They are lost in the waking, dream and deep-sleep states of consciousness. And totally involved in the temporal existence of these states. Ignorant and indifferent towards their absolute state of the divine Self. But those who seek the Self within enjoy peace and bliss progressively. Pursuing the spiritual path they finally attain the absolute bliss of Enlightenment.

Relating to the proximity of the goal a seeker pursues, he experiences four progressive stages of happiness:

Salokyam	Inhabiting the same location as the object of pursuit.
Samipyam	Getting nearer, approaching the object.
Sarupyam	Seeing the form of the object.
Sayujyam	Merging with the object of pursuit.

A common experience in life illustrates this progressive joy. A couple in Pune awaits the arrival of their son after long years of study in a foreign country. They hear that his plane has landed in Mumbai, more than a hundred kilometres away. Yet the news of his arrival in the country, in the same location as theirs, gives them the first taste of joy. That is *salokyam*. An hour later they hear that he is driving down in a car to Pune. The fact that he is coming nearer, approaching them provides greater joy, *samipyam*. The car reaches their home. They see him from the balcony. The sight of their son excites them furthermore, *sarupyam*. Then they rush down for the final embrace. The culmination of their joy, *sayujyam*.

A spiritual seeker goes through a similar experience in his pursuit of the Self. He too passes through these four stages of happiness. Shifting his focus from the external world to the Self within gives him the initial happiness. Withdrawing from the affairs of the world and locating himself in the realm of the Self. Occupying the same realm is the joy of *salokyam*. And by pursuing the Self, getting closer to the Self, he experiences greater peace and happiness. Which is *samipyam*. Further, with sustained spiritual experience he gains a glimpse of the brilliance and bliss of the Self. Though the Self is not an object of perception, he sees Its radiance in all his experiences of life. Feels a deeper contentment and happiness. That is *sarupyam*. Finally, with determined and concerted effort his individual self merges with the supreme Self. He gains *sayujyam*. The absolute bliss of spiritual Enlightenment.

Thus must you give your personality a lift to your real Being. You will then lift the whole world. Move to the central core of your personality. Become the axle around which the world revolves. Scores of sages have done that. The secret of their success is that they sought the truth within themselves. They did not rely on outside forces. Nor attach themselves to any institution. To any mission. Buddha was not a Buddhist. Nor Christ a Christian. Swami Rama Tirtha relied on no mission. Yet, institutions and missions were built around their personalities. People who belong to institutions and missions raise dollars, put up buildings, buy up materiality. Such conquest has little to do with spiritual growth.

Reflect for a moment. Who form congregations? Associations and institutions? Who meet in large numbers? Form great assemblies? Not stalwarts. Not the real masters of the world. No spiritual colossus lives in numbers. He does not find the need for an association or mission. He lives alone. All by himself. Only weaklings gather crowds around them. Just mark the animal kingdom. Sheep and deer move in herds. Sparrows and pigeons flock in numbers. But a lion moves majestically all alone. An eagle soars in the sky all alone. Yet a single lion or eagle can put to flight the congregations. Such is the might and power of your Self. Gain that inner strength. Move to the core of your personality. Get to the fourth state of Self-realisation. You become the King of kings. The God of gods.

Path of Reality

Vedanta leads you to your original state of Being. The fourth state of God-consciousness. The state of the absolute Reality. You attain that state by exhausting your desires, *vasanas*. As long as you possess *vasanas* you are caught up in the limited worlds of the waking, dream and deep-sleep. With the eradication of *vasanas* you regain God-consciousness. A human minus *vasanas* equals God.

Vasanas manifest as desires and tarnish your personality. Your Godhead, the supreme Self within is encrusted with the impurity of desires. In truth you have not lost your divinity. You can never lose it. The divinity only remains covered by impurity. Like a brass pot is tarnished when exposed to the outer atmosphere. A pot remains bright, brilliant if preserved and polished. The difference between a saint and a sinner is the difference between the bright and tarnished pots. The surface of the tarnished pot is oxidised. Which is the coating of impurity. It turns dark, black. The impurity however can be removed. The pot needs polishing. Apply any polishing material like Brasso. Rub it all over the surface until the impurity is removed. Wipe it clean. Finish it with a polishing cloth. The pot regains its original lustre. Lustre is its inherent nature. Not something obtained from elsewhere. The Brasso has only removed the impurity.

Similarly, the divinity is obscured in people by their *vasanas*, desires. Vedanta provides the Brasso-technique.

Removes the encrustation of desires. The technique comprises the three main disciplines of *Karma*, *Bhakti* and *Gnana Yogas*, the Paths of Action, Devotion and Knowledge. Apply this technique regularly until the desires drop off. When the desires are reduced considerably you develop mental concentration. With the growth of concentration you could practise meditation. And through sustained meditation the last trace of *vasana*, the desire for Self-realisation vanishes. What remains is your Self. The Self unfolds Itself. You become the Self. Attain spiritual Enlightenment.

The above three disciplines are seen reflected in William Wordsworth's famous poem:

The Daffodils

I wandered lonely as a cloud
That floats on high o'er vales and hills,
When all at once I saw a crowd,
A host, of golden daffodils;
Beside the lake, beneath the trees,
Fluttering and dancing in the breeze.

Continuous as the stars that shine
And twinkle on the milky way,
They stretched in never-ending line
Along the margin of a bay:
Ten thousand saw I at a glance,
Tossing their heads in sprightly dance.

The waves beside them danced; but they
Out-did the sparkling waves in glee:
A poet could not but be gay,
In such a jocund company:
I gazed — and gazed — but little thought
What wealth the show to me had brought:

For oft, when on my couch I lie
In vacant or in pensive mood,
They flash upon that inward eye
Which is the bliss of solitude;
And then my heart with pleasure fills,
And dances with the daffodils.

— William Wordsworth

The first line of the poem suggests *Karma Yoga*, the spiritual Path of Action. It is selfless action performed in a spirit of detachment. The word 'wandered' signifies a sense of detachment. A wanderer moves about with no particular place or person to return to. And 'lonely' confirms that he is not attached to anybody. He relates to the world with a true spirit of renunciation. While the comparison to a cloud reveals his dedication to service and sacrifice. A cloud symbolises the extremity of service and sacrifice. The cloud gives rain, produce, prosperity. The extremity of service is not just giving all that one possesses but giving oneself away. That is what a cloud does. In providing rain a cloud gives all that it has and gives itself away. That is the calibre of service rendered by one who practises *Karma Yoga*.

A person who does selfless service to the community rises above the influence of the pairs of opposites he encounters. He remains peaceful and happy, unaffected by fortune or misfortune, joy or sorrow, honour or dishonour and the continuous fluctuations in the external world. This idea is well portrayed in the second line: *That floats on high o'er vales and hills.*

A feeling of ecstasy comes to him as a result of his selfless dedicated service. The result is not sought after. The experience of jubilance, the flood of all-embracing love takes him unawares at the sight of the golden daffodils. This is highlighted by placing a comma after the word *host*. The pause indicates that unexpected experience.

The subsequent lines describe that exuberance. His intoxication of pure love for nature. He remains enraptured by the objects and beings of the world. That universal feeling of oneness specifies the Path of Devotion, *Bhakti*.

Karma, selfless action and *bhakti*, devotion purifies the mind. When the mind is pure, the intellect is poised to reflect and contemplate upon the higher truths of life. Hence he *gazed – and gazed –*. With that the poet deftly introduces the third discipline of *Gnana Yoga*, the Path of Knowledge.

The ultimate practice of meditation culminating in spiritual Enlightenment is evidenced in the last stanza. In meditation, the mind is *vacant* of worldly thoughts while it is *pensive* in deep thought of Reality. That practice opens up the *inward eye*. Gives the insight of the supreme Self within, referred to in the *shastra* scripture as the opening of the *gnana chakshu*, the eye-of-wisdom. He becomes one with the All. *Dances with the daffodils*. The individual merges with the all-pervading Reality.

CHAPTER XII

THE FOUR *YOGAS*

Four Spiritual Disciplines

Human beings are separated from Godhead, the supreme Self by *vasanas*. *Vasanas* manifest as thoughts and desires. Root out your desires, thoughts, *vasanas* you become one with Godhead. The union of your individual self with the supreme Self is *yoga*. The merger of the conditioned-consciousness, the ego with the pure, unconditioned Consciousness. *Yoga* is derived from the Sanskrit root *yuj*. *Yuj* means *to join*, *to unite*. The *shastra* scripture has prescribed four *yogas* for the eradication of *vasanas*:

Bhakti Yoga	Path of Devotion
Gnana Yoga	Path of Knowledge
Karma Yoga	Path of Action
Hatha Yoga	Path of Compulsion

These four spiritual disciplines have been designed to suit the four distinct categories of humans. Classified according to their inner nature. Their natures depend upon the relative strengths of their mind and intellect. Thus there are the *emotional*, *intellectual*, *active* and the *indolent* classes of people. Following the respective discipline an aspirant can gradually reduce his desires. Prepare himself for meditation leading to the ultimate state of Self-realisation.

The one who belongs to the *emotional* cadre has the mind more pronounced than the intellect. His heart predominates over his head. He is more impulsive, emotional, devotional. Less rational, intellectual, contemplative. He gives in to his feeling and emotion. The mind rules his personality rather than the intellect. Such a person is designed for the Path of Devotion, *Bhakti Yoga.* He would need a form, an altar, a personal God to pour out his love. His mind revels in the remembrance of the Lord-of-his-heart. The devotion to his Lord displaces all other feeling and thought. Consequently, his mind is focussed upon the higher. With sustained devotion the devotee becomes free of his desires.

The second type is the *intellectual,* whose intellect is more developed than the mind. His head predominates over his heart. He is more analytical, rational. Less impulsive, emotional. His intellect controls the passions of his mind. He remains objective. Does not succumb to his feeling and emotion. Is logical in his approach to life. An enquirer. Perceives the distinction between the terrestrial and the Transcendental. But he will not be satisfied in merely postulating, positing a personal God. Does not take things for granted. He needs logic and reason to accept anything. A person of such calibre is suited for the Path of Knowledge, *Gnana Yoga.* Following this path he becomes rooted in the contemplation of the Reality. Consequently, his mundane thoughts and desires drop off.

The third type, classified as *active,* possesses a mind and intellect more or less equally developed. He could be sometimes emotional and at other times rational. He has a mixed temperament. The Path of Action, *Karma Yoga* caters to such a person. Where both the mind and intellect are engaged. The mind surrenders to the higher ideal he works for. While his intellect channelises action towards that ideal.

191

Thus with the mind and intellect set on the higher goal he sheds his worldly thoughts and desires.

The last category is the *indolent*. The indolent lacks both head and heart. His intellect is poorly developed. He can hardly think, rationalise. No way conceive the existence of the transcendental Reality. Nor does his mind possess feeling, emotion. Far from having devotion to bow down to any altar, deity or personal God. Hence he cannot take in spirituality either through the mind or the intellect or a combination of both. That leaves him unfit to take up any of the above three courses. The only recourse left for him is to administer discipline forcibly through his physical body. Through the Path of Compulsion, *Hatha Yoga*. *Hatha* means force, oppression. *Hatha Yoga* is therefore a discipline administered through force. It covers a schedule of physical exercises known as *asana* and *pranayama* and a series of other practices involving self-torture. Such as standing on one leg or holding up arms for long periods, inhaling smoke and other such torturous practices. These are undertaken as spiritual practices. They help to draw the practitioner out of his indolence. Help the mind to start feeling. The intellect start thinking. He gradually grows to qualify for the other three spiritual courses.

The four categories of human beings only indicate the preponderance of their respective nature. None would be wholly intellectual or emotional or combined or wholly lacking in emotion and reason. Hence each category of persons would comprise a major portion of their respective nature with minor aspects of the other three. An aspirant has to primarily analyse and assess the proportions constituting his nature before he chooses his spiritual discipline. Thereafter he needs to proportion the four *yogas* to suit his composite nature. Thus the one categorised as *intellectual* would need pre-eminently *Gnana Yoga*, the Path of Knowledge along with graduated portions of the other three *yogas* to fulfil the proportions of his remaining minor natures. So do the *emotional* and *active* categories need to concentrate mainly on their respective *yoga* and proportionately combine with the other *yogas*. While the *indolent* has to plunge into *Hatha Yoga* with traces, practically nothing of the higher three disciplines. If an aspirant follows this methodic procedure his spiritual development would be meteoric. But hardly anyone understands the logic and reason for such an integrated discipline. And none follows any method or system in their spiritual life. Hence the world bitterly complains of lack of spiritual development despite their efforts in the spiritual field.

The human mind is congested with selfish thoughts and desires. Like cotton clogged with impurities. Bits and pieces of extraneous matter stick firmly to cotton. One cannot pull them out easily. There is a special process for purifying cotton of its impurities. It is known as carding. The impure cotton is beaten with a card, an instrument used for the purpose. The mass of clogged cotton is thinned out with the beating. Fine fibres of cotton separate and fly about. The impurities sticking to it drop down by gravity. The pure fluffy cotton is collected. The same phenomenon takes place in the mind. The human mind is plagued with egocentric desires. They cannot be easily removed. The practice of *yoga* helps to free the mind of its desires like carding frees cotton of its impurities. *Yoga* sets up a high ideal for self-development culminating in Self-realisation. The mind is drawn towards the ideal. It expands into the vastness of the ideal. As a result the selfish desires drop off. The mind becomes purified.

Thus with constant practice of the *yogas* the mind is rid of all desires except the ultimate desire for Self-realisation. It no more rushes to the world. It turns introvert. An introvert mind alone is qualified to meditate and attain spiritual Enlightenment.

Meditation is the final gateway to Self-realisation. The practice of the *yogas* takes you up to the gateway. The different disciplines purify your mind of worldly thought and desire. The mind becomes qualified for concentration and meditation. Without preparing the mind the practice of meditation is a mockery. You cannot run before you can crawl. One cannot really meditate unless the mind is cleansed of its desires. This is a law. Both the preachers and practitioners of meditation are ignorant of this fundamental law. And plunge into meditation without the initial preparation. They are lured into it because of the apparent, initial feeling of peace it creates. Not realising that the peace gained is temporary. It soon wears away. Another reason for people rushing into meditation is that its procedural details are simple, easily communicable. Far removed from the protracted, deep study and reflection on Vedantic truths. Which are difficult to convey and whose effects are slow, practically indiscernible. Hence the temporary effect of meditation has been exploited to a point of absurdity. Which has resulted in a worldwide craze, a mania for meditation.

Few realise that meditation is the highest technique that a human being can learn and practise. It is the most specialised art, skill. Which requires a well prepared mind freed from worldly attachments and desires. Only a qualified mind can be trained to meditate. Meditation is the art of keeping the mind in sharp focus upon a single thought to the exclusion of all other thoughts. The mind maintains a silent chant of a *mantra* word-symbol under the supervision of the intellect. The intellect does not allow the mind to slip into any other thought. The steady, single pointed, conscious mental absorption in a single thought is meditation. Meditation practised thus leads you to the ultimate state of Self-realisation.

Bhakti Yoga Path of Devotion

Bhakti means devotion. And *Bhakti Yoga* is the Path of Devotion designed for persons in the emotional category. Generally misconstrued as a path of blind faith, superstitious belief or mechanical ritual. *Bhakti* is not merely a fanatic attachment to a personal God to the exclusion of other Gods. Nor does it mean a zealous upholding of a cult or creed against others. Yet people throughout the world follow these practices without probing into their validity. And religious prayer and worship is directed merely to gain either material benefit or mental solace.

Prayer is not beggary. Moreover, mere asking will not help. Yet people make selfish demands in their prayers without paying the price for them. They want to harvest without sowing seeds. Eat without producing. The law of life is that you get what you deserve, not what you desire. You are rewarded *by* your work, not *for* your work. Work performed brilliantly need not solicit any gain. The work itself earns the reward. The same law holds good in the spiritual field as well. People make selfish demands in their prayers. Beg for favours. Implore with tears. But the unrelenting law of life has no room for weak pity.

Devotion today has come to mean mere superstitious centering of love in personalities, blind reliance on rituals and unquestioning faith in idols and places of worship. People are attached to their own creeds. Involved in their own sects. They restrict themselves to their particular idols. And have lost the catholicity of religion. The minds of so-called religious people are plagued with a strange fear, an uncalled-for anxiety and a vain hope centering around an unknown God. And they direct their desperate feelings towards holy bodies and idols, relics and rituals. Such devotion reaches one as far as those outward forms and places go. No further than that. Idols have no doubt a place and purpose in spiritual practice. But few realise that an idol is meant to reach the ideal. And that an idol is not the ideal. The idol has no meaning or purpose without an ideal. It is a means to an end, not an end in itself. Not realising this, most practitioners in the devotional path are stuck to their idols. With no concept of the ideal it stands for. A devotee may use an idol only to reach the ideal. But he must go beyond the manifest form or person to gain the unmanifest Reality.

An idol may be a living person or an inert object, substantial or insubstantial. It is meant to represent the ideal that is sought. Like a national flag for a nation. The flag is the idol used to develop national consciousness, the ideal set for the people. Imagine a person with a deep regard and respect for his flag. He uses it faithfully for national ceremonies and conventions. While he engages his time in anti-national activities! Such is the state of devotional people today. They stick to idols. Hang on to personalities. Get addicted to ceremonies and rituals. Run after pilgrimages to places of worship. With no sight of an ideal. They miss the soul of prayer and worship. They take the husk and throw the grain away!

Cast aside all these meaningless practices of devotion. And probe into its quintessence. Devotion arises when the intellect fails to comprehend an unknown realm. Where the mind surrenders to the area of ignorance. You surrender to a doctor when you are ignorant of your illness. You surrender to a lawyer when you are ignorant of the law related to your problem. But you have not cared to scan the vast areas of ignorance in your life. And thus remain totally unaware of the expanse of ignorance that shrouds your personality. Yet you sport an ego of I-know-it-all.

It is time you examined the crevices in your personality. You know not where you come from. You know not the purpose of your sojourn in this world. Where and when you go from here. The day you are born, mother's milk is programmed for your sustenance. Your oxygen supply assured. Your temperature and pressure within maintained meticulously to this day. The atmospheric temperature and pressure outside maintained punctiliously for your survival. Your alimentary canal, respiratory organs, nervous system and countless other functions service your personality day and night, from birth to death. The unseen functions are not confined to mere maintenance of beings. They extend further as a constant vigilance over any intrusion by predators. The moment a foreign matter enters your body or you bruise yourself there is an instant release of forces within to mend the damage done to the body. You must realise the boundless benefaction lavished on beings. Hardly anyone is aware of it all. Much less grateful for what is received and enjoyed.

To this vast realm of ignorance of an unseen hand functioning, must you surrender. An acute awareness of the infinite blessings showered everywhere followed by gratitude would constitute the fundamentals of devotion. Devotion therefore is to cognise the splash of Divinity manifested in every being, everywhere. To identify and merge with that omnipotent, omniscient, omnipresent Reality.

The *Upanishads* in the *Vedas* have given humanity the highest, ultimate philosophy. Which takes you to the threshold of the supreme Reality, *Brahman*. One of them entitled *Kenopanishad* roars the staggering truth in five consecutive verses: *That supreme Reality, Brahman is your Self within and not what you worship here in the world.* Though the *Upanishads* are known for their brevity, their terse, cryptic language. It marvels in its profound explanation of God. God is the supreme Omnipresence while He resides within as your Self. The Self that enlivens your eyes to see. That enlivens your ears to hear. Your limbs to function. Mind to feel emotions. Intellect to conceive thoughts. That is the supreme God. And not what people worship in the external world. Remember That. Realise That.

To attain God-realisation a devotee must qualify himself with sterling qualities. The *Bhagavad Gita* in its twelfth chapter, verses 13 to 20, enumerates thirty-five divine qualities that constitute a true devotee. For a detailed study you may go through the author's commentary on the *Gita*. However a brief statement of those qualities is given below for your ready reference:

Hates no being, friendly, compassionate, not possessive, free from egoism, balanced in pleasure or pain, forgiving, ever-content, uniting with Self, self-controlled, of firm conviction, mind and intellect dedicated to Self, who does not agitate the world, who is not agitated by the world, free from joy-envy-fear-anxiety, free from want, pure, dexterous, unconcerned, untroubled, not arrogating any activity as one's own, neither rejoices-hates-grieves-desires, balanced in pleasant or unpleasant happenings, alike to friend-foe, heat-cold, joy-sorrow, honour-dishonour, free from attachment, equal to censure and praise, silent, content with anything, free from possessions, firm-minded, endued with faith, regards Self as supreme.

A devotee of God is one who is endowed with the thirty-five qualities. True devotion means faith in good rather than faith in God. The general concept of devotion, *bhakti* does not seem to have any bearing on these qualities. A person with none of these qualities is still reputed to be a great devotee, *bhakta*. The non-essentials of devotion are blown up at the expense of the essentials. People in ignorance accept fanatic attachment and following of a particular deity or personality, creed or cult as devotion. Devotion is not as simple as that. The devotional path requires a high level of discipline and training to develop the divine traits.

The real and earnest part of devotion is seen in the annihilation of the ego, self-effacement. A true devotee considers himself a spoke in the wheel of life. Surrenders his individuality to the totality. To the general plan of nature. Recognises and feels the divinity in and around.

Devotion and love are the same emotion. Differing in direction, not in nature. When a feeling of affection, fondness is directed to your equals or lower beings or objects it is called love. The same directed towards the higher is known as devotion. You love your friend, your child, your pet. But you are devoted to your parents, guru, God. Therefore one cannot claim to have devotion to God if he has no love for his fellow-beings. This idea has been well captured by James Henry Leigh Hunt in his poem *Abou Ben Adhem*.

The poem narrates Abou Ben Adhem's encounter with an angel in his dream. Abou dreamt one night that he saw an angel writing in a book of gold. Abou asked the angel as to what it was writing. The angel replied that it was the names of those who love God. Abou enquired if his name was in that list. The angel replied it was not so. Then Abou cheerfully implored the angel to put his name down as one who loves his fellow-men. The angel wrote and vanished. The next night it returned to show the names of all those

whom God really loved. And that list had Abou Ben
Adhem's name right on top! The poem:

Abou Ben Adhem

Abou Ben Adhem (may his tribe increase!)
Awoke one night from a deep dream of peace,
And saw, within the moonlight in his room,
Making it rich, and like a lily in bloom,
An Angel writing in a book of gold:
Exceeding peace had made Ben Adhem bold,
And to the Presence in the room he said,
"What writest thou?" The Vision raised its head,
And with a look made of all sweet accord
Answered, "The names of those who love the Lord."
"And is mine one?" said Abou. "Nay, not so,"
Replied the Angel. Abou spoke more low,
But cheerily still; and said, *"I pray thee, then,*
Write me as one that loves his fellow men."

The Angel wrote, and vanished. The next night
It came again with a great wakening light,
And showed the names whom love of God had blessed,
And, lo! Ben Adhem's name led all the rest!

— James Henry Leigh Hunt

Gnana Yoga Path of Knowledge

Gnanam means knowledge. And *Gnana Yoga* is the Path
of Knowledge designed for persons in the intellectual
category. It is meant for those who enquire into the mystery
of life and the world. Who am I? How did this world come

about? What is the origin of beings? Who is God? The Path of Knowledge finds answers to these questions. *Gnana Yoga* is not mere erudition and scholarship in religious literature. Not cramming spiritual knowledge from textbooks, precepts and preceptors. True knowledge arises out of an internal discipline of reflection and contemplation on the eternal truths. Scriptures and sermons would play a vital part in your spiritual development provided you think originally on the subject, reflect upon the truths therein until you assimilate, absorb them. As you absorb the knowledge you apply it practically in all walks of life. You begin to question what is permanent and impermanent in life. What is eternal and ephemeral. Distinguish the Real from the unreal. This discipline has been brought out by one potent advice by the poet-philosopher Shankaracharya: *nitya anitya viveka vichara* which means reflecting on the distinction between the Eternal and the ephemeral.

You must therefore examine what is unchanging in the changing phenomena of the world. What remains constant in the inconstant factors of life. Observe your own life's journey. How it passes through various facets from childhood through old age. Your personality is in a constant flux of change. Never static. Yet you point to yourself and say, "This is me. This height, weight, this name, fame is me." Little realising that the moment you point your finger at yourself you have already changed. There can be no fixation of your personality. Nevertheless you go on declaring, "I am a child, I am a boy, I am a man, I am an old man." The personality moves on. But the *I* remains constant.

The same *I* assumes three distinct states of consciousness. As a waker, dreamer and deep-sleeper. These are three different personalities. But you declare: I am the person-in-the-waking-state, I am the person-in-the-dream, I am the person-in-sleep. That *I*, the constant Factor which runs through the three states is the supreme Self.

The Path of Knowledge helps you develop the awareness of that one Reality in the kaleidoscopic patterns of life. Recognise the unity in diversity. The one Self pulsating in every facet of life. You must develop an awareness of the divinity that pervades everywhere. Make good use of scriptural study and reflection to probe into the Self that you are. Keep your thoughts in your divine centre while you function in the world. Never let yourself slip out of your Self. Just as fishes live in the medium of water. Birds in the medium of air. So do you live in the medium of the divine Consciousness. That Consciousness is your real Self. Remember you are the Self at all times. Revel in your Self. You will soon rise above your worldly attachment and entanglement. And reach the state of Self-realisation.

In actual practice you must make sure that you study the scripture daily. You derive the best result if you do so in the *sattvik* time, between 4 a.m. and 6 a.m. Reflect upon what you study. Contemplate on the truths therein. Apply them in your life. Be consistent in your effort. The results of your endeavour show up gradually. You need to exercise a great deal of patience and perseverance before you become established in the eternal Being that you are.

Most people lack this discipline of studying the scripture or listening to spiritual discourses. They seek instant ways and means to Self-realisation. And they believe that by directly plunging into meditation they could attain Enlightenment. Such people are far removed from divinity. Their intellect is obscured by a cloud of ignorance. And the mind infested with desires. Whereas the pursuit of knowledge frees your mind of its desires. Clears the cloud of ignorance.

Your intellect begins to distinguish the Eternal from the ephemeral. And you perceive the play of divinity in all walks of life. There is far more power in your disciplined way of living than in most men in their assumed state of meditation.

The *Bhagavad Gita* in the thirteenth chapter, verses 8 to 12, gives out twenty qualities that define the Path of Knowledge. They are virtues that go with the person endowed with spiritual knowledge. For a detailed study of those qualities you may go through the author's commentary on the *Gita*. For your ready reference they are enumerated below:

Humility, unpretentiousness, harmlessness, forgiveness, uprightness, service to preceptor, purity, steadfastness, self-control, dispassion towards sense-objects, absence of egoism, insight into the pain and evil of birth-death-old age-disease, non-attachment, free from infatuation to son, wife, home etc, constant balance of mind in desirable or undesirable happenings, unflinching devotion to Self through steadfast *yoga*, resorting to solitary place, disinterest in gathering, constancy in Self-knowledge, perception of the end of true knowledge.

A seeker must develop these twenty qualities to ensure his advancement in the Path of Knowledge.

Karma Yoga Path of Action

Karma means action. And *Karma Yoga* is the Path of Action designed for persons in the active category. Action is inevitable as long as one is alive. Since every human being is constituted of *vasanas*, desires. One's *vasanas* forcibly manifest themselves as thoughts, desires and actions. A human is bound to act. But is free to choose the type of action he executes. *Karma Yoga* provides the course of right action leading one towards spiritual evolution.

All creatures except human beings have a built-in programme to conduct themselves in the nature of their particular species. Just as the carnivore and the herbivore merely display their distinct and different natures. Only human beings have the choice of action. No other creature is faced with the dilemma of choice. Since humans are confronted with this problem the Path of Action is laid down for their guidance to a better life, towards evolution.

The physical body executes action. But the body cannot act on its own. It is either the mind or the intellect that propels the body to act. The mind is riddled with likes and dislikes. The intellect is that which reasons, judges, decides. In practical life you either operate as per your mind's likes and dislikes or let your intellect reason and decide the course of action. In which case your intellect may approve and go along with what your mind chooses to do. Or disapprove and decide a course of action opposed to your mind's fancy. The problem with the mind is that it has no direction or dimension. It can prove detrimental, even fatal to you. The mind entertains boundless desires. It can never be satiated. Hence, you cannot afford to let your actions be driven by the indiscriminate demands of the mind. Your intellect must maintain a constant vigilance over the mind's activity. That does not mean that you discard all that your mind likes and court what it dislikes. Your intellect only makes sure that you take to the right course of action regardless of the pressures exerted by your likes and dislikes.

Your like and dislike, your attraction and aversion, attachment and revulsion for things, beings and actions turn out to be the greatest enemy working against you. Few realise their impact on one's life. If not governed by the intellect they could lead you to destruction. People are unaware of the devastating nature of the mind. Worse still, they nurture and nourish their likes and dislikes. Pamper them. And go through suffering and sorrow. The practical way to circumvent the impact of your likes and dislikes is to rise above them. By pitching up an ideal in life. An ideal is a higher goal, a common cause that you choose to work for, above your self-centred interest in life. Wherein your interest and attention is focussed towards the higher values of life rather than your selfish ends. If you do not dedicate your life to an ideal you will remain enslaved by your likes and dislikes.

Hence carefully study and reflect upon the importance of fixing an ideal in life. As high an ideal as you can reach within your capacity. Make sure you choose a realistic ideal and work towards it. When your intellect is fired with an ideal, your mind's likes and dislikes slowly lose their persuasive influence. The ideal that you set for life could be relative or absolute. A relative ideal is that which is directed to the welfare of your community or country, to humanity or all living beings. The absolute ideal would be to realise the supreme Self, attain the ultimate spiritual Enlightenment.

Karma Yoga, the Path of Action envisages an ideal in life. One who follows this path, a *karma yogi*, dedicates his life's activities to the ideal he has set. His mind is focussed on the noble cause for which he works while the body is engaged in constant action. All along his intellect ensures that the mind and body do not slip away from the path set for the purpose. When the mind and intellect are thus pursuing a selfless ideal the body becomes energised to work. The more he works the more energy it releases. And with greater energy work turns out dynamic.

The Path of Action further ensures that the energy gained is not dissipated through unproductive channels. There are three distinct ways through which energy drains away. One way is by the mind worrying about the past. The second is through its anxiety over the fruit of action. And the third, its excitement in the present action. However lofty the ideal be, your mind tends to slip into these channels. It loses its concentration on the present action. Your intellect must exercise its strength to hold the mind on to the action whenever it strays away. You must learn to clip the past, clip the future and plunge into the present activity. Then your action becomes perfect be it in the material or spiritual field.

With the pursuit of the appropriate *yogas* the mind is freed from the bulk of desires. You develop a sense of dispassion, a feeling of renunciation. Your mind withdraws from its involvement in the affairs of the world. Indicated in the diagram as *uparati*, withdrawal.

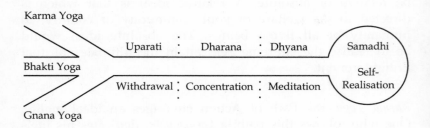

When *uparati* sets in, you develop mental concentration, *dharana*. With sustained abstraction from the world and concentration upon the higher, you enter the last stage of meditation, *dhyana*. And in deep meditation, the single pointed thought ultimately dissolves in absolute silence. In that silence, you attain *Samadhi*, spiritual Enlightenment.

CHAPTER XIII

RENUNCIATION

What is Renunciation

Renunciation is the quintessence of spirituality. The sap of religion. The spirit of renunciation instilled by Vedanta paves the way to Enlightenment. Yet the subject of renunciation is seldom spoken of in religious institutions. A topic which hardly finds a place in spiritual discussions. And the concept of renunciation is totally misconstrued. The idea of renunciation is repulsed by the modern society. The thought of it is dismissed by people as something repugnant. The beauty and grandeur of renunciation has been transformed into an ugly caricature. The general misconception is that it means resignation and retirement from life. To go barefooted and bareheaded. Live in the seclusion of forests. This is far from the truth. Had it been so then renunciation would be of no practical use to people. And only cater to a few social recluses who shun any form of pleasure or material comfort.

Ironic as it may seem, renunciation is meant for one and all. It has to be practised in business and home, in everyday life, in the din and roar of the marketplace. It is the solace of life, it will be the solace of death. In its true form, renunciation provides the greatest consolation to those who suffer from worldly attachment and desire. And when intensified it draws out the divinity in a human being. Animates him to bring about a reintegration, a reunion with the supreme Being. Renunciation is the fragrance a spiritually evolved person releases while performing his obligatory duties and responsibilities. The sublime trait of renunciation ought not to be reduced to weak resignation. Those equipped with this great trait stood out as spiritual stalwarts in the world.

Hence, a thorough understanding of this human quality is of prime importance in one's life and living. No progress is possible without renunciation. As you advance to the higher echelons of life you drop the lower. It is a natural progression. Your childhood traits fall off as you reach your teens. So do your teenage fascinations drop with advancing maturity. The flower is sacrificed when the fruit emerges. Thus renunciation is a mark of growth, a symbol of progress in life. Below is a careful and methodic analysis which provides a clear picture of renunciation.

1. *Does renunciation mean isolation from society? Retiring to secluded places?*

It cannot mean that. If so, it would be of no use to people to practise and live by. Renunciation is an essential ingredient of religion. Designed for every human being for his evolution. He needs to apply it in all facets of life while interacting with the world.

2. *If association with the world is permissible, does renunciation then mean abstaining from individual possession and enjoyment of worldly objects and beings?*

It cannot mean that either. In the past India was the home of many royal-sages. They were kings who were highly evolved souls living a life of renunciation. King Janaka was one such royal-sage. He reigned over a kingdom. Enjoyed the comforts of royalty. Yet was a man of renunciation. Rooted in the thought of the Supreme, never was he enmeshed in the affairs of the world. Tradition apart, it would be impractical to allow one to contact the sense-objects but not enjoy their pleasures. To stimulate the appetite for sensual pleasure through contact and stifle enjoyment therefrom. That would be far more frustrating than total abstinence from them. Hence there is no objection to enjoyment of sense-objects. The practice of renunciation therefore does not taboo worldly possession or enjoyment.

3. *Does renunciation then mean restricted possession and enjoyment? Fixing limits to the quantum of your possession and extent of your enjoyment of sense-objects?*

No, not even that. Had it been so, the practice of renunciation would mean merely following charts with fixed limits for material possession and sensual enjoyment. Moreover, it is not possible to fix such limits in practical life. What is excessive for one may be insufficient for another. Both in terms of material possession and sensual enjoyment. Hence renunciation cannot be defined by such arbitrary boundaries. This truth has been highlighted in the scripture by two extreme examples. Lord Krishna was known to have kept the company of many *gopis* milkmaids. Yet he was acclaimed as a *nitya brahmachari* meaning perpetual celibate. So too was Sage Durvasa known for freely consuming food. And he was known as *nitya upavasi*, one on constant fast. These apparent contradictions are meant to drive home the truth that possession and enjoyment do not determine one's stature of renunciation.

4. *If the quantum of possession and enjoyment also is not related to renunciation, then what is renunciation? What is*

the difference between a materialistic, sensual person and a renunciate?

This is the crux of the problem. Go over the above analysis carefully. It becomes evident that renunciation is not severance from the world. Nor does it mean abstinence from possession and enjoyment. Nor restriction and limitation imposed upon the quantum of possession and enjoyment. Hence, you could remain amidst people and prosperity, you could acquire, possess and enjoy objects and beings without imposing any restriction or limitation and yet be a renunciate. If one is allowed to enjoy all these liberties what then does confer the status of renunciation upon an individual? You can find that out by studying your own past experiences in life.

In your childhood you were attached to playthings. You spent your time then acquiring and enjoying toys and trinklets. Now that you are grown up you no longer value them. You treat them as trifles. You are preoccupied with other attractions. Caught up with your family, name, fame, wealth, power. The childhood playthings do not hold your interest any more. They drop off. You are said to have renounced them. What determines your dispassion towards your childhood interests? What ascertains that spirit of renunciation? Carefully analyse the cause. It is not your physical parting from playthings. Not your dispossession or non-enjoyment. Nor limitation in their possession or enjoyment. You may possess them. Even join your children at times, enjoy playing with them. And yet claim to have renounced them because you do not treasure them any more. They are not worth anything to you. You have no value for them. No longer credit them with any merit. Your interest has risen to greater heights. Thus, as you graduate to higher values of life you automatically drop your interest, value for the lower. You grow out of it. That spirit of inner abstraction or resignation is the crux of renunciation.

Renunciation therefore is growth in one's personality. Founded by knowledge established in the higher values of life.

The highest value, the greatest mission in life is the discovery of the supreme Self within. He who has set Self-realisation as his goal in life, pursues it with faith and conviction, has no attraction for worldly possession and enjoyment. Name and fame mean nothing to him. Wealth and power do not lure him. He does not get enmeshed in family affairs. He understands the ephemeral nature of all that the world offers. Be it wealth or enjoyment. If he needs to possess or contact them he does so with inner abstraction. Others may not recognise his mental resignation towards them. Thus renunciation could be defined as disinterested interest, dispassionate passion towards the world. The Tamil scripture refers to that state in striking terms *Thungamal thungi: Asleep, yet not sleeping.*

One takes this supreme stance in life when one sets the right value for the world. Considers object and being, action and perception, emotion and thought to be ephemeral, transient. Renunciation therefore is a mark of spiritual growth. Emanating from knowledge of the eternal Self. A spiritually evolved person commands a true spirit of renunciation. He runs his family with love and affection, possesses property, enjoys the senses. While he goes through these experiences his mind remains anchored in the supreme Self within. With the mind rooted in the Self he understands the futility of the world. Feels that inner dispassion towards the events and experiences of mundane existence.

Few in the world today have a proper understanding of this magnificent stand of renunciation. The ignoramuses feign this illustrious state of being by their outward practices. They live in seclusion. Discard property and possession. Avoid sense contact. Put on an act of celibacy. With all that, their minds entertain material and sensual thoughts. They still harbour mundane values. Their appraisal of the world remains high. Such impersonators are far removed from the state of renunciation.

The above dissection of renunciation clears the general misconception of a materialist and sensualist. A person is adjudged a materialist or not by the value he confers upon material wealth regardless of the quantum he possesses. When he understands material objects as trivial and trifling, as valueless and a potential impediment to spiritual growth, he is no materialist. Whereas another who carries much value for material wealth, regards it as a primary aspect of life would be a materialist, whether or not he possesses it. Similarly a sensualist is not judged by the extent of his contact with or enjoyment of sense-objects but by his mental attitude towards them. When a person places sense-objects and the pleasures thereof in their proper perspective, realises their clear limitation, considers them the harbinger of future sorrow and misery and maintains a suzerainty over them, he is no sensualist even if he were to enjoy them. Whereas the one who considers sensual pleasures as an all-important part of life, succumbs to the pleasures of the senses would be a sensualist, even if he physically abstains from them.

Renunciation therefore is the measure of spirituality. The yardstick of spiritual evolution. As an aspirant evolves to the higher, subtler realms of his personality he becomes freed from the lower, grosser levels. He no longer identifies with the grosser. He grows out of the desires associated with them. In effect, renounces them. As he reaches the height of spiritual evolution, identifies with the supreme Self, he attains total renunciation. When his desires completely fall off.

The Self within, *Atman* is enveloped by concentric layers of matter comprising thoughts and desires. As you move away from your divine centre your ego develops. Your thoughts and desires turn grosser, they multiply. And at the farthest point, your ego is maximised. Your thoughts and desires become grossest, countless.

Thus, when you live at the lowest level of your personality, your thoughts and desires are gross and numerous. But as you acquire spiritual knowledge you begin to entertain higher and nobler values. You move up to the higher realms of your personality. Your thoughts and desires improve in quality and reduce in quantity. Consequently, you renounce the lower. Thus, through daily study and reflection on spiritual literature, you identify with the supreme Self, the core of your personality. At that stage your only desire is to realise the Self. All other desires vanish. You reach the state of total renunciation.

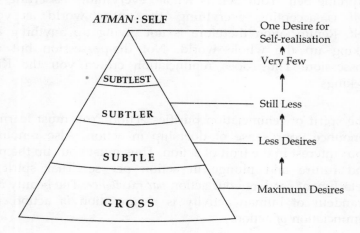

True renunciation therefore means delivering everything to the supreme Reality. Not considering the body, mind and intellect as yours. Dropping the false idea of your personal self. Casting aside your vain, accumulative and possessive attitude. Not arrogating anything to yourself. Resigning everything to the Reality. Appropriating everything to the real Self in you. You then rise above the little self, the ego. It is your ego that becomes involved, enmeshed in the affairs of the world, obsessed with mundane duties and responsibilities. Rising above the ego and identifying with the real Self, you remain above worldly care and anxiety. You remain detached, free from the persecutions of the ego. Maintaining that exalted state you plunge into single pointed meditation. Attain spiritual Enlightenment.

The practice of negating the little self and asserting the real Self helps in rising above your false personality. Subduing your ego. Effacing your copyrighting spirit of 'me' and 'mine'. These feelings and thoughts engender, feed your little appropriating self, the ego. You must negate your ego to attain the state of renunciation. Remember you are the supreme Self. Your Self is whole, everything. Asserting the Self is accepting everything, the entire world as your Self. Renunciation therefore is not giving up anything but taking up the whole world. Not dis-possession but all-possession. Thus does renunciation crown you the King of kings.

The spirit of renunciation purifies action. You must learn to renounce your sense of doership in action. Also renounce your interest in the fruit of action. Thus must you clip the past and future and plunge in action per se. That spirit of detachment renders your action *par excellence*. The beauty and grandeur of human activity is renunciation *in* action, not renunciation *of* action.

Renunciation has further been classified under three broad categories. Known as *sattvik, rajasik* and *tamasik. Sattvik* renunciation is the highest, true renunciation. *Rajasik* is conditioned, temporary state of renunciation. And *tamasik* is the lowest, no renunciation at all.

Tamasik renunciation is relinquishment of obligatory action out of delusion. A human being has to fulfil his obligation to his family, his business, community, country. Etcetera. Relinquishing duties and responsibilities out of ignorance, indifference is considered *tamasik*. Also discarding things out of ignorance of their value, because one is not aware of its pleasure-content, would fall under *tamasik* renunciation.

Rajasik renunciation is relinquishment of action because of fear of physical or mental pain that it may cause. In that case, the person claiming to have renounced action would willingly take to it if the strain or pain part of it is removed. Such pseudo-relinquishment is considered *rajasik*.

Ironically, true renunciation does not mean giving up action. *Sattvik* renunciation, acclaimed as of the highest order, speaks of performance of action. A human has to perform his obligatory functions in life. He cannot give up his duty and responsibility. He must do what he ought to do without being involved in his action or entertaining a profit motive in it. Just carry out work objectively. With no desire driving action. And no craving for fruit. Thus *sattvik* renunciation means acting without the mind's attachment to action or anxiety for the fruit thereof.

Way to Success

The spirit of renunciation is the secret of success. The lives of some of the outstanding personalities in history have demonstrated this truth. The secret of their success lay in keeping themselves above attachment, above worldly worry and anxiety. Their mind was set on a high and noble ideal beyond any trace of the selfish ego and its demands. Their energies were directed, dedicated to the lofty goal. Their power arose from that stand they took. Their mind reached above self-aggrandising, egoistic living. That was their state of abstraction. A spirit of renunciation. Wherein the world and its attractions meant nothing to them. Renunciation is the sap that flows in the tree of success.

Vedanta provides you with the knowledge to live that exalted life. Renunciation is synonymous with the knowledge of Self. Knowledge and renunciation are two sides of a coin. The *rishis* great sages of the past retired to the forest to contemplate, discover the fundamental truths of life. Just as scientists isolate themselves in the laboratory to discover the laws governing the world. The truths of life that the sages unearthed constitute the knowledge meant for the people to apply in their day-to-day living. In the same manner as the scientific laws found in the laboratory are applicable to the outside world. Vedanta therefore is not designed for resignation or retirement. Yet people wrongly believe it to be so. And have unwisely alienated it from the modern society, especially the youth. Sadly, the youth have been brainwashed to believe that Vedantic knowledge promotes renunciation meant for superannuates who are done with life or for idle recluses.

Renunciation has nothing to do with place, position or profession. It flows from knowledge which refines you. Places you on vantage ground. Puts you right on top. Renders you peaceful and blissful. Free from anguish and anxiety. Few realise the grandeur and power of renunciation. Through renunciation you gain everything. Its spirit leads your actions to success. Also supports your enjoyment of the world.

There is a stern law of life concerning attachment: *Attach you lose detach you gain*. None seems to be aware of it. Much less follows it. It means that if you cling on to any material form, selfishly attach to a person or object, you shall go through suffering and sorrow. Either something terrible happens to that relationship or you lose the object of your desire. Whereas, when you live a life of mental detachment, in a state of renunciation, you will find objects and beings reaching you. Swami Rama Tirtha has proclaimed this truth to the world: *The way to gain anything is to lose it*. It is an inexorable law of life. Observe it in your surroundings. Learn it from your experience. Realise this truth from personal knowledge.

Renunciation paves the way to prosperity and peace in life. The more you renounce, the more peaceful you are, the more the world courts you. Leave the world alone, you gain it. You run after it, you lose it. The phenomenon of colour illustrates this truth. Physics explains the principle underlying perception of colour. Light consists of seven vibgyoric colours. You see an object only when it is bathed in light. By the light it reflects. A rose appears red because it reflects red colour only. It absorbs the other six colours and rejects red. Strange as it may sound, the rose is red because it gives away red. Thus an object appears in the colour that it relinquishes. There is a story depicting this striking truth of life.

The king of a state was anxious to meet a *sannyasi*, a recluse who has renounced everything in life. He enquired of his minister if he could find one such person. The minister took the king's wish lightly and averred that there were many around. The king waited for a while. There was no response. One day he summoned the minister and gave him a week's time to fulfil his wish. The minister then realised that the king was serious. He tried hard to find one. But his attempts were all in vain. In utter desperation he devised a clever plan. He chose a young man to put on an act of a *sannyasi* in return for a large sum of money. The man readily yielded to his request. He was dressed in ochre robe with other spiritual accessories to adorn his faked religiosity. He was asked to sit under a tree in a secluded place. The stage was set. The minister announced that he had located the *sannyasi*. The king and his retinue was brought to the scene. The king was inspired at the sight of the feigned *sannyasi*. He prostrated at his feet. So did the queen. The king looked enquiringly at the minister. He had to prostrate too! The king offered trays of money, clothing and food. The *sannyasi* would not accept any of them. The king was amazed at his spirit of renunciation. He reverentially took leave of the holy man and returned to the palace with his retinue.

The minister rushed back to the scene. He commended the young man on his great performance. And offered him the promised payment. The *sannyasi* refused to accept it. The minister was confused. He told him that the play was over and bade him accept the money. The young man gestured to the minister to sit down and spoke these words of wisdom, "Dear sir, did you not witness the beauty and grandeur of life in our episode? Have you not learnt a great lesson today? Do you realise I feigned an act of renunciation for a short while. The king, the queen and the entire retinue were at my feet. Just an act of abstraction, a show of renunciation showered so much wealth and reverence upon me. What then would be the power of true renunciation? Realise that sir, and take back your money."

Renunciation is Bliss

There can be no peace, no happiness unless you renounce your little self, give up your self-asserting ego, drop the idea of 'I' and 'my', 'me' and 'mine'. E. Carpenter, an Englishman of great spiritual experience says, "Never before could I have believed it but I see it all now. There is no happiness unless you have clean dropped thinking about yourself; but you must not do it by halves. While even there is a least grain of self left, it will spoil it all. You must just leave it all behind and vouchsafe the personality and mind that much sympathy as to any stranger, no more, no less." Hence must you banish all attachment and anxiety. Brush aside fear of censure and hope of appreciation. Consider yourself as you would a stranger. Cast aside your cherished personal ego and pass disembodied out of yourself. Pass through the gate of indifference, through the door of knowledge into the palace of peace and bliss. The *Ishavasya Upanishad* proclaims this truth: *May you enjoy bliss through renunciation.*

Bhoga in Sanskrit means enjoyment. And *yoga* means renunciation. People construe these two words as antonyms. Consider *bhoga* to be opposed to *yoga*. But that is not so. If you study them carefully you will conclude that they are not different. *Bhoga* enjoyment is nothing other than *yoga* renunciation. It may sound revolutionary. But it is the truth. There can be no real enjoyment unless you are poised in the mental state of renunciation. No sooner you renounce the arrogating ego than you become the personification of joy, happiness, bliss. You turn spiritual. The path to the supreme Self, the way to the bliss of Self-realisation is the crucifixion of the little self.

Attachment is the prime cause of mental agitation and sorrow. When you are attached to material objects, to wealth you are riddled with worry and anxiety. Anxiety to procure more and more. And worry about preserving or losing it. Thus a newly fixed carpet in your house, a china you value or any such prized possession can cause mental agitation, suffering and sorrow if you are attached to it. Similarly a boy attached to a girl, a mother attached to her child would cause the mind to be disturbed. When you are driving your personal, expensive car on a rough and rugged road your heart throbs. Whereas the same ride in a hired car becomes enjoyable! Thus when you are detached you enjoy the world. That explains why you enjoy a tragic movie, a horror movie.

Shakespeare's play *Hamlet* was filmed with the famous actor Sir Lawrence Olivier. It depicted a great tragedy. Every bit of it was very sad. Melancholic, yet magnificent. It drew millions of admirers. They enjoyed the movie thoroughly. Many saw it over and over again. There was a charm about it that kept everybody spellbound. Notwithstanding all that, would anyone desire to be Prince Hamlet in the movie? Would anyone like to be involved in those tragic circumstances? Everyone may enjoy the movie but none would like to get anywhere near those scenes, much less get mixed up with them. If that be so, what makes it so attractive, so enjoyable? How does a sad movie make millions happy? On a careful study you find that the enjoyment arises from one's aloofness from the happenings on the screen. It is one's detachment from it. Not being involved or entangled in it.

When you look upon a movie as a witness, you enjoy it. When you get directly involved in it, you suffer. Some even sob. So it is with the world. Keep your mind anchored to the divine Self within and look at the world as you would see the movie. You must learn to live in your home, with your family, run your office with your associates, meet the world impersonally as a *sakshi* witness, without getting attached to them, entangled with their affairs. When you look at the phenomenal world thus from an impersonal angle as a *sakshi*, view it objectively, it lends a charm. It is beautiful. Wonderful. You enjoy every bit of it. But if you view it personally, lose your objectivity and get involved, entangled in it you suffer. Your life turns miserable. It is a universal law.

Almost every human being suffers from the nagging weakness of attachment. To rise above it you need to strengthen your intellect with spiritual knowledge. A knowledge which exposes the absurdity of your personalised relation with the world. Your immaturity. You begin to understand the futility of such relation. With knowledge seeping in, you gradually develop a sense of detachment towards the world. The dawn of detachment drives away the mist of worry and anxiety. Leaving you in peace and bliss.

Two childhood friends happened to meet after a long lapse of time. One of them was a successful businessman. The other a spiritual mendicant, *sannyasi*. Engrossed in conversation they lost track of time. And reached the bank of a river late in the evening. They had to cross over to the other side. The boatman refused to ferry them across as it was past his working hours. Their side of the river was infested with wild animals. The businessman offered the boatman a chunk of money. The latter yielded. They were ferried across to the safer side where the businessman's mansion lay. That night after entertaining his guest with supper, the businessman enquired, "Tell me friend, of what use is your stand of renunciation? If I had not possessed the money, both of us would have been devoured by wolves. Has not your way of life proved to be impractical?" The *sannyasi* replied with these wise words, "Dear friend, undoubtedly your money has helped us today, but was it its possession or its dispossession that really saved us?"

The problem with renunciation is that it has a detestable front. People find it hard to accept the concept of detachment. The very thought of it sends a shiver down the spine. The idea of detachment stings you. Little do you realise that the sting of renunciation transports you to a higher plane, to permanent peace and bliss. It relieves you from all worry and anxiety associated with the world. The initial feel of renunciation acts like a wasp's sting in a dream. The dreamer's pain is momentary for it wakes him up. He is freed from all trouble, worry and anxiety pertaining to the dream-world. Practising detachment therefore may be initially painful but it is all gainful. It ushers you to greater planes of happiness, leading you to the bliss of the supreme Self.

Renunciation heralds Meditation

The mental state of renunciation is an essential prerequisite for practising concentration and meditation. You need to first free yourself from your mental bondage to the world. The mind is riddled with desires. The unfulfilled desires cause the mind to be agitated, disturbed. Such a mind remains enmeshed in the affairs of the world. It cannot rise to the subtler realm of contemplation and meditation. You need a calm and composed mind to do that. And the way to achieve that state is through reduction of desires. The three *yogas*, *karma* action, *bhakti* devotion and *gnana* knowledge, have been prescribed from time immemorial to eradicate desires. *Karma Yoga*, the Path of Action is the spiritual discipline directed to the body. *Bhakti Yoga*, the Path of Devotion to the mind. And *Gnana Yoga*, the Path of Knowledge to the intellect. Thus must you intelligently proportion these disciplines to suit the constitution of your personality. You then gradually reduce the bulk of desires. Your mind is freed from agitation. It becomes calm. A calm mind alone can be directed to meditation. And through meditation you attain spiritual Enlightenment.

The above traditional procedure has been scientifically designed. You cannot short circuit this procedure and plunge into meditation. The mind requires to be prepared by the practice of the *yogas* to free it from the bulk of desires. A practice that involves time. A procedure that may be slow but sure. But people lack the patience and perseverance. They look for immediate results. This human weakness has been widely exploited. Self-appointed spiritual leaders have been hawking physical exercises as *yoga*. Also selling meditation indiscriminately to unprepared minds all over the world. The innocent masses have been led astray. Scores of pseudo-spiritual courses are marketed everywhere. Some of these courses enjoy a large following because they lend an immediate peace, solace. The ignorant do not realise that their experience is temporary, transitory. And that they fall back into their state of sorrow and misery. These courses do not help you to grow spiritually.

The divine Self is lost in spiritual ignorance. The mass of desires veils the Self. You cannot recognise your Self through this mass. Just as you cannot see your reflection in a pond filled with moss. The green mantle covers it completely. There are two ways of seeing your reflection in the pond. The simple, easy way is to plunge your fingers into the water and push the moss aside. The moss separates forthwith to give you a glimpse of the reflection in the clear water beneath. But, before you can register the sight of the reflection below, the moss reunites. It reassumes its mantle masking the reflection. This way of recognising your Self is futile. The popular spiritual courses adopted by the masses is akin to pushing the moss to get a glimpse of the reflection. These practices lead you nowhere.

The effective way of seeing your reflection is by removing the moss gradually. The moss is cleared little by little. It becomes thinner and thinner. Ironically, you gain no glimpse of the reflection yet. But with sustained effort the moss is rendered so thin that it separates for good. You see your reflection in the clear water below. Similarly, you need to clear the mass of desires in the lake of your mind. This is achieved through study and reflection on spiritual literature. As you gain more knowledge the mantle of ignorance becomes thinner, the mass of desires reduces. Thus by your determined, sustained effort the veil of ignorance splits to let you realise the divine Self within.

CHAPTER XIV

MEDITATION

Technique of Meditation

A human stands out supreme amongst all living beings by virtue of possessing both gross and subtle intellects. The intellect is the faculty of thinking, reasoning, judging, deciding. It is designated as gross when this faculty operates in the terrestrial realm. As the thinking is confined to the precincts of the world. And when it transcends the terrestrial world to conceive the transcendental, it is termed subtle. The subtle intellect distinguishes the Eternal from the ephemeral, the Real from the unreal. It is used in meditation to attain spiritual Enlightenment. No other being possesses this unique faculty. At best, animals can claim to have a rudimentary gross intellect. That with which a dog distinguishes its master from a stranger. Food from dirt. Etcetera. But it cannot stretch beyond that. Beyond the miniscule part of the terrestrial world. No animal possesses a subtle intellect.

The mind is merely a continuous flow of thoughts. It acts like a film in a movie projector. The film consists of a series of pictures. These pictures passing through the light in a projector project the movie on the screen. The rapid movement of the pictures produces the solidarity of the projection. A similar projection is this world. Your mind is like the film. And your thoughts, the pictures. The rapid movement of thoughts through the light of Consciousness, the Self creates the solid, substantial world. Where there is no thought flow, no mind, there is no world. Even when the mind is temporarily cut off, the world is no more. As in deep-sleep. When the thoughts are completely eradicated from the mind, the world disappears. The light of Consciousness alone remains. You realise your divine Self.

The mind of the present generation is in a chaotic state. People's thoughts run wildly in all directions. Seeking material gain and sensual pleasure. Which causes the mind to be agitated. An agitated mind cannot concentrate. Much less meditate. The strategy of meditation is to converge the mind to single thought and ultimately annul it. The practice of meditation therefore requires a mind free from the pressures of extroverted pursuits. A mind that remains calm, composed and has turned introvert. One attains that state through sustained physical, mental and intellectual disciplines. By practising *Karma*, *Bhakti* and *Gnana Yogas*, the Paths of Action, Devotion and Knowledge. A mind thus turned introvert is made to chant a *mantra*, a word-symbol representing the supreme God, *Brahman*. The chant is known as *japa*. You could choose a *mantra* that inspires you most. In *japa* the mind repeats the *mantra*. The intellect observes, witnesses the single thought flow. During the chant the mind may slip into other thoughts. It has the tendency to wander away. The intellect is employed to pull the mind back to the chosen line of thought. Thus, by repeated effort the mind is kept focussed on the chant.

Meditation is the art of maintaining the mind in focus upon a chosen thought to the exclusion of all other thought. In the process of meditation, the chant is gradually brought to mental whisper to finally end in silence. The intellect remains aware of the entire proceeding until the moment of silence is reached. The silence is cessation of thought flow which indicates extinction of the mind. The intellect which has been observing the chant also ceases as there is nothing for it to observe. What remains is pure Silence, pure Awareness, pure Consciousness. The absolute Reality, *Brahman*.

Meditation is a scientific technique to exhaust your thoughts and expose the supreme Self within. The intellect plays an all-important role in it. Maintaining its control on the mind during the entire procedure. Meditation therefore is not a mere mechanical repetition of a *mantra*. The human mind has a tendency to be drawn to a particular object or being, tangible or intangible, even towards a deity. And its thoughts start to flow in that direction. If the intellect does not exercise its control over the mind, the thought flow continues. The mind has its way. It can cherish the thought of the object continuously for a period of time. As young lovers do. This is mere emotional indulgence. Mental infatuation. When the mind runs in the direction of its desired object without the awareness of the intellect. Whereas, meditation requires a disciplined effort by the practitioner. The intellect needs to be alert. To keep the mind's focus on the chant. Prevent it from slipping into any other thought. Such programmed, disciplined concentration on the chosen *mantra* is meditation.

Uncontrolled, indisciplined thought flow is mental indulgence. Whereas controlled, disciplined thought flow is concentration, is meditation. Both are flow of thoughts but of opposite nature. They produce conflicting results. Mental indulgence increases your desires. While meditation razes your desires. They act like diarrhoea and purgative. Seemingly the same, but with a distinct difference. Diarrhoea is a disease while purgative is a remedy. Likewise, thoughts running after the world unchecked by a discerning intellect increases your desires. Creates mental instability. Whereas, disciplined thought flow governed by the intellect decreases your desires. Finally, the practice of meditation annihilates your last desire and regains your supreme Self.

You cannot practise single pointed meditation until you have risen well above attachment and desire. When your mind becomes free from worldly attraction and entanglement. Remains under the control of the intellect. And you are objective in your transactions of life. The progress and success in meditation is therefore directly proportional to the preparation of the mind. Your mind must be cleansed before you reach the seat of meditation. The purer the mind the easier it is to practise meditation. Purity of mind means rendering it free of desire and expectation. Means renunciation. Nothing less. "Blessed are the pure in heart, for they shall see God," assures Christ. You must first gain the purity of mind. But people directly try to meditate without the initial preparation. Without purifying their mind. They will not give up their attachment and desire, their hope and expectation, yearning and craving. They will not pay the price for what they seek. Those extroverted people, living a material and sensual life, wish to become the Buddha overnight.

Meditation is the highest spiritual practice. It requires pre-meditative preparation. Your mind must be rendered equanimous to be able to meditate effectively. To plunge into meditation directly without preparation is futile, even detrimental. The time spent in meditation is a small part of the day. The rest of the day you are preoccupied with worldly activity. Your activity during the day tells upon your practice of meditation. Egocentric, selfish activity agitates your mind. And an agitated mind cannot meditate. Whereas selfless, sacrificial activity makes your mind calm and composed. Renders it conducive for meditation. The human mind is ulcerated by self-centred activity. Meditation cannot help heal the ulcerated mind if the activity during the day continues to be selfish. Just as a wound treated by a surgeon can never heal if you keep scratching and irritating it the rest of the day. This is the sad plight of those who claim to practise meditation. Who sincerely try to meditate every day. While all day they indulge in desire-ridden, selfish activity. That ruins their effort in meditation. Continuing this way, their mind develops frustration, bitterness. They turn into ugly caricatures in life.

Principle of Meditation

The principle underlying meditation is: *As you think so you become.* Thinking is conscious thought force. Not mere mental indulgence when your mind on its own flows towards an object. Instead, let your intellect set an objective, a goal in your life. Let it constantly channel your thought and effort toward the goal. You shall gain your objective. The same principle works in the spiritual field. Set Self-realisation as your objective in life. Let your intellect shift the mind's focus from the world to the Self within. Keep the mind steady in single pointed meditation upon the Self. You then become the Self. You attain the state of Self-realisation.

Realisation of the Self is defined as desirelessness, thoughtlessness. If that be so, how can the thought of Self in meditation bring about the state of thoughtlessness? It seems paradoxical. But it works in actual practice. When you hold the mind focussed in single pointed concentration upon a *mantra* word-symbol, the thought ultimately dissolves into silence. Into the enlightened State of thoughtlessness. Shankaracharya explains this phenomenon in his text *Atmabodha*. By the simile of purifying water with a cleansing agent known as kataka-nut powder. The powder acts in the same way as alum does for cleansing water of its impurities. The powder is sprinkled on the surface of the impure water. It forms a slimy film on top. Fine particles of suspended impurities stick to the bottom of the film. The film becomes heavier. It goes down gradually. More impurities stick to it. In the process all the impurities settle down to the bottom along with the film. The significant part of the process is that the cleansing agent itself settles down along with the impurities. Pure water stands above it. So it is with the process of meditation. The divine Self is polluted with thoughts. The thought of the *mantra* displaces all other thoughts and itself disappears in the heat of meditation. Exposing the supreme Self that lies beyond thought.

The Symbol ॐ Om

ॐ Om is acclaimed as the most powerful word-symbol of *Brahman*, the supreme Reality, God. It is known as *pranava*. *Pranava* means that which pervades life. Om is used in meditation by spiritual seekers. *Brahman* is the ultimate Goal a human being can aspire to reach. One cannot reach It directly through the body, mind or intellect. *Brahman* is not something that your sense organs can perceive. Nor is It an emotion your mind can feel. Nor a thought your intellect can conceive. It remains unknown. Most people need a known idol to reach an unknown ideal. Some need a gross idol with a form. A stone, metal or any solid substance. Others can do with a subtler form like fire. Thus fire has been a common idol of worship in many religions. The subtlest idol is sound. It is considered subtlest since only one of the five sense organs, ear, can contact it. And of all sounds, Om is acclaimed the most natural, most potent. There are reasons for the choice:

1. Sound can be classified under two categories: inarticulate and articulate. Inarticulate sound, also known as intonational, deals with feeling, emotion of the mind. Concerns the heart. Whereas the articulate sound, also known as alphabetical, can be recited in the letters of the alphabet. It deals with knowledge, understanding by the intellect. Concerns the head. However, articulate sound has a limited application. It

can be transacted only by those who have gone through the particular training, learnt that language. Imagine a Persian meeting a Russian. One tries to communicate to the other in one's language. Neither of them understands the other. But when one laughs or cries the other instantly knows he is happy or unhappy. Such communication is inarticulate, intonational. A universal way by which even babies and animals can communicate. Music is another example of intonation. The sound of music has a positive effect on beings. It produces great results.

The symbol Om has the distinction of being both articulate and inarticulate, alphabetical and intonational. It has a deep philosophical significance. While the chant of Om has an extraordinary effect on human beings. The two aspects together help an individual attune with the eternal Being.

2. Om, ॐ is constituted of three sounds, three letters A अ, U उ and M म् . In Sanskrit grammar अ A and उ U coalesce to form ओ O. Thus अ A, उ U and म् M together is pronounced as Om, ॐ. Even the mute can produce the sound of ॐ, Om, Aum. अ A is a guttural sound. It emanates from the throat. There is no sound below the throat. उ U is the sound produced when it courses through the mouth. And म् M is where it ends, when the lips close. There is no sound beyond that. Thus Om covers the full range of sound. Represents the entire phenomenon of sound. The chant of Om produces peace and harmony around.

3. ॐ Om symbolises the pure Consciousness. The Consciousness that pervades the waking, dream and deep-sleep states. अ A represents the world experienced in the waking state of consciousness. While उ U represents the world of the dream state of consciousness. And म् M, the nothingness of the deep-sleep state of consciousness. While

chanting Om the meditator must focus his concentration on that pure Consciousness, the supreme Self that supports the three states all through life.

4. The *mantra* word-symbol Om does not belong to any religion. It is merely a symbol of the ultimate Reality. It represents the pure Consciousness, the supreme God. It is nature's word. Not subject to conjugation, inflection or grammatical manipulation as other words are. Om occupies a very special place with reference to God. God is said to be omniscient, omnipotent, omnipresent. These words begin with Om. Even prayers in different languages end with Amen, Ameen which again is a reference to Om.

In the practice of meditation the mind chants the *mantra* Om. Between every two successive chants there is a momentary silence. That silence is known as *amatra*. The intellect discriminates between sound and silence, between *mantra* and *amatra*. As long as the chant lasts there is thought flow, which establishes the presence of the mind. And with thoughts flowing, the pair of thought and silence exists for the intellect to continue operating. In the peak of meditation the chant ends in silence. The thought flow ceases. The mind becomes extinct. There is no longer the pair of thought and silence. Consequently the intellect ceases. Thus the meditator transcends both the mind and intellect. His individual self merges with the supreme Self. Gains spiritual Enlightenment.

Procedural Details

The process of meditation starts with the withdrawal of the mind from its preoccupation with the affairs of the world. The meditator must then ensure that all external factors are conducive for the plunge into the inner Self. Before starting the practice of meditation, one must try and eliminate all that could possibly disturb the mind. The disturbances spring from the environment, physical body, from breathing, mind, intellect and even the time chosen for the practice. These impediments must be eliminated to create the best atmosphere for meditation.

The first impediment is the external disturbance arising from the environment. Hence you must choose a quiet, peaceful place for practising meditation. If it is difficult to find a peaceful place, you may choose a peaceful time of the day. The early hours of morning, the *sattvik* time is distinctly silent and peaceful even in an otherwise noisy environment.

The next preparatory step in meditation is to attend to the disturbance caused by the physical body. To avoid any such disturbance you need to sit cross-legged in the appropriate physical posture. Use a thin flat cushion, not too soft or too hard. The recommended posture is to sit on your hams with legs folded to form a maximum base. Keep your vertebral column erect with a slight forward bend at the pelvic region. Your arms resting in front with fingers interlaced. In this posture the physical body remains in maximum equilibrium. With its centre of gravity falling at the centre of the base. You may take time to get accustomed to the posture. If however, you are unable to adjust your body to the posture due to some physical defect or other reason, you may sit on a chair or other comfortable position that suits you. Keep your eyes gently closed looking nowhere in particular, as in sleep. Having positioned in the meditative posture your limbs may still be stiff, your muscles tense. That again could disturb your mental concentration. As they may relax on their own during meditation. To avoid this you should release the tension in the muscles. By mentally inspecting the parts of the body from head to foot. That would relieve all stiffness and relax the body.

Needless to mention, the relaxation of the physical body will not be effective unless your body has been kept in perfect fitness prior to meditation. That would require regular physical exercises, *asanas* practice of yogic postures and *pranayama* breath-control.

Pranayama tunes up your breathing. Proper, controlled breathing is conducive to mental equanimity. When your breathing is properly regulated it is easier to keep the mind peaceful. Conversely, when your breathing is hard especially after a long run, it would be difficult for the mind to remain calm and composed. *Pranayama* is a simple technique of breathing practised as follows. With the little and ring fingers of your right palm extended and the other two folded, press the thumb against your right nostril and inhale slowly through your left. When you have inhaled fully, close the left nostril with the two smaller fingers. With both nostrils closed, hold your breath. After holding the breath for a while, keep the left nostril closed and exhale slowly through the right. After exhalation is complete, keep the air out with both nostrils open. These four steps form the first half of *pranayama* – inhaling, holding the breath inside, exhaling and keeping the breath outside.

For the second half of *pranayama*, follow the same procedure in the reverse direction using your left palm. With the fingers of your left palm arranged in a similar manner, press the left thumb against your left nostril and inhale through your right. After inhaling fully, close your right nostril with your two smaller fingers. With both nostrils closed, hold your breath. After holding the breath for a while, keep the right nostril closed and exhale slowly through the left. After exhalation is complete, keep the air out with both nostrils open. With this the second half is complete. Thus one round of *pranayama* consists of eight steps. *Pranayama* is merely an exercise for the lungs. With no spiritual connotation. It is false logic to claim that control of breath can control the mind. The gross cannot control the subtle. The truth is just the opposite. Control your mind, your *prana* breath will be controlled.

Now reverting to the seat of meditation, with effective relaxation of the muscles and a little *pranayama,* your body and *prana* breath are set for meditation. The next source of disturbance is the mind itself. Some thoughts may linger and disturb your mind. Let your intellect examine the mind and keep it vacant of thoughts. If however they enter the mind, gently dismiss them. When the mind is relatively free of thoughts start the *japa,* the chant of the chosen *mantra* word-symbol. Your mind does the chanting. Your intellect observes, witnesses the chant. And maintains the focus on the *mantra* to the exclusion of all other thought.

The most conducive time for the practice of meditation is *brahma muhurta,* between 4 a.m. and 6 a.m. If that be inconvenient, choose a time as close to it as possible or any other time suitable to you. Sit in the recommended meditative posture in the selected place. Repeat the *mantra* mentally without causing any movement of your limbs, throat, mouth or tongue. During the chant the mind would stray away from the *mantra.* And your intellect may not be aware of the mind's digression. For the intellect to effectively hold the mind's concentration on the *mantra* you may use a *japamala* rosary for the chant.

The technique of telling-the-beads with a rosary is common to most religions. The *japamala* has beads strung together in a single cord with a little space between the beads to facilitate its movement. One of the beads is designed to protrude from the rest. The protruding bead is known as *meru.* In meditation you suspend the *mala* rosary from the ring and little fingers held together. Hold a bead with the tips of the middle finger and thumb. Let your index finger stick out of the rest. With the *mala* positioned thus, rest your palm on the calf muscle on the same side of the body. And the other palm on the other thigh. With each chant of the *mantra* turn a bead with your middle finger in the clockwise direction i.e. towards your body. Let the chanting synchronise with the rotation of the beads. Proceeding thus you will reach the *meru*. At that point turn the *mala* in the opposite direction, without disturbing your posture or opening your eyes. And continue the chant with the rotation of the beads. The moment your mind wanders away from the chant, the rotation of the beads stops. You then feel a jerk. That alerts the intellect to put the mind back into meditation.

In the initial stage of meditation you may choose to chant aloud. Even keep your eyes open. As you advance in the practice of meditation you would feel more comfortable to chant mentally with eyes closed. You practise meditation every morning after adequately preparing the mind. Continue the chant until you bring it to mental whispers. Allow the chant to die away in silence. The silence does not remain for long. Thoughts would prop up and disturb the silence. That indicates you have done enough for the day. Following this procedure daily, try to elongate the period of silence. You then delve deeper into it. Ultimately, in the depth of that silence the supreme Self reveals Itself.

Self-Realisation

In the silence of meditation all your *vasanas*, thoughts and desires are eradicated. Your mind and intellect are extinct. That is the sacred moment when your supreme Self reveals Itself by Itself. You attain the ultimate state of Self-realisation. The fourth state called *Turiya*, beyond the waking, dream and deep-sleep. A state wherein your individuality merges with the all-pervading Reality. You become *Brahman*. Like the dreamer becomes the waker. The dreamer loses his personality in the higher experience of the waking state. Similarly, the waker loses his finite personality in the infinite experience of Self-realisation. An experience that is beyond the highest pleasure the body could ever sense, beyond the greatest happiness the mind could ever feel, beyond the subtlest knowledge the intellect could ever conceive. That is spiritual Enlightenment.

The state of Self-realisation confers absolute power, bliss and knowledge. Yet the Self-realised conducts himself as any other human being in the external world. Though inwardly he has become a *Sakshi* Witness of the entire phenomena of life. Nothing in the world can either enhance or diminish his State of absolute fulfilment. Besides, his presence radiates peace and bliss to one and all.

CHAPTER XV

THE STATE OF SELF-REALISATION

Self-realised Person

A Self-realised person is one who has discovered his Godhead. Realised the supreme Self, *Atman*. Attained that divine state by shedding all his *vasanas*, thoughts, desires. He no longer identifies with his physical body, mind and intellect. Consequently, becomes free from the persecution of action and perception, emotion and thought. Transcends the limitation of the waking, dream and deep-sleep states to merge with the limitless Reality. Spiritually Enlightened he becomes omniscient, omnipresent, omnipotent.

A human being is constituted of the pure Consciousness combined with the gross, subtle and causal bodies. The Consciousness functioning through these bodies becomes the waker, dreamer and deep-sleeper respectively. The waking, dream and deep-sleep are the three conditioned states of consciousness. Your entire life is restricted to these states. At any time of your life you assume only one of the three personalities. When you enter the waking state, you assume the personality of the waker. The waker experiences the waking world alone and rejects the dream and deep-sleep states. So do the dreamer and deep-sleeper experience their respective states and reject the other two. Each state exists only for the respective personality experiencing it. Who alone attributes a reality to it. But not the other two personalities. Hence each one has a relative reality.

The Consciousness runs through all the three states of waking, dream and deep-sleep. Furthermore, the Consciousness exists beyond the three states in Its original purity. Free from conditioning. That supreme Consciousness is eternal, all-pervading, infinite. The Self-realised merges with the Consciousness. Becomes one with the absolute Reality.

The Consciousness is the substratum of the microcosm as well as the macrocosm. The centre around which both of them revolve. The microcosm and macrocosm merge with the eternal Consciousness.

His Intrinsic Being

A Self-realised person has merged with the supreme Reality. He manifests divine characteristics. Displays exceptional power. Bears universal love. Possesses boundless knowledge. Enjoys absolute self-sufficiency. Revels in total fulfilment.

His power

Selfish activity has limited power. If you work with ego and egocentric desires, if your actions are directed towards personal gains, your work becomes limited. Lacks efficiency, dynamism. Drop your selfishness. Renounce your egoistic tendency. Pitch up a higher goal in life. A nobler cause, an ideal beyond your self-centred interests. Let your activities be directed to the set ideal. Let your work turn impersonal. Your actions then become efficient, dynamic. They produce results. You command power, strength.

Let an employee approach his employer for a personal favour. With a selfish desire to fulfil. He hesitates, falters, fumbles. He lacks strength to put forth his case. Let the same person take up a common cause to serve the interest of his fellow employees. He then approaches the boss with a higher purpose. With no personal motive in it. His impersonal attitude provides him courage and strength. His action becomes powerful. His effort fruitful. Apply this principle in life. Annihilate your ego. Get rid of your little self. You gain power and strength. Your activity assumes infinite proportions. That determines the power of a Self-realised person. In the invocation to the *Gita* a verse describes the power of the spiritually evolved: *It makes a mute speak. A lame scale mountains.*

His love

The love that people claim to possess is restricted to the area they identify with. Beyond that area they engender bitterness, hatred. The area of identification starts with a dot, increases in concentric circles only to get lost in its boundless, infinite expanse.

The lowest, meanest character confines his love to the dot. To his own personality. No more. He is selfish to the core. In his lifetime he caters to his welfare only. He does so even at the expense of his family. His love starts and ends with his personality. The next grade of humans moves up to the first circle defined by one's family. A person in this category pours out love for the members of his family. He cares for their welfare. Serves and sacrifices for them alone. His love stops there. It does not extend beyond the circumference of the domestic circle. All other families save his present a competition, conflict, bitterness. Higher than this cadre is the individual who identifies with the larger circle, his community. His love reaches beyond the family to embrace the members of his community. His interest is confined to this boundary. Within his circle he feels a sense of fraternity and friendship. That is his limit of love. Beyond the limit he engenders hatred, jealousy and other negative feelings. Thus does love reach further to the citizens of his country, to humanity, to all living creatures. Yet the love in all these cases is confined to its area but turns bitter beyond its boundary.

Far above all these cadres lies the divine love of a Self-realised soul. In him there is no trace of selfishness. His identification, attention, interest is everywhere and nowhere in particular. His love has no boundary. No division or demarcation. No limitation. It is love in its purest form with no qualification or modification.

His knowledge

Brahman, the supreme God is all-pervading. Brahman alone exists. Nothing else. That is your real Self. You know not your Self. The ignorance-of-Self projects the world. Just as ignorance-of-rope projects an illusory snake. So is this world illusory stemming out of your ignorance. Hence all knowledges pertaining to the world spring from the base of ignorance. Even the greatest scientific discovery and invention are within the realm of ignorance vis-à-vis the absolute Knowledge-of-Self. Pre-eminent scientists have declared that their findings are relative, not absolute. The Self alone is absolute, real. The world is relative, unreal. The Self-realised has found this truth. Is established in the Knowledge-of-Self. Knowledge of Brahman. Absolute Knowledge.

Spiritual ignorance is the cause of all sorrow in the world. There is only one way to eradicate sorrow and establish

enduring peace and happiness in life. That is to instil
the Knowledge of the inner Self. The Knowledge of the
absolute Reality.

His self-sufficiency

Living beings can be classified under three categories:
plant, animal and human. Of the three, the plant is most
dependent upon the world for its survival. The animal is
less dependent. Yet much dependent on the environment.
A human being alone is designed to be independent,
self-sufficient. A Self-realised person enjoys absolute
independence. He does not depend on anything in the world.
Nothing in the world can in any way affect his absolute
state of peace and bliss.

A plant needs attention. If you leave a plant unattended it
will perish. Water may be available a few metres away. That
will not help the plant. If there is no water at its root it will
die. So also, if it is denied direct sunlight. It cannot help
itself to the blazing sunlight just around the corners. A plant
is wholly dependent upon the world around.

An animal is not totally victimised by the rigours of the
external world. It can adapt itself to an extent to different
environment and circumstance. If food is not available at
its location the animal finds it elsewhere. If its dwelling
place is not suitable it moves to more conducive environment.
Birds and fishes are known to migrate hundreds, thousands
of kilometres for that purpose. Nevertheless, all these
creatures have a limited capacity to adapt themselves to the
changing world.

A human being enjoys far greater freedom. He is least
dependent upon the stern laws of nature. He can harness

nature by artificial devices. Conquer space by incredible speed. Annihilate time by electronic equipments replaying past events. Consume processed food in place of natural produce. Cure disease with medicine. Substitute virtually anything for what is found wanting in nature. Humans possess such phenomenal powers. Yet you find yourself persecuted by the ever changing world. The reason for victimisation is your unintelligent identification with the body, mind and intellect. Through your constant attention upon these equipments you have become one with them. Whatever happens to them happens to you. The outside world, constituted of objects, emotions and thoughts, can affect your body, mind and intellect but not your Self. The Self within is immaculate. It is transcendental. Nothing terrestrial can influence It, affect It.

To live up to the status of a human being you must shift your focus of attention from the body, mind and intellect to the real Self. To the extent you identify with the Self, thereby detach yourself from the material equipments, you shall be freed from the persecution of the world. You shall gain your independence. A Self-realised person, having merged with the Self, becomes totally self-sufficient. Enjoys absolute independence. Revels in supreme liberation.

People everywhere seek liberation in the world. Every human craves for sweet liberty. Some leave their motherland and move to other countries in search of freedom. Battles have been fought all along human history in the name of liberty. Freedom fighters, liberty seekers attain their limited goals in the world. But none has found true freedom through external pursuits. All the successes that people claim fall within the boundary of the world. But the world itself is one large prison. They are limited, restricted to the prison-house of the body and its perceptions, mind and its emotions, intellect and its thoughts. In effect, they still remain bound to the world. So the desire to liberate, to free oneself persists.

Such persistent yearning for independence actually emanates from the supreme Self within. Your real Self is boundless, infinite. Hence, you can never find satiation until you realise your original Self. Not knowing this truth, the ignoramuses seek freedom in the world. In the past, people believed that the sun revolved round the globe. The truth is to the contrary. The scientist who declared that the earth was round and not flat, was done away with. Likewise, spiritual ignoramuses the world over reject, condemn the wise who declare that true freedom lies within oneself, not in the external world.

It is no doubt difficult to straightaway attune to the inner Self for attaining ultimate liberation. People take to the easy way to find freedom in the external world. Such freedom is of an impermanent nature. You cannot rely on the world wholly for your liberty. Realising the uncertainty of the changing world, you must gradually shift your reliance to the eternal Self rather than the world for peace and bliss. You must attain absolute self-sufficiency. The following episode drives home the need for the shift in focus.

A village was submerged in a deluge. A man managed to climb a tree. And cling on to one of its branches. A bird was also perched on a neighbouring branch. Torrential floods continued to flow below. Both man and bird were resting on the branches. But their statuses were different. The man was totally dependent on the branch. If the branch were to break he would perish in the waters below. Whereas, the bird was not dependent on the branch. Even while sitting there, it relied on its wings, not on the branch. So it is with human life. In the flood of desires people make use of the world for their pleasure and joy. Few realise that they have become wholly dependent upon the changing world. They suffer from mental tension, stress and strain. And when the world breaks down, they perish. Like the man hugging on to the branch. But a person endowed with Self-Knowledge is free from tension like the bird with wings. Though he makes good use of the world, he never relies on it. He remains ever attuned to the supreme bliss of his own Self. Remains wholly self-sufficient.

His fulfilment

The bliss of Self-realisation is infinite. A person who revels in that state of bliss remains absolutely fulfilled. The greatest happiness that the world can provide cannot enhance his bliss. Nor can the deepest sorrow diminish it. That state of supreme fulfilment is inconceivable. It cannot be captured in words.

Revelling in absolute bliss within, the Self-realised remains wholly satiated, fulfilled. He requires nothing. Aspires for nothing. No physical pleasure, no emotional joy, no intellectual satisfaction can augment his state of supreme bliss. Alexander the Great, Emperor of Greece, came to India. He had a desire to meet one such sage. He was led to the bank of river Indus. He found a sage lying on the ground. Basking in the sunlight bare-bodied, barefooted. The Emperor was thrilled at the sight of the holy man. He requested the sage to accompany him to his country. Offered him wealth, power, pleasure for acceding to his request. The sage smiled at him. He told him he had everything. He was everything. He was everywhere. And did not need anything. Nor wished to go anywhere. Alexander insisted that he accede to his request. The sage laughed at his immaturity. The Emperor felt insulted. Acting impulsively he imprisoned the sage. The wiser counsellors warned the Emperor of the consequence of such a sacrilegious act. Alexander took the advice. He realised the seriousness of his offence. He went up to the prison. There was the man relaxed, gazing at the sunbeam coming from an opening above. The Emperor sought the good man's pardon. And beseeched him to accept a boon. The sage reiterated that he required nothing. Now the Emperor reverentially pleaded with him to accept it just to satisfy his conscience. The sage was impressed at his devotion. He complied, "In that case, dear king, please take a step aside and let the sunbeam fall on my eyes!"

His Extrinsic Conduct

Self-realised Souls have demonstrated a wide range of extrinsic conduct. Their post-realisation lives have been distinct and different. Yet they all remained intrinsically as the one Self. Like the brilliant spectrum of colours emerging from colourless light. Each colour exhibits a beauty of its own. So does every Enlightened One display a distinct magnificence. Beautiful and graceful. Their actions however differ widely. Though they all spring from the depth of spiritual Enlightenment. From the one divine Self. Thus you find a marked difference in the external manifestation of divine Souls from time immemorial. Even the recent sages like Swami Rama Tirtha, Saint Tyagaraja or Ramana Maharshi were poles apart in their manifestations. Ramana Maharshi observed silence practically all his lifetime. He hardly moved out of his small town of Tiruvannamalai in South India. While Saint Tyagaraja gave out the divine Carnatic music. He sang all through his life. Distinct from these two, Swami Rama Tirtha was dynamic. He enthralled the world with his electrifying discourses on Vedanta.

You ought not to judge sages and saints from what you see them act. Their expressions in the world may confuse you. And you would perhaps gather wrong impressions. Perfection in a human is assessed not from his external action but from internal attunement with the supreme Self. The test of perfection is his merger with the inner Self. Not his expression. Whatever be the mode of living, the Self-realised leads humanity through the path of righteousness to the goal of Enlightenment. Some sages have lived in seclusion observing austerity. While others lived in company amidst material comfort. However, both were totally detached, disinterested in their mode of living. Revelling in the bliss of realisation their lives only promoted universal welfare, redeemed humanity.

The Enlightened One lives in his home, with his family, amidst his environment with perfect objectivity. Established in the divinity within, he remains absolutely detached. He takes the position of God. He is in the world, yet out of it. Like a lotus leaf unattached to the water all around. He looks at every being and every thing happening in the world from an impersonal angle. As you would watch a movie on the screen. When you look upon the world as a detached witness, the world becomes a source of enjoyment. But when you get involved, entangled in the affairs of the world, the same world becomes a source of misery. The Enlightened is ever positioned as a *sakshi* witness. Never attached to anything. Never enmeshed in the world. He stands out as a picture of renunciation. Revelling in absolute bliss.

The ignoramuses do not look into people's intrinsic nature. They are carried away by external demonstrations. They make a great blunder in considering pseudo-spiritual persons as evolved souls. Some of these charlatans perform all sorts of fantastic feats. They are known as spiritualists. Who read a book blindfolded, repeat another's thoughts, communicate with departed souls, demonstrate such sensational acts. All that does not render them holy, spiritual. They are just as worldly as others, except for having learnt a special art. It may be admired as a skill, technique. There is nothing more to it. A spiritualist can claim no more divinity, knowledge-of-Self than a brilliant technician can.

Some *hatha yogis* are known to have buried themselves alive in a coffin. Others have swallowed razor blades, drawn needles through the skin, performed many such feats. But these men are far from being spiritual. And their feats have nothing to do with the divine state brought about by the Knowledge-of-Self. There have been instances of such men having committed crimes. Even convicted by the state. However, history has shown some true sages possessing this art, the skill of performing great feats. They learnt it only to draw people to educate them in the knowledge of *Brahman*, the supreme God. However, the knowledge of this art is in no way related to their spiritual status.

Self-realisation is acclaimed as attainable in one's lifetime. And Self-realised Souls are those who have merged with the supreme unifying Self. If that be so, how is it they do not conduct themselves uniformly? Why is there so much difference in the lives of the Self-realised? This has baffled many thinkers. It is only the great Swami Rama Tirtha who has given the most lucid, perfectly convincing explanation of this phenomenon. The Swami described the life of the Self-realised sage with the help of the following law of physics.

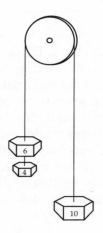

The circle in the figure is a pulley. Pass a fine thread over the pulley. Fasten 2 weights of 10 and 6 to the ends of the thread. Add an additional weight of 4 to the smaller weight. 6 + 4 = 10. The weights are balanced. 10 on each side. They remain motionless. Now, remove the weight 4. Then there is 6 alone on one side and 10 on the other. The weights are no longer balanced. As a result, 10 will go down and 6 will rise. After a lapse of one second, replace the weight 4 alongside 6. The weights equalise again on both sides. What would be the result of their equalisation? The layperson believes that they would become stationary. But that is not so. They will continue moving. Their velocity or speed will be 8 feet per second. In the beginning when the weights were equal they were at rest, the original rest was preserved. But when the motion started and the weights equalised later, the motion does not stop. At the end of the first second, the resultant velocity will be 8 feet per second. If you let the weights 6 and 10 move for 2 seconds and add the weight 4 to balance them at the end of the second second, then the resultant velocity will be 16 feet per second. If you let the same weights continue their motion for 3 consecutive seconds and add 4 to balance them at the end of the third second, then the resultant velocity will be 24 feet per second. At the end of 4 seconds, it will be 32 feet per second. Etcetera.

Study the above data. You will notice if the weights are kept unequal, the result is that at the close of each second there is an increase in velocity, 8 plus the original velocity. So the velocity that has already been acquired remains the same. If the weights are equal in the beginning, before the motion was started, they will be at rest. If the weights are equalised at the end of the first second, after velocity 8 has been acquired, then equalising the weights will prevent any further increase in velocity beyond 8. If however the weights are equalised at the end of the second second, after velocity 16 has been acquired, then equalising the weights will prevent any further increase of velocity beyond 16. Etcetera. The increase of velocity at the end of the second is called acceleration. Therefore, after equalising the weights there can be no further acceleration.

Go over this experiment carefully. You will notice that there is no force acting when the weights are equalised. If there is no force acting upon the bodies there can be no change produced in the state of rest or motion. Thus, equalising the weights at the very beginning when the bodies are at rest, the original rest will be preserved as there is no force acting upon them. But equalising the weights after the bodies have already acquired motion then, according to this law, the original acquired motion will remain. The equalising of weights does not disturb the original rest or the original acquired velocity. The equalising will only prevent further change in the velocity. Therefore, equalising weights at the beginning will keep the bodies at rest. While equalising at the end of the first second, the original acquired velocity of 8 will remain without further increase. And equalising at the end of the second second, the original acquired velocity of 16 will remain without further increase. Etcetera.

Now apply this law to the life of a Self-realised person. An individual is born in the world with a portion of the aggregate of his *vasanas*, unmanifest desires. The aggregate *vasanas* are known as *sanchita*. A portion of the *sanchita* which needs immediate manifestation forces itself out, to be born as a human being. That bulk of *vasanas* an individual is born with is termed *prarabdha vasanas*. The *prarabdha* is the original acquired *vasanas* which get exhausted only upon the death of the individual. But the individual can within his lifetime exhaust the entire *sanchita* when he attains Self-realisation. Thereafter, there is no individual propulsion for his life's activities.

Realisation equalises the disparity of demand and supply. The individual makes his demands. The world makes the supplies to meet the demands. The imbalance created by the inequality between his demand and supply lasts until Self-realisation. The unfulfilled desires cause the motion of life. When the *sanchita*, the aggregate of all unmanifest desires, is exhausted there is no more motion generated. No further acceleration. But the original acquired velocity remains. That is the state of the Self-realised. He lives on because of his original acquired *prarabdha vasanas*, desires. Like a car moving at 100 kilometres an hour runs out of fuel. It has no more acceleration as the fuel is exhausted. But its motion continues because of the already acquired velocity. So too do the Self-realised function differently because of the different *prarabdha vasanas* they are born with. If the original *prarabdha* was little, feeble then his manifestation upon realisation would be the same. Perhaps like Ramana Maharshi. If the *prarabdha* was of music, then he would perhaps turn out to be Saint Tyagaraja. And if made up of erudition and scholarship, he would emerge as Swami Rama Tirtha.

Impact of World on Him

The Enlightened person revels in the supreme bliss of the Self. He remains absolutely fulfilled. No more physical pleasure, emotional joy or intellectual satisfaction can enhance his bliss within. His state is like the ocean. Rivers pour millions upon millions of gallons of water into the ocean. Or you may draw millions out of it. Neither makes a difference to the ocean. So too the extremities of wealth, environment or situation make no difference to his state of absolute bliss.

Now observe the life of a layperson. He can take a loss up to a point. Beyond that point he cannot handle it. He collapses. Imagine a person losing a pen. What is the loss to him? Nothing. It will not break his heart. Stretch it a little. He has his pen with him. But, coming out into the car park he finds his car missing. What is the loss of a car to him? It may or may not upset him. Extend this thought further. The car is there but as he reaches home he finds his newly built house completely gutted. Everything reduced to ashes. How is that? Furthermore, his house remains perfectly intact but he hears the family, his dear wife and two lovely children, have met with a fatal accident. How would he handle that? Thus somewhere down the line, from a pen to a family, something can upset him, shatter him. In contrast, for the Self-realised the loss of everything in the world is no loss at all. It has no significance in the boundless bliss that he revels in.

Vedanta pronounces an astounding truth that the entire world is unreal. A mere imaginary projection. A figment of your mind. This rigid, stern world is just another dream. The waking and dream states differ only in degree, not in kind. You do not perceive this truth as long as you remain in the waking state. The moment you move up to the fourth plane of Consciousness, attain Self-realisation, this solid-seeming world disappears. It turns into a meaningless nothing.

You may get a glimpse of this staggering truth by comparing it with your personal experience of the dream-world. As long as you take the position of a dreamer, the dreamer finds the dream-world to be real. As solid and stern as the waker finds the waking world to be. No sooner the dreamer wakes up to become the waker than the dream-world disappears. The dream-world means nothing to the waker. Imagine the waker entering into his erstwhile dream. What impact will the dream-world have on the waker? Will the riches of the dream-world increase his wealth in the waking world? Will the joy and sorrow of the dream mean anything to the waker? The honour or dishonour meted out to the dreamer have any impact on the waker? The entire dream-world has no pith or substance, has no value to the waker. Just so, the waking world has the same impact on the Self-realised person. The waking world is a hollow, empty nothingness to him. He wants nothing from this world. Expects nothing. Has no interest in anything that the world offers. Nor is he dependent on anything. Heat or cold, joy or sorrow, honour or dishonour mean the same to him. In Shakespeare's words:

> All the world's a stage,
> And all the men and women merely players;
> They have their exits and their entrances.

That is the supreme stance of the Enlightened.

The waking world does not in any way affect the Self-realised person. It produces no effect on him. His state is comparable to the phenomenon of optical vision. A rugged landscape lies on the delicate retina of your eyes. It does not burden the eyes. Your eyes remain unaffected by the nature of the landscape. So does the Enlightened remain free from the impact of the world. He passes through life's affairs, the world's fluctuations and challenges without the least burden. He maintains his supreme state of peace and bliss through the undulation and altercation of life.

His Impact on World

The world is made up of good and evil. Righteous and unrighteous forces have been conflicting with each other from time immemorial. Neither of them has succeeded in destroying the other completely. There can be no good or bad alone since the world is constituted of pairs-of-opposites, *dvandvas*. Thus from the very inception, virtue and vice are the warp and woof that have patterned the world. These opposing forces have been in the past, are so in the present and will continue in the future. Religions symbolise them as god and the devil. The *Bible* speaks of the conflict between Satan and Christ. The epic *Mahabharata* recounts the proverbial war between the evil Kauravas and virtuous Pandavas. The *Ramayana* portrays the battle between the demon Ravana and Lord Rama. John Milton's epic poem *Paradise Lost* describes the war between the demons and gods. History has shown no God-person could exterminate evil and establish goodness alone. Nor could the devilish-person wipe out goodness and establish evil alone. At best, they have succeeded in strengthening their trait and weakening the opposite. Thus the role of the good and evil would perpetually alternate in the world. Whereas, yours is to rise above them and reach the divine Core of your personality.

The dual forces of good and evil that operate in the macrocosm do so in the microcosm as well. Material craving and sensual indulgence pull you down to the lower level of your personality. While your divine aspirations lift you to the higher, edify you. The lower temptations generally outnumber the higher aspirations. The strength of the lower lies in numbers while that of the higher is in its quality.

The human mission is to use one's higher nature to control and conquer the lower. Let your mind expand and accommodate the interest and welfare of fellow-beings. It elevates you. The mind behaves much like water. Water kept in a pot remains in it for days on end. Pour the water on the floor. Let it spread over a large area. It evaporates fast. Water vapour rises upward. It reaches high up in the sky. And when it becomes concentrated, constricted it forms into clouds. The rainwater falls downward. The sun draws water up. The earth pulls it down with its gravity. The same phenomenon is seen in your mind. When your mind remains selfish, self-centred restricting itself to the individual alone it lies low. Involved, attached, lost in the affairs of the world. The earth pulls you down. The Enlightened Soul acts like the sun to draw your mind to greater heights. The mind expands to become unselfish, selfless to soar to the height of perfection. Helps you evolve spiritually. It is a law.

In truth the sun does everything in the world. But remains unattached like a witness, *sakshi*. It sheds lustre, supports life everywhere. Provides vegetation. Causes the waters to flow. The winds to blow. The earth and planets revolve around it. It is the centre of everything. Such is the glory and grace of the God-person. His presence sets everything right. In his divine presence righteousness prevails over unrighteousness. The world is no longer gripped by worry and anxiety, stress and strain. People turn towards the Self within. Such is the impact of a realised Soul upon the world.

Section III

The Essence of Vedanta

CHAPTER XVI

USE AND ABUSE OF RELIGION

Individual Diagnosis and Treatment

The subject of religion has received a casual treatment the world over. Hardly anyone takes up religion seriously. Except perhaps the professionals who make a living out of it. And they too have no clue of what it is. Humans can ill afford to do so. Religion is a technology dealing with the development of the individual. Just as science is a technology dealing with the improvement of the world. Life is constituted of the individual and the world. Both of them need to be carefully developed, improved. If neglected, there can be no material or spiritual progress.

Even the intelligentsia have no idea of the role of religion in human life. In the name of religion some plunge into ritualistic practices without understanding what they represent. Others indulge in devotional prayer and worship soliciting material gain or mental solace for themselves. Yet others pick up religious books indiscriminately and read them to satisfy their curiosity. Few approach it methodically as one would pursue science or technology. And the world remains deprived of the value and worth of religion. Consequently, few can claim to have attained spiritual mastery.

Medicine or engineering is a scientific course. To gain the knowledge of either you need to go through a systematic process of study under proper guidance. You cannot become a surgeon or an engineer by merely reading medical or engineering books of your choice. The technical courses have laid down definite procedures to follow. You observe these disciplines as far as scientific technology is concerned. You would join a university. Follow the prescribed course step by step, year by year under qualified masters until you complete it. But you do not care to treat religion the same way. You do not seem to appreciate that religion is a technology far more scientific than any other known in the world. That there is a greater system and more rigorous discipline associated with the spiritual courses. The procedures laid down in them are far more exacting. You will have to follow them meticulously like the other sciences. Besides, you need guidance, supervision to enable you to adhere to the right channel for your spiritual evolution. Needless to mention, you must put in the all-important effort on your part to observe these disciplines to gain spiritual evolution.

Spiritual disciplines are varied. The fundamental requirement though is to choose the aspect of training compatible to one's person. Every individual has a distinct constitution. The inner nature differs from person to person. One's own inner constitution is known as *svadharma*. And a constitution of an alien nature is *paradharma*. You must make sure you choose your spiritual discipline in accordance with your *svadharma* and not *paradharma*. This applies even in the material field. You must select a career which conforms to your basic nature and temperament. If your inner nature is inclined towards mathematics you should choose your study and career in mathematics. Or it could be music, sport, any other field. Thus, basing your career on your inherent nature you would meet with success and progress in your chosen field. The same rule holds good in the spiritual realm as well. Your inner nature could be emotional or intellectual or balanced in both. Seldom does one find a person lacking both emotion and intellection. You must therefore take up the spiritual discipline compatible with your particular nature. That would escalate your spiritual development.

The first and foremost phase of spiritual training is the diagnosis of one's inner constitution. Before you take up a spiritual path you must ascertain the nature of your constitution. The inner nature is determined by the varying strength of the mind and intellect. When your mind is more developed than your intellect you are classified as *emotional*. Whereas, when your intellect is more developed than your mind you are *intellectual*. Balanced in both, you are *active*. And there are the broad disciplines of Devotion, Knowledge and Action prescribed for the three categories.

Spiritual disciplines are imparted to the mind and intellect to rehabilitate them. Chasten your mind's emotions. Subtilise your intellectual thoughts. To achieve this you need to administer appropriate spiritual practice in accordance with the nature of the inner constitution. One medicine cannot take care of all diseases. The *emotional* need to take to the Path of Devotion. The *intellectual* need the Path of Knowledge. And the *active*, Path of Action. But in the world today these three classes of people take up courses at random. And the spiritual practices in vogue are all indiscriminately mixed up. They have no method, system supporting them. People usually follow a religious practice because they are born into it. Or because of environmental influence. Or certain circumstance or opportunity that came their way. Rare indeed are they based on analysis and choice as per their individual requirement. Consequently, religion has produced little effect upon humanity.

Furthermore, even those classified as *emotional*, *intellectual* or *active* do not carry each one's particular trait only. No person is wholly emotional, wholly intellectual or wholly active. Each has his own trait in predominance and the other two traits as well in less degree. Hence the three spiritual paths must be followed in the proportion of one's constituent nature. For instance, a person who is 70% intellectual, 10% emotional and 20% active must put in 70% of his time and effort in the Path of Knowledge, 10% in Devotion and 20% in Action. Thus programming your diagnosis and treatment methodically, your progress in the spiritual path would be meteoric. Failing to observe a systematic procedure, your progress will be slow. Or you may remain stagnant, perhaps deteriorate.

Meditation is the final part of the spiritual course. Not meant to be practised by initiates. You do not start religious practices with meditation. You end with it. A spiritual seeker has to prepare the mind before he enters the final stage of meditation. The preparation is through consistent practice of the prescribed disciplines. An ill-prepared mind plunging directly into meditation could harm itself. Suppress, frustrate the individual.

Religious practices the world over have been indiscreet with no scientific bearing. Not planned, programmed to suit individual requirement. With hardly any correlation between a person's constitution and his religious observance. An emotional person would take to the Path of Knowledge though he is least designed for introverted study and reflection. So too, an intellectual person would plunge into the Path of Devotion indulging in prayer and worship least suited for his spiritual progress. Thus most people, if not all, err in taking to religious practices by sheer accident of birth or circumstance.

Above all, a great blunder committed throughout the world is that people try to meditate with a load of desires heavily hanging on them. Minds infested with desires are most disturbed. And using an agitated mind to meditate is like a plane trying to take off with a load of weight more than it can carry. It can never take off and is bound to crash. So will a disturbed mind if it pursues in meditation without offloading the bulk of desires. Vedanta cautions people against beginning at the wrong end. Desires are your weakness. You must get rid of the weakness through proper disciplines. Keep your bosom free of desires. Then alone would you be able to meditate and realise your Self.

A careful study and analysis of today's religious beliefs and systems would reveal how they have become a mockery. As a result people have lost the vital instruction, guidance in their lives. And the world has led itself to anarchy. The concept of religion has to be revolutionised. The world has to look at it from a totally different perspective. Religion is not just a balm to soothe your nerves. Nor an intellectual companion to relieve your boredom. Nor a physical pastime to recreate yourself. Religion serves a different purpose. It provides you with the knowledge of the spiritual disciplines and their respective values. You must gain that knowledge. Correlate your individual needs with the disciplines. That would ensure your evolution. A community with such self-developed individuals is the need of the hour. But the world today is steeped in ignorance. People are fanatically attached to age-old ritualistic practices without any reference to their meaning and worth. That has caused disruption in the society. The human race has turned inhuman. And people have become bitter, hostile, militant in the name of religion.

Therefore the gravest problem facing humanity is stark ignorance of the Reality. Ignorance of your supreme Self. Ignorance is the source of endless desires. People, replete with desires, go into the world seeking their fulfilment. Little do they realise that their desires can never be satiated through external pursuit. Ignorance can be overcome only through knowledge. The Knowledge of your Self. Your Self is supreme. Realise your Self. You attain Enlightenment. Through individual Enlightenment the world shall be redeemed.

Positive Religion

Religion provides you the technique of discovering your supreme Self within. Every step you take in life toward your union with the Self would be positive religion. Your desires are responsible for the gulf created between you and the real Self. Hence, you would be practising positive religion when you use it to eliminate your desires. The spiritual courses help you achieve this. *Bhakti Yoga*, Path of Devotion improves the quality of desires. *Gnana Yoga*, Path of Knowledge changes their direction. And *Karma Yoga*, Path of Action reduces their bulk.

Bhakti Yoga is the course of devotion. Where your mind surrenders to the supreme Being that seems to hold the world together. When your feelings rise from the secular to the sublime. The thoughts engrossed in the affairs of the world get gradually displaced by the thought of divinity. The change in the quality of thought helps to eliminate your mundane thoughts and desires.

Gnana Yoga is the course of knowledge which maintains the thought of the supreme Reality in all transactions of life. Wherein the intellect keeps the mind focussed on the Eternal while it is engaged in the ephemeral world. As a result, the direction of thought shifts from the finite world to the infinite Self. Here again your varied thoughts get slowly absorbed into the one powerful thought of Reality. And your thoughts and desires pertaining to the world drop off.

Karma Yoga is the course of action dedicated to a high ideal beyond your self-centred interest in life. The highest ideal being Self-realisation. The mind is fixed on the ideal. The intellect directs all actions towards the attainment of the ideal. Consequently, the thoughts and desires for the world do not sustain themselves.

The general idea therefore is to fix your attention and concentration upon the inner Self in and through your transactions of life. Let the body be employed in your obligatory functions. Your mind feel its various emotions. Your gross intellect entertain multifarious thoughts of the world. But your subtle intellect must remain anchored to the Self within. Thus, one part of your intellect should be ever glued to the Self while your equipments are engaged in their respective activities. One wonders how this could be put into actual practice in life.

The practicality of this discipline is brought out by the example of Indian classical music. In a public concert, the musician has a background note playing behind him all through his performance. It is called *shruti*. He renders a variety of songs with different *ragas* tunes and *thalas* beats. But all along his performance he is attuned to the *shruti*, the note behind. One part of his concentration is always on the note. He keeps that invariable while he goes through the variable songs, *ragas* and *thalas*. A classical musician will not sing without the *shruti*. Whereas a layperson would find the background note disturbing while he sings. Similarly, you would bring out the chaste music of life if you adopt this classical method of living. Let your subtle intellect be attuned to the supreme Self while your body, mind and gross intellect are engaged in their activities. Fix your concentration on the unchanging, pure Consciousness while you go through your changing perceptions, emotions and thoughts. That is classical living. It brings out the melody, harmony in life.

Adopting the proper spiritual discipline you command peace and happiness. Apportion the spiritual courses according to your personal requirement. Make sure the quantum is not too much or too little. The proportion of the exercises is as important as the dosage of medicine is to cure a disease. The medicine prescribed may be proper but it will not cure the disease if the dosage is improper. As you progress in your self-development pitch up higher ideals, Self-realisation being the ultimate. Continuing your spiritual practices thus in accordance with your nature and capacity, your desires should drop off gradually. When the mind is freed from desires it becomes balanced, prepared for meditation. You can then apply your mind to single pointed meditation. With sustained meditation you shall attain Enlightenment.

In the geometrical centre of the *Bhagavad Gita*, Lord Krishna declares this impeccable truth in verse 22 of Chapter IX:

To those who are attuned to the Self with constant and unswerving focus, spiritual progress and Enlightenment is assured.

Negative Religion

Most spiritual practitioners employ religion for mere worldly gains. Use religious means to serve their personal ends. With no thought of eradicating their desires. No attempt at spiritual evolution. No idea of attaining the ultimate state of Enlightenment. People in every faith go to religion just to satisfy their material, emotional or intellectual demands. Their approach is purely utilitarian. Selfish and self-centred. All that is negative in character.

One class of people go on pilgrimages, conduct religious ceremonies, perform various rituals for their material wellbeing. They pray for riches, higher status, better health and other mundane benefits. Their motives rise no higher than that.

A second class of persons seeks religious asylum for emotional solace. They are the ones who are mentally disturbed. Who are not able to handle their life's problems. And go through sorrow and suffering. Such people approach religious avenues to ease their mental woes and gain peace. They also have utilitarian motives with no higher goal in mind. They are selfish in nature, far from being religious.

People in the third category pursue religion to satisfy mere intellectual curiosity. To clear their doubt and confusion about the world. They consume various literature which provides them a satisfaction to their general queries. No sooner they find their intellectual solutions than their pursuit of religion ends. Their subtle intellect remains dormant. It lacks the strength or conviction to delve deeper into the quintessence of life. They have practically no spiritual urge to realise the supreme Self within, attain spiritual liberation.

Religion is not meant to cater to your physical, mental and intellectual desires. It is designed to rehabilitate the inner personality. Reconstruct the fallen mind and intellect. The modern mind and intellect have deteriorated to an alarming extent. And they lie dilapidated in spiritual ruins. The role of religion is to pull the human race out of the ruinous state it has plunged into. The mind is bereft of all chastity. Human emotions have turned base, vulgar, violent. While the intellect has hit an all-time low. Thinking has lost its originality. Reasoning is no longer free and clear. The need of the day is to chasten human emotion. Cultivate the art of thinking. Strengthen the intellect. Educate people on the higher values of life.

Regenerate their inner personality. Guide them inward to recognise the supreme Reality. That calls for consistent effort in a planned course for evolution. A role that religion is meant to play. The process of true spiritual education is gradual. Slow but sure. Since its results do not show up immediately hardly any take to it. People do not want to strive and struggle. Pay the price of peace and bliss. Instead, look out for instant relief and remedy.

The present religious practices the world over are far removed from spiritual education. For generations people have become averse to spiritual study and reflection. None realises that human beings need specific direction in life and living. All other creatures, save human, have their respective instructions built into their lives by nature. With little choice to live apart from their built-in directives. Human beings alone are left with the choice of action. Either to get involved in the terrestrial or turn towards the Transcendental. Again in the terrestrial field, what is to be done and what not. The same dilemma prevails in the spiritual arena as well. Is one to gain true spiritual knowledge through an authentic course of study and reflection or blindly follow the senseless rituals and ceremonies imposed by religious fanatics. People are totally lost, adhering to some blind faith, sheer superstition or routine ritual. These are purposeless practices maintained by spiritually illiterate masses. Apart from these, two other fads have been spreading the world over in the name of religion: *yoga-asanas* physical-exercises and meditation. These are the viruses that have killed the spirit of religion.

These two faddish practices are simple and easy for teachers to communicate and masses to follow. That makes them even more popular. In sheer ignorance people take to these practices through hereditary or peer pressure. They lack the intellect to steer themselves away from these pressures and observe a disciplined, methodic procedure for their spiritual evolution.

Yoga has a worldwide market today. It has been reduced to mere *asanas* physical-postures and *pranayama* breathing-techniques. These are good exercises which tune up the physical body. No more. But people are led to believe that they are mystical, divine. And the ignorant have accepted *yoga-asanas* and *pranayama* as a spiritual course. This spiritual merchandise has earned the promoters wealth, name and fame. While leaving the followers in confusion and chaos. *Yoga* exercises are gross. They can no doubt shape the gross body but not the subtle body. The subtle body consists of the mind and intellect. You could build your physical structure through *asanas* and *pranayama*, but in no way develop your inner personality. The gross can never control the subtle. It is the law.

The second fad sweeping the human race is meditation. Meditation has become the bestseller in the world today. Self-appointed religious heads are hawking meditation like Swiss watches and Japanese cars. It has turned into a multi-million dollar business. The innocent masses do not know what they are buying. They are swept away by publicity campaign. Unaware of the adverse results that meditation can bring about to ill-prepared minds cluttered with desires.

Meditation is specialised training carefully administered to advanced spiritual practitioners. Yet millions flock to meditation halls without a clue of what it is and the consequence it leads them to. A simple reason for its mass appeal is the initial solace it gives to a novice. It is usually people suffering from stress and strain that take to meditation. A mind with considerable mental agitation is suddenly brought to the thought of divinity. The mind experiences a certain solace. A temporary feeling of peace. Which is comforting. As a result one is led to believe that meditation can directly bring about peace and bliss. Therefore the practitioner plunges into it more seriously. And finds himself losing his mental equilibrium. He gradually becomes more agitated, frustrated in life. Few realise where the mistake lies. Some believe that they are not putting in adequate effort. They even try harder and cause themselves greater harm.

The instant effect of peace caused by meditation can be explained from a common phenomenon experienced by people. A metropolitan businessman is generally infested with worry and anxiety. His mind is agitated. With no peace and harmony. He spends sleepless nights in his luxurious mansion. On one rare occasion he joins his family for a picnic to the woods. The wife is organising a meal. The children are chasing butterflies. The man rests his head on the protruding root of a tree and falls off to sleep. The very same man who could not sleep on the cushioned mattress in his air-conditioned bedroom! The reason for this phenomenon is that the environment lends a temporary charm to the disturbed mind. But the effect of the environmental peace does not last long. If, however, he repeats his visits to the same place he will lose that temporary influence. He will sleep no more. On the contrary his mind becomes more agitated, frustrated without the luxury of his home.

The effect of meditation on a beginner is just the same. A mind congested with thoughts and desires, worries and anxieties is drawn to one line of thought. It is removed from the congestion of thoughts for those moments. It experiences a temporary peace. This practice thus lends the charm to an agitated mind. That feeling is lost with repeated attempts at meditation. Some understand its futility and drop the practice. But the ignoramuses are led to believe that the instant relief is a permanent transformation of their personality. They pursue doggedly only to be disappointed and frustrated in their lives.

Thus the general trend everywhere is to abuse religion. Rather than use it for the redemption of humanity. The unauthentic, superstitious practices in the name of religion have taken root because of the temporary solace they produce. People seem content with the ephemeral effects of religion. They do not realise, with the effect wearing away, their old nature of stress and strain returns. This resembles a strange phenomenon which occurs in the Himalayan ranges year after year. In winter when it is biting cold snakes become cold-stricken. A snake lies coiled as if lifeless. For all purpose it appears dead. People handle it as a rope. The same snake with a little warmth stretches itself. It regains its nature. Similarly, the wrong ways of religion may subdue the desires and ego for a while. But the moment the environment and situation turns conducive the self-same desires and ego rise again to the surface. Hence, the true spiritual way of life is to exterminate the desires, not just subdue them. And extermination of desires alone unveils the supreme Self.

Impediments in the Spiritual Path

The true spiritual path is a scientific, methodic process for human redemption. Human beings are steeped in spiritual ignorance. Everywhere people grope in darkness to find peace and happiness in the world. What they need is the Light of Consciousness that shines within every living soul. The Knowledge of the divine Self. The process of redemption is clear and simple. Analyse the nature of your inner personality. Assess your spiritual need. Treat it with the compatible spiritual courses. Practise them diligently, consistently until you gain that supreme Knowledge.

However, while pursuing the course of spirituality you must carefully avoid, overcome two main impediments that confront you. The first is at the mundane level which is common to all. While the second is encountered by those who take up the spiritual practices seriously. The common factor in both impediments is the human weakness of becoming attached to the objects of experience. The mind craves for sensual pleasures, emotional feelings and intellectual concepts. It gets you involved in and attached to the mundane affairs. As a result of your attachment to the world you lose sight of the spiritual goal. This impedes your progress in the spiritual path.

The second impediment you face is your attachment to spiritual courses. Your involvement in *Bhakti* Devotion, *Gnanam* Knowledge and *Karma* Action. The courses themselves turn out to be most entertaining. They provide you with much greater peace and joy than that provided by your mundane activities. Your mind develops a fascination for the courses themselves. And begins to revel in them. Gradually you become involved in, attached to the practices. It is far more difficult to pull yourself out of spiritual involvement than from mundane involvement. Hence you continue to merely indulge in their enjoyment. You lose the very purpose of the spiritual path you have undertaken. With no thought of spiritual unfoldment and enlightenment. That becomes a greater obstacle in the spiritual path. Since the entertainment derived from spiritual practices is far superior to that of mundane activities, you become more bound to them. The attachment to the spiritual revelry is more binding than the attachment to worldly pleasure and joy. That explains why the attachment to spiritual courses turns out to be a greater obstacle in the path. You become more deeply rooted in ignorance. You grope in denser darkness. The *Ishavasya Upanishad* in verse 9 cautions humanity of this imminent failing in the spiritual path:

Those who are involved and attached to the material world grope in blinding darkness, ignorance while those who are attached to spiritual courses are lost in greater darkness, ignorance.

You must overcome these main obstacles in your spiritual path. Get over your attachment by gaining objectivity in life. You gain objectivity by strengthening your intellect through daily study of Vedantic knowledge. Reflect upon the truths therein. Use that knowledge to maintain objectivity in your material as well as spiritual life. You would then rise above all attachment and involvement. Remember, you take to the spiritual course for your evolvement, not your involvement. Never lose sight of the goal of Enlightenment through your life.

The spiritual courses are undertaken to unfold the divinity within you. They pertain to the terrestrial realm. They can reach you only to the point of terrestrial perfection. But cannot take you directly to the transcendental Reality. The Reality lies beyond the terrestrial realm. Hence, you will have to ultimately go beyond all terrestrial effort and cross over to the Transcendental. A phenomenon strikingly similar to an athletic event known as the pole vault. In this event, the pole-vaulter uses a pole to gain the height required to cross over a bar set for the purpose. The athlete runs with the pole, pegs one end of it on the ground, heaves himself up with the other end to the height of the bar, discards the pole and rolls over to the other side. No pole-vaulter can jump that height *without* a pole. Equally so, no pole-vaulter can jump that height *with* the pole. If he clings on to the pole after reaching the height he will dislodge the bar. Only by discarding the pole at that height can he cross over to the other side.

In the same manner, you cannot gain Enlightenment without the aid of the spiritual courses. Ironically, if you are attached to the courses, cling on to them you cannot gain It either. The spiritual courses can lift you to the zenith of terrestrial perfection. Thereafter, you must leave them and plunge into the silence of meditation. Then alone would you be able to cross over to the Transcendental. Attain spiritual Enlightenment.

CHAPTER XVII

LAW OF CAUSATION

The Supreme Law

The universe is an expression of innumerable laws of nature. They are physical, chemical, biological, psychological, philosophical and several other laws. These are all impeccable, infallible, each having a cause-effect relationship. A cause for an effect and an effect for a cause. The meticulous functioning of the countless laws is the law of causation. They seem to bow in obeisance to some mysterious controller, governor. That unknown, unseen governor is indicated as *Brahman*, the supreme God. The infinite power that holds the laws together. Acting like a monarch to whom obedient subjects pay homage. The English poet John Milton puts this idea across succinctly in his sonnet *On His Blindness*:

> *His state is kingly: thousands at His bidding speed*
> *And post o'er land and ocean without rest.*

The phenomenon of this world is therefore an endless expression of cause and effect. The incessant play of the law of causation. Which has been functioning from the very beginning. A coconut seed always produced a coconut tree and a coconut tree produced a coconut seed. A chicken produced an egg and an egg, a chicken. Where there is no cause and effect, there is no world.

The law of causation governing the macrocosm applies equally to the microcosm. Every human being is subject to this law. It operates at the physical, mental and intellectual levels. If the physical body has gone through a proper discipline of *yoga* and exercise it would presently be hale and healthy. And if the body has had no proper physical training, been sensually indulgent it would be pale and sickly. Similarly, the flow of thoughts and emotions towards the positive or negative would determine the nature of the present inner personality. So what you are now is a result of what you have been doing in the past, dating back from this moment. And what you would be in the future would depend upon what you do from this moment. It is an irrefragable law.

The above law has no sway over the supreme Self. It can only control the material equipments, affect your physical, mental and intellectual personalities and not the Self within. Your real Self is above the law of causation. It is not subjected to cause and effect. You must therefore leave the precincts of your body, mind and intellect and get to your divine centre. Be your Self. You will then govern the world instead of the world governing you.

The law of causation governing humanity falls under two categories. They are known as the law of destiny and the law of *karma*. The law of destiny deals with your past and present status. Whereas, the law of *karma* covers your past, present and future. It covers the law of destiny and goes beyond, into the future to explain your life in its entirety. Study it on its own merits. Examine the logic and reason that supports it. By a thorough grasp of the immaculate functioning of the law you can steer your personality to the highest order of life.

Law of Destiny

The constitution of each human being is a cumulative effect of his past thoughts, desires and actions. His past activities are the cause. His present personality is the effect. The effect is called destiny. Your destiny at any time is therefore the result of your past. Your past activities are *fait accompli*. You have no control over what you have accomplished earlier. You cannot alter them now. You will have to face the result set by those causes. Hence your present destiny is fixed. You naturally become a victim of your own past activities. If you have had a proper course of education you would be a literate now. If not, if you have neglected your study and learning you would be an illiterate. Likewise, if you had gone through a proper course of spiritual discipline you would command success and peace in your life. If however, you had chosen a material and sensual life you would be mentally agitated and sorrowful. You reap what you sow. This is the law of destiny.

People are not aware of this imposing law of nature. In their ignorance they believe destiny is something which is predetermined. Some accept it as a plan ordained by God. Others presume it is a play of stars and planets. Yet others hold it as a stratagem of luck and accident. These are all preposterous presumptions.

Destiny is ruled by a scientific law relating to cause and effect. You are the creator of your destiny. There is no extraneous power controlling your life. No God shaping your destiny. God has nothing to do with the type of thought, desire and action emanating from you. He does not determine their nature. No doubt God is the supreme power which enables you to think, desire and act. But the quality of your activities is entirely your making. You are the architect of your life.

You are responsible for its positive or negative character. You make or mar yourself.

Spiritual ignoramuses believe that God does everything. That whatever happens, happens with the will of God. That God has created the world and determined the course of each one's life therein. And consider a human being a victim of God's determination. They do not believe that he has any part to play in moulding his life. Whereas, the atheists aver that a human being is wholly responsible for whatever happens in life. That human effort is everything. And there is nothing else to it. Vedanta resolves the difference in their points of view. God is, no doubt, the substratum, prime mover of all activities. As petrol is to movement of all cars. But petrol does not determine the mode and course of their motion. It is the engine that provides the power in the car. The driver determines its direction, course. Similarly, the human mind and intellect determine the nature and direction of activities. And they in turn fabricate his destiny. Not God.

The responsibility of your life therefore lies in your hands. Entertain positive thought and feeling. Perform positive action. You meet with fortune. Whereas with negative thought, feeling and action you bring about misfortune upon yourself. You mould your destiny. You get what you deserve. It is an unfailing law. Richard Chenevix Trench puts its across beautifully: *The stone that is fit for the wall is not left in the way.*

Law of *Karma*

The law of destiny defines the status of a person at any moment of his life with reference to his past from that moment. Whereas the law of *karma* is an extension of the law of destiny into the future. Both the laws are based on the principle of cause and effect. The law of destiny states that you are at present the product of your past. The law of *karma* reaches further to state that you are not only the product of your past but the producer of your future as well. Destiny covers only the past and present while *karma* covers the past, present and future. With reference to your past you are a product, a slave. But with reference to your future you are a producer, a master. You are the son of your father, as well as the father of your son. You are a son-father, product-producer at the same time. Looking back into your past you develop pessimism. Looking ahead into your future you gain optimism. With the knowledge of the law of *karma* you begin to realise that your shortcomings and difficulties are the creation of your past unintelligent activities. And that you have now the opportunity to create a better future for yourself. That you are the master of your destiny.

A human being therefore is bound by his own past while he is free to act as he wills. Freedom and bondage seem to coexist in one person. Thus you are a product of your past. You also possess a free will to act as you please. There are two forces operating in your life. The one from the past that has shaped your destiny, known as *prarabdha*. The other which gives you the freedom to choose your action, *purushartha*. Your *purushartha* chooses your course of action. And the actions executed already by your *purushartha* self-efforts result in your *prarabdha* destiny. Your destiny is thus the cumulative effect of all your past self-efforts. Whatever has been the nature and quality of your effort in the past, the same will be reflected in your present destiny. If your physical, mental and intellectual activities have been positive you meet with a positive destiny. If negative, you meet a negative destiny. If partly positive and partly negative, your destiny takes the same proportion.

Destiny is similar to your bank balance. And self-effort
to your capacity to earn or lose money, to credit or debit
your account. Your bank balance at any point of time is
the aggregate of all your credits and debits prior to that
moment. Regardless of your balance showing credit or
debit, your capacity to earn or lose remains independent
of it. You could earn more and increase your balance. Or
withdraw more and decrease it. Likewise, regardless of your
present status you could put in positive effort and evolve
spiritually. Or indulge in negative effort and devolve. The
law of *karma* goes on.

Hence it is your effort that makes the difference to
your destiny. Few understand this law. They meekly attribute
their success or failure to God. Not realising that God
is merely the substratum of activity. And has nothing to do
with the nature or quality of activity. God is like the
sun above. The sun is the source of activity. Sinner or saint
draws his vitality from the sun. The sun provides them both
the energy to act. The sinner in a vicious way. The saint
in a virtuous way. Thus beings act according to their
independent nature. You cannot commend or condemn
the sun for their particular deeds. The sun stands clear from
vice and virtue of the world. So does God though supporting
everything remain immaculate, free from the happenings
in the world.

Your destiny at present is the effect of all your past
self-efforts. For example, if you had exercised your free will
in the past in merely gratifying your senses and leading
a sensual life, then you would be a sensual person at present.
That is your destiny. Instead, had you chosen to live
a disciplined life and practised the higher values you would
now be a spiritually evolved person. Moreover, regardless
of what state you are in at present you tend to continue the
same way. A sensual person pursues his sensual activities.

A spiritual person continues to be spiritual. Which gives the impression that your present choice of action is influenced by your past. If that be so, how can self-effort be free? Where does free will fit into the law of *karma*? An alcoholic is addicted to alcohol because of his heavy drinking in the past. If the past were to influence his present action he will continue as an alcoholic. How then can he claim to have the freedom to choose to drink or not to drink? Likewise a person is benevolent, noble because of the virtuous life he has led. Here again, if the past influences his present action he will continue to be virtuous. Thus if it is accepted that one's past completely influences one's present, then the good will continue to be good and the bad will continue to be bad. But this is not so in practical life. People are subject to change. The good are known to have turned bad, so have the bad turned good. What then is the relationship between *prarabdha* destiny and *purushartha* self-effort? A question that has been disturbing the spiritual lobbies for long. The exact relationship between the two is easier understood with the following two illustrations.

The first comparison is to a motorboat. The speed of the motorboat is 16 kilometres per hour in still waters. The boat is in a river moving downstream. The water in the river flows at a speed of 2 kilometres per hour. The speed of the boat downstream will then be 18 (16+2) km/hour. While moving upstream the speed of the boat will reduce to 14 (16-2) km/hour. Thus the speed of the boat varies from 18 to 14 km/hour depending upon its movement down or up. But all along, the actual speed of the boat remains the same at 16. The original speed of the boat is independent of the speed of water. Yet when it moves in the river it becomes 18 downstream and 14 upstream.

Now, compare the original speed of the boat to your *purushartha* self-effort. And the speed of water to your *prarabdha* destiny. Your self-effort is ever free. Your destiny cannot alter your self-effort. Just as the speed of the water cannot change the original, independent speed of the motor. Nevertheless, in effect the boat gains 2 km/hour downward and loses 2 upward. Similarly, even though your self-effort is independent, it is in effect altered by your destiny. When you apply your self-effort in the background of your destiny, the effect produced is different. Your self-effort makes its free choice in the background of your destiny. The combination of your effort and destiny produces a different effect.

Consider the case of the alcoholic. One day the alcoholic may choose not to drink. He exercises his free will to abstain from liqour. And yet he may be found consuming it. The reason being that his destiny, the background of indulgence, is more powerful than his effort to abstain. When both these forces operate the resultant effect will lean towards the more powerful. That explains why he drinks even if he chooses not to do so. If however, he continues to exercise his choice not to drink, he would gradually neutralise the effect of his destiny and stop drinking.

The second example again illustrates how *purushartha* self-effort functions in the background of *prarabdha* destiny. A wall is painted in yellow colour. Apply a little blue paint on it. The blue mixes with yellow to turn green. Those who look at the wall do not see blue. They see green. In fact, you are applying blue but it appears green. Keep applying blue over and over again. The yellow gets neutralised and the colour turns blue. The yellow wall has now become blue. The blue paint is free will, your self-effort. The yellow paint on the wall is your destiny. Just as the blue in the hand is free from the yellow on the wall, your self-effort is independent of your destiny. But when you apply your self-effort against your destiny the effect produced is different. Keep on applying your self-effort in the same direction.

In course of time your destiny changes in the direction set by your effort.

Birth and Death

The universe displays a graceful progression of events. All evolution follows a perfect sequence of rise and fall. A rhythmic motion of construction and destruction. Night follows day and day follows night. The seasons appear and disappear in regular succession year after year. Birth, childhood, youth, old age and death make a progressive chain. Cause and effect project themselves endlessly. The law of causation works with mathematical precision. Yet people hold fanatical beliefs that there is no life after death or that there is. Such irrational beliefs lead you nowhere. The subject of birth and death is deep, unfathomable. You cannot dismiss it thus by such speculative notions. You must study the subject carefully. Death and birth are merely a change of state. A movement from one experience to another. There is nothing terrible, abominable about death as people view it.

Birth and death are two sides of a coin. There can be no birth without death. And no death without birth. Morning dies. Evening is born. Evening dies, night is born. Night dies, morning is born. This chain of birth and death goes on perennially. So does the chain of birth, growth, decay and death continue. The phenomenon of birth and death brings about change. The world is in a continuous flux of change. Creation and destruction are the warp and woof of the world. The play of these two powers maintains the mineral, vegetable, animal and human kingdoms.

Creation, destruction and maintenance are three facets of the same phenomenon. They are not separate from one another. In the chain of creation and destruction of the different facets in the day, the day is maintained. Likewise in the appearance and disappearance of the seasons, the year is maintained. In the progressive ages of life, the individual is maintained. The entire universe therefore is an expression of the three powers of creation, destruction and maintenance. The devotional people find it difficult to conceptualise the precise manifestation of nature. So the scripture has personified these powers as gods. Brahma as the god of creation. Shiva as the god of destruction. Vishnu, god of maintenance. Also indicated to the intellectuals that they are one by combining the three gods in the form of Dattatreya.

Some believe that when a person dies nothing remains. That death is the end of the personality. And that there is no trace of him thereafter. Others disagree with this view. They do not consider death as finality. They believe in the continuity of life. And that the present incarnation is only a link in the chain of his entire life. Yet others posit the existence of imaginary realms of heaven and hell where they believe humans go to after death. These beliefs are not based on rational analysis and derivation. Instead, you must collect relevant data, study them carefully and draw intelligent conclusions from them. Only then would you get a clearer idea of the phenomenon of birth and death.

There is another strange phenomenon concerning death. Though death is inevitable and everyone knows that all living beings are certain to die, none believes it in practice. Young or old, healthy or unhealthy, even the terminally ill feel that death is far away. It is a wonder that nobody practically believes in death. Even at a ripe old age people keep amassing wealth, enlarging their worldly relations, behaving as though death would never take hold of them. Intellectually they may concede. But from a practical point of view they ignore their imminent end. It seems paradoxical. On the one hand a person is so certain of his end. The very thought of death sends a quiver through his entire frame. His body turns cold at the mere mention of death. While on the other hand it does not seem to bother him at all. He writes poetry, flourishes his art portraying death! What could be the reason for this paradox? How is it that the looming danger of death does not actually impede, disturb his life? Everyone expects to live on and on without being concerned about the end. The reason for this innate assurance of longevity is the immortal nature of the Self within. Every human being is quintessentially the Self. That being so, Its immortal nature colours his material layers. Which makes his individuality assume a sense of immortality. And keeps him free from the thought of death.

Theory of Reincarnation

What happens when a person dies? His gross body perishes in that form. The material of the body merges with earth. Science declares that something cannot pass into nothing. The law of indestructibility of matter, the law of conservation of energy states it. The same law would apply to the subtle body as well. The subtle body of the person comprises his thought, feeling and desire. The resultant of his mental and intellectual forces. His inner energy comprising subtle matter. Applying the same law to the subtle body, you would realise that its energy cannot vanish into nothing at the time of death. In this world there are innumerable deaths occurring everyday. And innumerable births. The mental energies of those persons cannot disappear or appear all of a sudden. That would be against the established law of science.

Life is a series of experiences. The progression of life is determined by desires. Desires drive you from one experience to another. In philosophic terms an experience is dead and another born at every moment. Thus your desires drive you through a continuous procession of birth and death. This procession will continue in perpetuity until the desires are eradicated from your personality. Desires are the cause and the experiences of life are the effect. At the moment of death a person is left with innumerable, unfulfilled desires. He may vanish from your sight but that does not mean that his desires are extinct. The desires have to be eradicated to prevent further manifestation. The cause has to be removed to erase the effect. When the desires are completely exhausted the cycle of birth and death ends. That is the state of Self-realisation, God-realisation.

Thus numerous desires of different sorts remain unfulfilled when people die. At the time of their death these desires have not been exhausted. It would be irrational to presume that all of them disappear into nothing. Now, look at the world from another angle. Different types of people are born with distinct tendencies, inclinations, desires. Every human being enters the world with his pattern of thought, feeling, desire. And people are born with a variety of desires. These variegated desires could not have emerged from nowhere. To accept that they have come out of nothing would again be as irrational as to presume that they disappear suddenly. Such presumptions would be violating the code of science.

Hence the great thinkers of the past made a careful scrutiny of this world and found hordes and hordes of desires disappearing and appearing perennially. After a thorough investigation of this phenomenon they brilliantly connected the unaccounted gain of desires of the born to the unaccounted loss of desires of the dead. A sheer audit of the accounts of life. They applied the law of causation which governs the entire universe at all times. Took the desires of the dead as the cause and linked them to the desires of the born as the effect. This observation is in accordance with the law of indestructibility of matter, the law of causation, the law of *karma*. This ingenious correlation of cause and effect projects the theory of reincarnation. It is only a scientific deduction from the available data. But cannot be proved experimentally. Hence presented as a theory.

Another popular belief is that the newborn inherits the tendencies of its parents. That the law of heredity establishes it. The law of *karma* does not oppose the concept of heredity. It corrects the general misconception that the equation between parent and child emanates from the parent. It is not the parents that determine the nature of the child. It is vice versa. The child determines the parents. The law of *karma* explains how the resultant effect of one's mental and intellectual energies would find the right body, parents and environment. With no extraneous power deciding this choice.

If desires are the cause for the continuity of life, how can one take birth in an environment or circumstance not to his liking? Take a form of life different from his desire? Why would a person be born poor when he desires to be rich? Why would anyone desire to be born physically handicapped? If desires decide your life's pattern how is it not so in actual fact? The world that you experience does not seem to always relate to your desires. This apparent paradox arises when you do not correlate cause and effect properly, fully. Your desires no doubt decide the course of your life. But then it is not a particular desire that decides it. It is the compound of all your desires. The total effect of your desires decides the course. It is called the resultant desire.

The parallelogram law of forces in physics explains this phenomenon as illustrated below in figures 1 and 2. Consider an object in position O free to move in all directions. Two equal forces act upon it. One force horizontally along

OA. The other vertically along OB. The object will then move, neither in the direction of OA nor OB, but diagonally along OR. There is no force operating along OR. Yet the object moves in that direction. The force that drives the object along OR is called the resultant. The resultant force is the effect of both the forces.

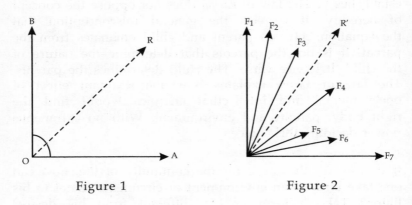

Figure 1   Figure 2

Let more forces OF_1, OF_2, OF_3 etc, be applied on the object. Several forces of varying strength and direction. Then the resultant would be the total effect of all those forces. Let it be OR'. Then the object will move along OR'. Here again the resultant force may not be in the direction of any one of the forces acting upon it. Yet the object will move in that direction. The same phenomenon takes place in your life. Your life is ordered by your resultant desire. The total effect of all your desires. Innumerable desires operate in you. Each has its own strength and direction. But you will move in the direction of your resultant desire. Which may not be in the direction of any one of your desires. That should explain why your life may not always be in line with any particular desire. That is the law of life which applies to every individual throughout the world.

Besides the above analysis and conclusion, it would be interesting to observe what exactly happens to a person at death. To his gross, subtle and causal bodies and *Atman*, the Self within. It is obvious that the physical body has not gone. It lies there. And the *Atman*, of course, cannot go anywhere since It is all-pervading. It exists everywhere. Being so, It should exist in the dead body as well. Besides, movement of an object is possible from a place where it exists to a place where it is not. As the *Atman* pervades everywhere there is no place where It does not exist. Hence It cannot move. Thus, the physical body of the person and the *Atman* are very much there at the time of death. It is only the other two components of the individual viz. the causal and subtle bodies that move out. Therefore, the transference of the causal and subtle bodies from one gross body to another is designated as the death of the former body and the birth of the latter.

The concept of birth and death becomes clearer with the example of the sun and its reflections. The sun's rays are all-pervading. Wherever there is a reflecting medium there will be a reflection of the sun. Hold a mirror in a frame in broad sunlight. You will find a reflected sun in it. Remove the mirror from the frame and fix it in another frame. Instantly, the reflected sun in the first frame vanishes and appears in the second. The image is *dead* in the first and *born* in the second. The reflected sun moves from the one to the other. Brought about by the transference of the mirror.

Equate the example to the phenomenon of birth and death. The sun above represents the *Atman*. Its all-pervading rays would then be the pure Consciousness everywhere. The frame would be the gross body. The glass and the reflecting material composing the mirror would represent the subtle and causal bodies respectively. The *Atman* functioning through these bodies projects the individual. Thus, the transference of the subtle and causal bodies from one gross body to another determines the death and birth of the individual. Until the *vasanas*, desires get completely exhausted, the causal and subtle bodies eliminated, the cycle of birth and death will continue for him. The moment the *vasanas*, desires are eradicated the individuality is dissolved. His cycle of birth and death ends. He attains spiritual Enlightenment.

Without the cognition of the law of causation and a clear understanding of the consequent theory of reincarnation, you could run into trouble. Here is a true story. A lady in her advanced age developed cataract in her eyes. She was losing her eyesight. At that time of her life a misfortune befell her. Her only daughter expired. She was terribly upset. She lost all her interest in the world. She would not meet anybody or go anywhere. Meanwhile her cataract ripened. She was practically blind. Her family and well-wishers appealed to her to undergo surgery. She refused to do so. She chose to deny herself eyesight for the rest of her life. She would say, "Am I to restore my eyesight to gaze at emptiness? The beauty in my home is gone. I have nothing more to see." They were all confused. And did not know how to persuade her to go through the surgery. They approached a *swami*, a sage for help. The *swami* met her personally. The wise man explained to her how the resultant desire works. "Remember, you are entertaining a powerful desire not to see the world," the sage said to her. "You are old. Death may overtake you any day. If you continue to deny yourself eyesight, there is a fair chance you will be born blind." The lady sprang to her feet. And went through the surgery the same day.

The significant part of the episode is that a person could be born blind even though he does not desire it. The resultant of all his desires becomes the cause leading to that effect. Therefore, it would be in your interest to scrutinise at all times the type of desires you entertain. Avoid negative thoughts and desires. Try to turn them positive. If you practise that, you would not be a victim of self-inflicted complications in life. Your life would then become more meaningful, purposeful.

Imagine a person who is brutal, bloodthirsty. He develops a passion for destroying, killing. He becomes a dangerous killer. The society does not allow him to manifest his destructive nature. The law prohibits it as well. His desires are frustrated. The frustrated desires must find their way out. This is not possible in his present embodiment, environment. Hence his resultant desire will forge itself into an appropriate embodiment for fulfilment. Thus his own desires could possibly cast his next incarnation as a tiger or a lion. Wherein the embodiment and environment becomes befitting, conducive for fulfilling those desires. No doubt, a human being cannot easily fall into an animal incarnation. A human possesses fine emotions and subtle thoughts which animals lack. Those thoughts and desires in him would strongly influence the resultant desire towards human incarnation. Notwithstanding it all, he could still force himself into a lower species by persistently indulging in such destructive passion.

There is also a powerful conjecture in spiritual lobbies that a person may not be reincarnated immediately after death. That his causal-subtle body may take a while before it finds the appropriate gross body and environment. The interim period after death and before the next birth would resemble sleep or dream. This observation again has certain validity since it is seen happening to other living species. The seed fallen from a tree is not always subject to immediate germination. An egg laid by a bird takes time to hatch. So too a human may experience a period of sleep or dream before his next incarnation.

People the world over are unaware of the relentless law of *karma*. They entertain all sorts of desires indiscriminately. Plunge into action in pursuit of their passions. Thoughtless of the dire consequences. And end up with calamities in their life. Unaware of their responsibility for the misfortune, they bewail the stars and planets. Blame everything, everybody in the world except themselves. In desperation some go to astrologers, palmists and spiritualists for help. Others pray to the gods to mend their fortune. Not realising they have brought the misery upon themselves. And that they have to redeem themselves.

CHAPTER XVIII

THEORY OF PERCEPTION

Phenomenon of the World

What is the world like? What is its exact nature? Is the world what it appears to be to the senses? If the perception of the senses were to determine that, then whose senses are to do it? The senses of different beings interpret the world differently. Ants perceive the world in a particular way. While elephants do so in another way. And humans perceive it different from ants and elephants. Then whose senses are to be relied upon? Whose accepted as the standard? That of human, animal or plant? Living beings view the world as children view their images in convex and concave mirrors. These mirrors produce ludicrous images. They appear long as pine trees or flat as pancakes. Thus there are multifarious versions of the world. The question arises as to the exact nature of the world. What is right and what is wrong? It has provoked philosophers to investigate and reach distinct conclusions. They have laid down conflicting theories. Vedanta reconciles these divergent views and presents the Vedantic Theory of Perception. It needs to be carefully studied and reflected upon.

One set of thinkers laid down the theory of Idealism. According to the Idealists the world is not what it appears to your sense perception. The world as it appears to you is false. Illusory. Unreal. Idealism again has different branches spearheaded by eminent philosophers like Berkeley, Plato, Hegel and others. Another set of thinkers laid down the theory of Realism. According to the Realists the world is real. The world is as it appears to you. Things and beings are just as they seem to you. Real in themselves. Baine and Mill are among the philosophers who support Realism.

Most people find it difficult to tune in to these abstruse, speculative theories. They dismiss them as mere theoretical enunciations of little value. They do not realise that theory plays an essential part in practical life. That all activity in the world is backed by thought. Vedanta provides you with the knowledge to explain the phenomenon of the world with its theory of perception. A theory founded on the laws of science.

Before launching into the study of the theory of perception the two terms commonly used, *subject* and *object*, need to be defined. In the context, the word *subject* means the perceiver, knower, experiencer. While *object* means that which is perceived, known, experienced. Take the example of perceiving a landscape. You are the perceiver and the landscape, the perceived. You are the knower, experiencer and the landscape the known, experienced. You are the subject. The landscape, the object.

Here again the concept of the subject varies. Western philosophers take the mind as the subject. Consider the mind to be the perceiver, knower, experiencer. Whereas, Vedanta states the mind itself to be an object, known, experienced. You can conceive your mind. Know it. Experience it. It fits into the definition of an object, not subject. Anything perceived or conceived, known or experienced ceases to be the subject in the true sense. Vedanta declares the inner Self, *Atman* to be the subject. To be the real perceiver, knower, experiencer. Hence, from the absolute point of view the *Atman* is the subject and the mind, the object. While in the relative sense, from a practical angle the mind becomes the subject and the rest of the world, the object. However, in the theories of perception discussed below the mind is taken as the subject, perceiver, knower, experiencer. And what is perceived, known, experienced by the mind as the object.

Idealism

Idealism is a theory which makes the subject responsible for the phenomenon of the world. The Idealists say that this world is not what it appears to be. The world perceived is produced by the subject's activity. The mind projects the entire phenomenon. Thoughts create it all. The thoughts are the reality according to the Idealists. The world, a mere illusory projection. With no reality of its own. The Idealists have advanced their arguments in support of this theory. Two of their main contentions are:

1. You perceive the world. Claim that the world is real. That it exists on its own. You do not seem to realise that the same world disappears no sooner you fall off to sleep. In deep-sleep you do not perceive the world. Even in the waking state when your mind is totally absorbed in some activity, like being engrossed in a novel, you do not see someone standing in front of you or hear him calling you or even feel his pat on your back. The Idealists thus maintain that you do not perceive the world when the mind is absent, when the subject does not participate. Your mind alone, your thoughts perceive the world. Therefore, according to the Idealists the entire world is but a projection of your mind, thoughts. Your senses no doubt perceive the world but they cannot do so without the mind. No mind, no world. That is the Idealist's law.

Examine the case of hypnotism. The hypnotist suggests powerfully to a protégé that the floor on which he stands is a lake. The thoughts in his mind are changed from the floor to a lake. The person does not see the floor any more. Sees a lake instead. He starts fishing in it! So it is your mind, your thoughts that create the world. The world has no reality of its own. This is one argument that the Idealists put forward.

2. The second contention of the Idealists is that the reality of the world cannot be based entirely on the senses. People attribute reality to the world relying merely on the evidence of the senses. Senses are surely not reliable. Your own senses interpret the world differently at different times, places and circumstances. Then there are the variety of senses of humans, birds and beasts. Submarine and subterranean creatures have senses too. Each set of senses has its own interpretation of the world. They differ widely. Now, whose senses are to be taken as authoritative? Whose senses fixed as the standard? They vary from being to being. Even in one being the senses change. You cannot treat a variable factor as invariable. It would be a mistake to do so. Hence the Idealists have concluded that the world is not what it appears to be. The world as it appears is false, illusory, unreal.

The Idealists give all-importance to the subject, none to the object. They take the subject to be everything. As the creator of the phenomenal world. Little realising the subject is variable, changeable, impermanent. They make the world depend entirely upon the subject. They fail to understand that the subject itself is a part of the created world. A part of the creation cannot be held responsible for the creation. Just as a dreamer is a part of the dream. An aspect of the creation of the dream. The dreamer, the dreaming-subject has not created the dream. The responsibility for the creation of the dream-world cannot therefore be placed on the dreamer. Similarly the waker, the perceiver-in-the-waking-world is a part of the waking world. It would be incorrect to hold the waker responsible for the creation of the waking world. That is what the Idealists have done. The waker and the world that he experiences are parts of the same creation. Hence the world cannot emanate from the waker, perceiver, subject. There lies the fallacy of the Idealists.

Realism

Realism is a theory which makes the object responsible for the creation of the world. Which considers the world real as it appears. The Realists believe things are real in themselves. You see the sun shining above. A hill standing yonder. A brook flowing across the meadow. They say all these have a reality of their own. Independent of your thoughts. Realists also advance arguments in support of their theory. Their main contentions are:

1. You perceive things and beings right before you. Because they are all there. Not only you, everyone perceives them. You see a horse. You see the same horse over and over again, day after day. The horse does not transform itself into a mule. It never does. Your mind may undergo change but the horse remains a horse. Just because it is real in itself.

2. The Idealists contend that everything is a creation of the mind. If that be so let their minds create what they wish. Let their mind produce a horse or a mule. They can never do that. They cannot produce substantial things out of insubstantial thoughts.

The Realists treat the object all-important and disregard the subject. Just the opposite of what the Idealists do. Realists believe the object to be everything. They consider the variable, changeable world of objects to be real in itself. They do not realise that the object also is a part of the creation. You cannot hold the object alone responsible for the creation of the world. But the Realists believe it to be so. That is where their mistake lies.

Thus the Idealists and Realists have been in constant conflict with each other. With their arguments and counter arguments. Quibbling and quarrelling with no meeting point. The Vedantic Theory of Perception takes both the subject and object into account. Reconciles the differences between the Idealists and the Realists. And presents a comprehensive formula for the phenomenon of this world.

Vedantic Theory of Perception

The theories of Idealism and Realism have accented the participation of the subject and object respectively in the creation of the world. They have exposed their limitation in their leaning entirely towards one of them. The Idealist has been rigid in holding on to the subject alone and the Realist, to the object. The Vedantic Theory of Perception softens their views to accommodate both their stands. It finds the meeting point to explain the phenomenon of the world.

The Idealists have observed that the world could not have arisen without the action of the subject. That there can be no world without the play of the mind. Without thoughts. That the mind's participation is necessary for perceiving the world. In the absence of the mind there can be no perception of the world. The Idealists assert that. So far as this observation is concerned they are right. But they take a step further to declare that there is nothing apart from the subject-mind responsible for the creation of the world. It is the action of the subject, mind, thoughts alone that produces the world. Nothing else. And that the object plays no part in it. Idealists are right insofar as they hold that the world could not have arisen without the subject, without the mind. But they err when they declare that nothing else, nothing other than the mind is responsible for the creation. They err in rejecting the participation of the object.

As opposed to the Idealists, the Realists have observed the creation of the world is due to the action of the object. That the object alone is responsible for the perception. In the absence of the object there can be no world. The Realists assert that. But they also further declare that nothing apart from the object is responsible for creating the world. The subject has no part to play in it. Here again, the Realists are right insofar as they hold that the world could not have arisen without the object. But they err when they declare nothing other than the object is responsible for the creation. They go wrong when they reject the participation of the subject.

The Vedantic theory states that neither the subject nor the object per se produces the world. It takes both the subject-perceiver and the object-perceived for creating it. The Idealists and the Realists have to come together to account for its creation. Neither of them can possibly do it alone. When the subject of the Idealists and the object of the Realists meet, there arises the phenomenon of the world. Action and reaction take place. The interaction between the subject and object, between the perceiver and perceived, between thought and thing produces the world.

Examine a perception. The perception of a flower. How does it take place? The Vedantic theory states that the quality, attribute of flower exists in the flower as the object. The thought of the flower exists in the mind as the subject. The subject impinges upon the object to bring about the perception of the flower. The union of the thought and quality of flower produces it. If either of them is absent there can be no perception. Say, the flower is not there. Instead, a stone is in the place of the flower. Then you will not perceive the flower. Likewise, if the thought of the flower is not in the mind, instead another thought has preoccupied the mind, you will not perceive the flower even if it were there. Therefore, it takes both the existence of the thought and the quality of the flower to bring about the perception of the flower. The creation of the flower.

The Vedantic theory reaches further to establish the underlying Reality in both. The supreme Reality, *Brahman* is all-pervading. It exists everywhere. In the subject and the object. The object-flower has certain quality. Which is variable, changing. Take away the quality from the flower. What lies beneath is not zero, not nothing but the changeless Reality. The quality is the structure. The Reality, the substratum. The union of the structure and substratum is the flower. Similarly, the Reality lies beneath the subject, beneath the thought of the flower as well. Thus the Reality, *Brahman* supports both the subject and object, the thought-of-flower and quality-of-flower. These facts defined and brought together gives the mathematical equation for the world.

Let the quality of flower be represented by QF.

And the underlying Reality by B.

Then the equation for the object-flower will be QF+B.

Which is the quality-of-flower and the underlying Reality put together.

Take the example of another object, a pen. The pen has its quality.

Let the quality-of-pen be represented by QP.

The Reality is the same, B.

Then the equation for the object-pen will be QP+B.

Similar equations can be made for the countless objects of the world. And the whole object-world perceived will be the aggregate of the qualities of all objects of the world and the Reality.

Let the entire range of objects of the world be marked O_1, O_2, O_3 etc.

The qualities of the objects be QO_1, QO_2, QO_3 etc.

The underlying Reality, B.

Then the equation for the object-world, for the entire perceived-world will be

$$QO_1 + QO_2 + QO_3 \text{ etc.} + B.$$

The subject is the mind. It consists of various thoughts. The thought of flower, thought of pen, thoughts of the entire range of objects of the world. When all thoughts are removed from the subject what remains is not zero, not nothing, but the underlying Reality.

Let the thought of flower be represented by TF.

The underlying Reality by B.

Then the equation for the subject-flower i.e., the thought in the subject-mind reacting with object-flower will be TF+B.

Similarly, let the thought-of-pen be represented by TP.

Reality by B.

Then the equation for the subject-pen i.e., the thought in the subject-mind reacting with the object-pen will be TP+B.

Again, the entire range of objects is O_1, O_2, O_3 etc.

And the thoughts-of-objects TO_1, TO_2, TO_3 etc.

Reality, B.

Then the whole subject-mind, perceiver would be the aggregate of the thoughts of all objects of the world and the Reality.

The equation for the whole subject, the entire mind, perceiver-of-world will be

$$TO_1 + TO_2 + TO_3 \text{ etc.} + B.$$

The Vedantic theory states the perception of the flower is a result of the combination of the subject and object, the union of thought-of-flower and quality-of-flower, TF+B and QF+B.

Therefore the equation of the flower is   TF+QF+B.

And the equation of the pen   TP+QP+B.

Likewise, the equation of the phenomenal world will be the combination of the thoughts-of-objects and qualities-of-objects and *Brahman*, the combination of the entire subject and object and *Brahman*.

Therefore, the mathematical equation of the world will be

$$TO_1 + TO_2 + TO_3 \text{ etc.} + QO_1 + QO_2 + QO_3 \text{ etc.} + B.$$

Thus the Vedantic Theory of Perception states the phenomenon of the world is brought about by the reaction of the subject and object in the medium of *Brahman*. A few interesting illustrations given below help to further elucidate the theory.

1. Two palms clapping produce sound. Either one of them on its own cannot. It is the play of both palms that does it. Similarly, the subject-mind alone cannot produce the phenomenal world. Nor the object-world. It is the impact between the two that accounts for the perception of the world.

2. Electricity has a positive and a negative pole. Neither of them produces a spark. But when the two poles come in contact with each other a spark is created. Though electricity as such has no spark in it. Likewise *Brahman*, the supreme Reality has no creation, no world in it. But when the two conditionings of *Brahman* come together there sparks off the phenomenal world. *Brahman* conditioned by thought becomes the subject-mind. Conditioned by quality becomes the object-world. The subject and object are like the two poles of electricity. When they come together there arises the perception of the world.

3. The ocean is a vast sheet of still water below with the waves on the surface. The water below is calm. Whereas the waves on top are ever disturbed. They produce ripples and bubbles, froth and foam all over the surface. Notwithstanding the varied expression, it is water and water alone. The sheet below, the waves, the ripples and bubbles, the froth and foam. The different manifestations are brought about by the collision of waves. One wave is like thought of the subject-mind. And the other like quality of the object-world. When these two impinge there arises the disturbed water, the phenomenal world.

Brahman is likened to water in the ocean. One wave, to the subject. Another, to the object. When the waves clash there arises the varied expression of water. Similarly, the clash of the subject and object produces the phenomenal world. However, *Brahman* remains the same, changeless Reality before and after the world emerges. Just as water remains as water in and through all its expressions.

4. The world projected upon *Brahman* is like a pattern of cloth woven from cotton. The pattern is made up of the warp and woof. The warp and woof are like the subject-mind and object-world. The combination makes the pattern,

produces the phenomenal world. Just as cotton pervades the warp and woof, the entire pattern, so does *Brahman* pervade everything, everywhere.

Thus *Brahman* remains ever the one supreme Reality. Absolute. Immaculate. Unaffected by the projection of the world upon It. *Brahman* is like space. Space cannot be conditioned, limited, divided. Yet it is referred to as pot-space, room-space, inside-space, outside-space etc. Nevertheless, space is one indivisible, all-pervading entity. Not subject to division. *Brahman* transcends even the subtlety of space. It is ever the illimitable, indivisible, infinite Reality. That Reality is your Self. Your *Atman*. Realise That. You will then realise the illusory nature of the world and rise above it. Become the supreme Reality.

CHAPTER XIX

THE ILLUSIONS: *MAYA*

When, Whence, Wherefore this World

The questions that bewilder the human mind concern the origin and purpose of the world. The mind remains beset with many baffling queries: When did the world begin? Whence the world? Wherefore? These are innocuous enquiries. But the layperson does not know what he is asking. The question when, whence, wherefore the world posits two ideas as separate from one another. It places the idea of when, whence, wherefore on one side. And the idea of the world on the other. But the ideas of when, whence and wherefore are an integral part of the world. They are not apart from the world. They emanate from time, space and causation respectively. Which are inherent in the world. Not beyond it. So the questions when, whence, wherefore of the world have no meaning. They pose a logical fallacy. A reasoning in a circle.

When you ask, when did the world begin, you place the world on one side and time on the other. You do not seem to realise that time is an essential part of the world. Your question segregates time from the world. You pull time out of the world and place it apart. In effect, you place the world before the world. You then create the world before it is created. Your question is the same as asking, when did time begin. If you say time began at a particular time, you posit time before the beginning of time. You produce time even before it is created. The questions, when did time begin, when did the world begin, therefore have no pertinence, no meaning.

In the same strain you ask, whence this world. Where did the world begin? You again segregate space from the world. You do not realise space also is an essential part of the world. When you ask that question you surround the beginning of space with space. For *where* cannot be conceived without the idea of space. *Where* denotes space. Hence your question produces space even before it is created. Your question 'where does the world begin' is the same as 'where does space begin'. It has no meaning.

The same reasoning holds good for causation as well. The idea of why, wherefore itself refers to causation. And the world is but a chain of causation. Your question, wherefore this causation, places causation before it is created. You cannot ask that either. Again, your question 'wherefore the world' is the same as 'wherefore causation'. It is meaningless.

Time, space and causation do not have a beginning or an end. Time stretches limitlessly both backward and forward. It can go back endlessly. Project forward endlessly. So does space extend on all sides without boundaries. It is all-pervading. Also, causation seems to have come from eternity and going into eternity. And time, space and causation constitute the world. Hence, there is no beginning or end to the world. The question of when, whence, wherefore this world does not arise. This question has no answer. It is beyond the scope of the intellect. Beyond human comprehension. Those who try to answer this question empirically are confused, confounded. They go round in circles. Get nowhere.

The world that you experience now in the waking state appears beginningless, endless. It is very much like your dream. The dream-world also has no boundaries. The dreamer views his world exactly as the waker, you view your world. The dreamer's intellect also cannot understand the origin of the dream-world that he experiences. Neither can it conceive the end of the dream-world. But the dreamer does not realise the limitation of his intellect. All the confusion and agitation that the dreamer goes through can be overcome only when he wakes up. When the dreamer becomes the waker. Then there is no longer the questioner and the question. The waker instantly understands the nature of the entire phenomenon of the dream. And the absurdity of the erstwhile queries and worries of the dreamer. The confusion and agitation that the waker experiences is much like that of the dreamer. You, as the waker now, question the origin, the meaning and purpose of the waking world. When, whence, wherefore this world. You are bewildered by the mystery of this world. This perennial problem can be completely solved only by spiritual awakening. On realising your supreme Self. The waking world is then seen just as another illusion, like the dream. All your ignorance and the consequent mental agitation vanish. You reach the Enlightened State of knowledge and bliss.

World, an Illusion

Vedanta declares that this solid-seeming world is not different from the dream-world. The waking world also is an imaginary projection upon the Reality, *Brahman*. A mere illusion. However, the world that a waker experiences is defined in time, space and causation. It is precise, accurate. Whereas the world that a dreamer goes through is imprecise, inaccurate. These two worlds therefore differ in degree, not in kind. But, both are illusions. The Reality supporting them is *Brahman*. When you realise your supreme Self, you get established in the supreme Reality, *Brahman*. The illusory worlds of the waking, dream and deep-sleep then disappear. What remains thereafter is *Brahman* alone.

When a person is hypnotised he sees a lake in his lounge. None else sees it. To the hypnotised the lake is real. When dehypnotised he does not see the lake any more. So too in the ignorance of your supreme Self, you have hypnotised yourself to believe you are the body, mind and intellect. In that self-hypnosis you see an imaginary world of things and beings. The world is just a hypnotic phenomenon. You must get off this self-hypnosis. Wake up. Realise your true Self. The supreme Reality reveals Itself. The world is no more.

Vedanta calls this world *maya*. *Ma* means *not*. *Ya* means *that*. *Maya* literally means *not that*. You ask if this world is real. Vedanta says it is *maya*, not that, no. How can the world be real when it is transient, fleeting, passing? The world does not exist at all times. It disappears in deep-sleep. It is also said to dissolve completely upon Self-realisation. The world does not stand the test of reality. Reality is something that lasts forever. Therefore the world cannot be real. Then is the world unreal? Vedanta says *maya*, not that, no. It is not unreal either. Cannot be called unreal. For, unreal means that which never existed, like the horns of a man. Man has never had horns. This cannot be applied to the world because the world exists for you now. Hence it cannot be unreal. If the world is neither real nor unreal can it then be partly real and partly unreal? Vedanta says *maya*, not that, no. World cannot be partly real and partly unreal. For the reason that reality and unreality cannot coexist. Thus the world you experience is neither real nor unreal nor partly real or partly unreal. It is *maya*. Just a dream. An illusion.

Analyse an erstwhile dream. The dreamer and the dream-world appear simultaneously. The dreamer would never accept that his life has commenced a few minutes back. The dreamer declares he is forty years old. He can account for those years in great detail. He goes over to his university and points out his name in the list of its alumni. He asks the principal of his high school to confirm his term therein. He even shows the municipal records wherein his birth was registered. Moreover, the dreamer swears the dream sun and moon, the hills and dales, rivers and lakes have been there for ages. The dreamer considers everything in the dream to be real. Yet with all those proofs, the dream has lasted only four minutes!

Now, carefully scrutinise your waking state. You as the waker and the waking world that you experience appear simultaneously. The waker declares emphatically that he is fifty years old. Like the dreamer, the waker also has a history of his own. And can account for his entire life. Bring up his university, high school and birth registration exactly as the dreamer had done. And substantiate the period of fifty years with proofs akin to those of the dreamer. With amazing similarity the waker also swears by the world of the waking state. That it has existed for ages. He pledges the sun and moon, the hills and dales, rivers and lakes in the waking state have all been there forever. The nature of the experience he goes through is not any different from that of the dream. Both the waker and the dreamer swear by the world that each experiences. Even as the one negates the other world. Vedanta declares that you, now as the waker cannot claim any more reality of this waking world than you, earlier as the dreamer had claimed of the dream-world.

Intrinsic and Extrinsic Illusions

People have observed a shoe being made by a shoemaker. A dress being made by a dressmaker. A pot by a potmaker.

They look at the world and conclude there must be a worldmaker. That there must have been a creator who created the world. They christened him God. Their conclusion sounds plausible, quite reasonable. But then, it is a mere theory. A supposition. Speculation.

If you maintain this theory that God created the world, you separate God from the world. You segregate God and the world. Thereby restrict the all-pervading nature of God. You place a limitation on the infinite Being. Moreover, by making God a creator you attribute motives, desires to God. You reduce God to the status of a shoemaker, a dressmaker, a potmaker. You must realise the origin of the world is well beyond the reach of the human intellect. The human intellect cannot conceive God. Give up that idea. Do not lead yourself to superstitious beliefs. Let your approach to the world be rational. Proceed from the known to the unknown. Do not take anything for granted. Through study, reflection and meditation you must gradually unveil your real Self. Realise your true Self. Discover your supreme Being. Attain spiritual Enlightenment. You will then realise the extraordinary illusion you were caught up in.

The Self-realised have declared from their own experience that the world that you perceive is just an illusory projection upon the supreme Reality. That there are two illusions playing in the world. Termed as intrinsic and extrinsic. Which have held the mass of humanity in total delusion.

An intrinsic illusion is one in which the real object and its illusion do not coexist. When the object is cognised the illusion disappears. And when the illusion appears the object disappears. The object and image do not appear together. For example, a child misapprehends a post in the dark to be a ghost. The child sees the ghost. It does not see the post. You see the post. You do not see the ghost. You then bring in light. Illumine the post. The child now cognises the post. Instantly the ghost is gone. You will notice that only one of them appears at a time. It is either the post or the ghost. They can never appear together to the same person at one time. That is an intrinsic illusion.

An extrinsic illusion is one in which the object, image and the medium which causes the image appear together. All three are present at the same time. An example of an extrinsic illusion is reflection in a mirror. You see your image in the mirror. The mirror is the medium that produces your reflection. In this illusion you, your reflection and the mirror all appear together. The object, image and the medium present themselves simultaneously. That is an extrinsic illusion.

There is yet another interesting phenomenon about these illusions. The possibility of both the intrinsic and extrinsic facets appearing simultaneously in a single illusion.

A boy treads on a rope in the dark. Mistakes it for a snake. He sees a snake. He does not see the rope. That is an intrinsic illusion. Where only one of the two is seen. The snake and not the rope.

Now follow carefully. You will find therein an extrinsic illusion created as well. Ask the boy to describe the snake he has seen. He says it is six feet long, four inches thick, black in colour. Examine the rope. You find the rope is six feet long, four inches thick, black. The boy's description of the snake fits exactly with that of the rope. The properties-of-the-rope have mirrored themselves in the illusory snake. The properties-of-the-snake is merely a reflection of the properties-of-the-rope. And the medium that has brought up this reflection is the illusory snake. The moment the snake was projected upon the rope, the snake becomes the medium for the properties-of-the-rope and the properties-of-the-snake to appear together at one time. Thus the two sets of properties and the medium present themselves simultaneously. All three coexist. That is an extrinsic illusion.

Human beings are caught up in both intrinsic and extrinsic illusions in their experience of the world.

The world appears to you as a pluralistic phenomenon of things and beings, as an infinite expression of time, space and causation. But the entire world is nothing but *Brahman*. *Brahman* alone exists. But you see a world. Not *Brahman*. Like the boy seeing a snake and not the rope. You see a world where there is *Brahman*. That is the intrinsic illusion.

In the same phenomenon there is an extrinsic illusion as well. *Brahman* is said to be eternal, all-pervading, infinite. You find these properties in the world as well. The world seems to have come from eternity and going into eternity. It is all-pervasive. And its chain of causation runs into infinity. Thus the world also appears to be eternal, all-pervading, infinite. You see the properties-of-*Brahman* clearly reflected in the properties-of-the-world. The medium that has caused this reflection is the world itself. The moment the world appears the three aspects of an extrinsic illusion show up. The two sets of properties and the medium all appearing at one time. That is the extrinsic illusion.

Brahman is the one Reality existing everywhere at all times. *Brahman* is *Atman*, the supreme Self within. It is ignorance of *Brahman*, the ignorance-of-Self that projects the two illusions. The non-apprehension of Self causes the misapprehensions of the world. You do not see the supreme

Reality. Instead you see the world. You also see the attributes of Reality in the world. The solid-seeming world is a play of the illusions. A meaningless projection. Strive hard to get out of these illusions you are lost in. Be it said to the credit of prevailing religions, that they have helped in removing one of the two illusions. At best they have succeeded in overcoming the extrinsic illusion. Undoubtedly approached the Reality. But that is not reaching the Reality. Vedanta takes you well beyond that. Removes not only the extrinsic but the intrinsic illusion as well. Provides you with the knowledge of the supreme Self within. Both the illusions disappear. You apprehend the ultimate Reality. Merge with *Brahman*.

Self-realisation, God-realisation comes in two stages. The earlier is partial realisation known as *savikalpa samadhi*. And the final is total realisation *nirvikalpa samadhi*. A spiritual seeker attains partial realisation when he removes the extrinsic illusion alone. In that stage he is on the verge, but not experiencing total realisation. Since the intrinsic illusion still lingers. When he sees Divinity in every object and being, all over. In a sinner or saint. He sees God alone everywhere. He experiences the unifying Divinity in the diversities of the world. No divisions. No demarcations. No denominations. Only Divinity. But the duality still remains. His individuality is there to recognise Divinity everywhere. It is the state of partial realisation.

Vedanta takes the seeker beyond the state of partial realisation. To total realisation of the supreme Self by overcoming the intrinsic illusion as well. To *nirvikalpa samadhi*. In partial realisation the seeker is in a state of duality. He has no doubt brought the entire pluralistic phenomena into a single mass of Divinity. He finds God all over. But then there is the duality of himself and God. He sees God different from himself. And when he realises the supreme Self within, his individuality merges with Divinity, the intrinsic illusion also vanishes. He becomes one with God. Attains total realisation. Absolute Enlightenment.

World is God

The world is not created by God. The world is God, *Brahman*. The elements that constitute the world are all *Brahman*. But when the component elements are brought together the resultant formation seems different. The resultant acquires properties different from those of the components. Here are examples to substantiate this truth:

Take the example of four triangles as in Figure 1. They are right-angled triangles. Place the four triangles with their vertices meeting at a point. They form a square as in Figure 2.

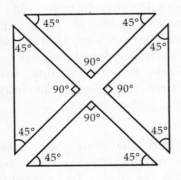

Figure 1

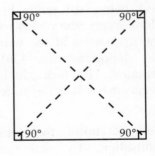

Figure 2

Study the two figures. The components are the triangles. They combine to form a square. The square is created as a result of

combining the triangles. The triangles have each two acute angles and a right angle. The hypotenuse is longer than the other two sides. Whereas the square has all right angles. And the sides are equal. The properties of the resulting formation are different from the properties of the original components. The new properties have risen from a new combination, a new formation of the components. The resultant is just a new name, a new form. No creator need be brought into this phenomenon.

In another example, two atoms of hydrogen combine with an atom of oxygen to form a molecule of water. Hydrogen is a combustible gas. Oxygen, a gas supporting combustion. Their combination produces water which extinguishes combustion. A combustible gas combines with a combustion-supporting gas to form a combustion-extinguishing liquid. It is incredible. But true. The resulting compound owes its status to a new name, new form, new configuration.

Another fascinating example is that of the element carbon. Charcoal is carbon. Diamond is carbon. Charcoal is black, dull. Whereas diamond is brilliant. Charcoal is soft and it can mark on paper. While diamond is hard and it can cut through metal. Charcoal is cheap, diamond precious. Notwithstanding all these differences both are made of carbon. The differences are in the structure of the carbon atoms in them. They differ only in the combination of the same component element. The different combinations create the wide disparity in the properties of the resultant form and name. Nothing else.

Vedanta declares therefore the difference between *Brahman* and the world is the difference between the triangles and square, between hydrogen-oxygen and water, between carbon and charcoal-diamond. The same Divinity that is *Brahman* is the world. The world is not any different

315

from *Brahman*. And yet they seem opposed in their nature. *Brahman* is eternal, all-pervading, infinite while the world is ephemeral, limited, finite. All the differences lie just in name and form, in combination and configuration. Resulting in a mere illusion. You must get off the illusion. Realise your true Self. Then there is Divinity alone. The supreme Reality reveals Itself.

Why heed an Illusion

If the world is a mere illusion, then all that goes with the world is illusory. That being so, then Vedanta and its philosophy also becomes a part of the illusion. How then can it carry any more credibility, any more importance than the rest of the illusion? What respect and regard can Vedanta boast of when it is just an aspect of an illusory projection? Why heed this part of the illusion? Why hang on to Vedanta alone? How can one part of the illusion pull you out of the entire illusion? It is a pertinent question. Vedanta provides a brilliant answer.

It is true that the knowledge and philosophy imparted by Vedanta is a part of the illusory world. But it has one distinction which all other parts of the illusion lack. Its unique character is highlighted in one potent simile *svapna simha vat* which means *like a dream-lion*. The philosophy of Vedanta is compared to the lion. Imagine a dreamer suddenly encounters a lion in the dream. The lion is a part of the dream-world. A figment of imagination like the rest of the dream. But the lion-in-the-dream has one distinct character which is denied to other parts of the dream. It is its faculty to catapult the dreamer from the dreaming state to the waking state. When the lion pounces on the dreamer he is startled, terrified. He jumps out of the bed. The lion wakes him up as it were. The dream-lion is no doubt a part of the dream. But it has the ability to swallow up the entire dream; itself vanishing in the act. Vedanta plays the role of the dream-lion in the world. Its chaste knowledge is admittedly a part of the illusory world. But it has the unique power to dissolve the entire world, dissolving itself in the process. That transports the waker to God-consciousness. To the ultimate spiritual Enlightenment.

CHAPTER XX

THE SUPREME REALITY

The Supreme God

The perceiver and the perceived, the individual and the world, the experiencer and the experienced, everything, every being, everywhere is the ultimate Reality, the supreme God known as *Brahman*. There exists nothing other than *Brahman*. The entire phenomenon of the play of plurality, of things and beings, of names and forms is a mere superimposition upon the one Reality. An illusory projection upon *Brahman*. But the superimposition does not make *Brahman* any less or more. It remains the same, immaculate, infinite.

An invocation in the ancient text of the *Upanishad* pronounces this truth:

Om purnamadah purnamidam purnat purnamudachyate
Purnasya purnamadaya purnamevavashishyate

Translation
Om. That is infinite. This is infinite. Infinite has come out of infinite. Take away infinite from infinite. What remains is infinite.

Adah means that. *That* refers to the supreme Reality, *Brahman*. *Idam* is this. *This* refers to the world, the pluralistic phenomenon projected upon *Brahman*. *Brahman* is supreme, infinite, inconceivable by the intellect. The world also appears infinite in nature. The world has emerged from *Brahman*. But *Brahman* is not any less. It remains the same, unaffected, unchanged.

This truth is akin to lighting many candles from a single flame. Numerous flames arise from that one flame. Yet the original flame is not any less. It remains the same, unchanged. So it is with *Brahman*. The universe has emerged from *Brahman*. Yet It remains ever the same. The infinite cosmos is drawn out of infinite *Brahman*. What remains is infinite *Brahman*. As in mathematics, infinite minus infinite is infinite.

Another example is that of numerous garments made of cotton. Cotton is spun into yarn. Yarn woven into cloth. And cloth made into garments. All these have come out of cotton. Nevertheless, cotton is not any less. Cotton remains as cotton be it in its original state or in the variety of garments produced.

These examples and illustrations serve as useful pointers to conceive *Brahman* though It is indefinable, inconceivable. They go a long way to explain the inexplicable. So that the human intellect can formulate some idea of Its magnitude and magnificence.

The most direct and practical example is the experience of the dream. The phenomenon of the dream proceeds from the mind. The dream consists of the dreamer and the dream-world. The dream-world also comprises infinite pairs of opposites, things and beings, names and forms. The creation of the dream-world does not render the mind any less. The mind remains just the same. Unaffected, unsullied by the projection of the dream. In fact all aspects of the dream are mere thoughts of the mind. The variety of thoughts have assumed these forms. As long as the dream lasts, the dreamer will not realise the insubstantial nature of the dream-world. The dreamer experiences the solidarity, reality of the dream-world just as the waker experiences that of the waking world. Only when the dreamer crosses the dream-world, wakes up into the waking world, the waker realises the entire dream-world to be a figment of his mind.

Similarly, the waking world and its infinite phenomena are nothing but different aspects of *Brahman*. The waker does not recognise this truth as long as he is in the waking state just as the dreamer does not realise the nature of the dream-world while he is in the dream. But the moment the waker recognises the Self, *Atman*, *Brahman*, rises from the waking state to Self-realisation, he apprehends the whole truth. That the waking world is yet another illusory projection. That *Brahman* alone is the Reality.

Reality is that which persists. Which exists in all periods of time. Remains the same in the past, present and future. Reality exists both as manifest and unmanifest. As structure and substratum. The world arises out of Reality. Exists in Reality. Merges ultimately into Reality. As waves arise, exist and merge into the ocean. The waves are nothing but water. So is the world nothing but the Reality, *Brahman*.

Brahman is the Eternities that cannot be conceived, defined, described. Yet, great Souls having realised *Brahman* have given various indications as to Its infinite nature. These serve as pointers to the unknown Reality. As arcs in geometry serve to fix the location of a point. An unknown point x is said to be 4 inches from a known point A and 5 inches from another known point B. You can then fix the location of x by striking two arcs with a compass measuring 4 and 5 inches respectively from A and B. The intersection of the two arcs would be the location of x. Thus the following indicative definitions help conceptualise to an extent the inconceivable *Brahman*.

Ekam **One:** *Brahman*, the supreme God is said to be one. There exists nothing but the one Reality, *Brahman*. The pluralistic phenomena is a superimposition upon that One. Yet *Brahman* remains the same. Just as the mind remains one even as the pluralistic phenomena of dream objects and beings arise from it.

Advayam **Non-dual:** The definition of the Reality being one creates the impression of a boundary around It. Which means that something exists beyond It. Since nothing exists other than *Brahman* It cannot strictly be defined as one. Hence said to be non-dual.

Nirakara **Formless:** An object takes a form where there is something other than the material of the object beyond its boundary. If there is nothing other than the object to define its boundary it can have no form. Anything all-pervading cannot have a form. Since *Brahman* alone exists, there is nothing other than *Brahman* to create Its form. Hence considered formless.

Sarvagatam **All-pervading:** *Brahman* alone exists. Nothing else. It pervades everywhere. If not so, there would be a place It has not accessed. That would restrict It, limit It. Since *Brahman* is limitless, infinite It has to be all-pervading.

Nirguna **Attributeless:** Substances have properties, qualities, attributes. They are perishable. If attributes are given to *Brahman* It would be reduced to a substance. And rendered perishable. Since *Brahman* is not a perishable substance, It is attributeless.

Aksharam **Imperishable:** Every object and being has a beginning and an end. Birth and death. The terrestrial world is an expression of creation and destruction. But *Brahman* is transcendental. Beyond the terrestrial. Not subject to birth and death. Hence, imperishable.

Aja **Unborn:** *Brahman, Atman* is not born when beings are born. Nor does It die when beings die. It always was, is and will ever be. With no beginning or end. Hence considered unborn.

Nitya **Eternal:** Eternal means beyond time. Time is the interval between two experiences. As distance is between two points. There can be no distance at a point. There has to be more than one point to create the idea of distance. A minimum of two points is necessary to measure distance. So it is with time. There can be no concept of time at the first experience. With the second experience alone is time born since two are required to measure time. That perhaps is the reason for the unit of time to be termed *second*. Time therefore arises with the second experience. But *Brahman* being the source of all experiences, existed at the very first. Hence, said to be before time. Trans-time. Timeless. Eternal.

Nirvikara **Changeless:** *Brahman, Atman* remains changeless in and through the changes occurring in the equipments It enlivens. The body, mind and intellect change continuously. These changes are perceptible because of the presence of the changeless substratum. The *Atman* that supports them all.

Nirmala **Stainless:** Stainless means pure, immaculate. A substance is pure when the material of the substance is not mixed with anything else. For example, a sample of gold is pure only when there is no material but gold in it. If other material is mixed with it, it becomes impure. *Brahman* is said to be ever pure since there exists nothing other than *Brahman*. There can be no contamination in *Brahman*. Hence stainless.

Anantam **Infinite:** Things and beings of the world have a beginning and an end. They are all finite. They arise out of, exist in and merge into *Brahman*. *Brahman* is the substratum upon which the worlds appear and disappear. It is beginningless, endless. Infinite.

Gnanam **Knowledge:** *Brahman* is absolute, pure Knowledge. The Knowing-Principle with which everything becomes known. People have the knowledge *of* sight, sound, smell, taste and touch. Also the knowledge *of* joy and sorrow. *Of* thought and idea. These are all conditioned knowledge. Knowledge defined by perception, emotion and thought. Whereas, *Brahman* is knowledge undefined, unconditioned. None can possess knowledge *of Brahman*. It is Knowledge per se. Unrelated to anything.

Anandam **Bliss:** The pleasures derived from objects and beings of the world are fleeting, ephemeral. Whereas the bliss of Self-realisation is absolute, eternal. It is the ultimate goal of human evolution. The Enlightened enjoys the uninterrupted supreme bliss.

Turiyam **Fourth:** Refers to the state of Self-realisation. The state of pure Consciousness beyond the waking, dream and deep-sleep. These three states are conditioned by the gross, subtle and causal bodies respectively. When one detaches oneself from the three bodies, rises above their conditioning, one merges with the pure Consciousness. Reaches the fourth state of *Turiyam*.

***Achintyam* Inconceivable:** *Brahman* is pure Consciousness. It is the supreme Self enlivening the senses to perceive objects, mind to feel emotions and intellect to conceive thoughts. It is the subject, not the object of experience. Your body, mind and intellect cannot reach *Brahman*.

The Self conceiving the world through the intellect is like a viewer observing a landscape through a telescope. The viewer uses the telescope to view everything except himself. He cannot see himself with the telescope. Likewise, the Self uses the intellect to conceive everything in the world except Itself. Hence the Self is said to be inconceivable.

Manifestations of *Brahman*

Brahman is one homogenous mass of Reality. But the manifestations of *Brahman* are manifold. Just as electricity is one while its expressions are manifold. The sun is one, its reflections manifold. Not knowing the unifying nature of *Brahman* the ignorant masses relate to Its multifarious expressions. They become involved in their differences. Divide themselves into various factions. And suffer the bitterness and misery arising therefrom. The wise rise above differences. Recognise the *Brahman* through Its manifestations. See unity in the diversity. Identify with the supreme Being. And revel in Its peace and bliss.

Brahman is the substratum of the microcosm and macrocosm that constitute the world. It is the centre around which both of them revolve. That supreme Being resides in your Self within. Discover your Self. The entire world will merge into It.

A highly evolved spiritual person finds the expression of divinity everywhere. He would go into raptures merely at the sight of a flower or fruit. William Wordsworth was in ecstasy when he beheld the daffodils. Whereas a less developed one not as spiritually evolved would need something more striking, perhaps a glorious sunrise or sunset to inspire him. And the least developed with hardly any spiritual insight would react only to spectacular sights like the snow-capped Everest or the mighty Niagara Falls. Anything less would not stimulate the divinity in him.

But then there are unspiritual extremists who do not react even to spectacular, breathtaking expressions of nature. They remain grossly inhuman, blind to the splash of divinity lavished all over. Those are the persons who need miracles to excite them. Only such unnatural gimmicks could stir them from their spiritual slumber. These barren characters lack the fundamental spiritual trait of the human species.

Everything in the world rests in your inner Self. All perception, emotion and thought proceed from the Self. The world has no reality of its own. But people look upon it as real in itself. Make a wrong evaluation. Give it false attributes. Which causes privation and pain, suffering and sorrow. They do not realise that the world has no status, substance, standing apart from the underlying Reality. You may give the world as much status as you would a picture of your family. The picture is valued, loved not for what it is worth but because of your family that it represents. The picture has no value apart from the family. Likewise the world is a picture of the Reality. It has no inherent value without the

Reality. Learn to regard the world as you would the picture. Understand the Reality alone exists. Recognise the Reality in and through all your experiences in life. Regard all happenings as a grand theatrical performance as Shakespeare has wisely advised.

Thus must you view the world from the balcony of your inner Self. Watch the procession of action and perception, emotion and thought go by. Do not allow yourself to become involved, enmeshed with them. Stand apart. Be objective. Be a witness, *sakshi*. All goes well thereafter. No friction, no frustration in life. You attain enduring peace and bliss.

The question remains, how does one extricate oneself from the worldly entanglement and identify with the Self within. Here is a simple parable which suggests a practical way to go about it.

There was a king who ruled his state to perfection. His subjects adored him. He was advancing in age. And had no heir to his throne. His ministers were concerned over the future of the state. They approached the king reverentially and laid the problem before him. The king resolved to nominate his heir. After reflecting over the matter he decided to organise a grand exhibition. With the finest exhibits from different parts of the world. In that exhibition he would be somewhere incognito. The subjects of the state would all be invited to the exhibition. He who finds him out shall be the heir to the throne. This was the royal proclamation.

The proclamation was publicised. The exhibition declared open. People thronged to it. Everybody searched for the disguised king. Soon their excitement and enthusiasm died away. They became involved in the variety of the fascinating displays. And quite forgot the search. They lost the very purpose of the exhibition. In that aimless mob one young man persisted with the search. Determinedly pursued the goal. Maintained consistency of his purpose. Put forth all effort to discover the king. And remained detached from the attractions around. He searched every nook and corner. At last reached the farthest end of the exhibition. There he found a small, neglected temple. It was a permanent structure in the vast exhibition grounds. Quite exhausted with the search the young man sat at the entrance of the temple. He heard a prayer chanted by a priest inside. Ignoring the ritual he promptly went in and examined the priest. And lo! There was the king disguised. The king commended the youth's determination and effort. And crowned him king of the state.

So it is with *Brahman. Brahman* remains incognito in the world. People are lost in the phenomena of perception, emotion and thought. Few care to search for the Reality that lies beyond the fascinations of the world. People are lost in the pleasures of life. They have virtually abandoned the kingdom of bliss. The wise one however rises above all terrestrial attraction. Searches and researches *Brahman* in the phenomenal world. That rare one finds *Brahman*. Becomes *Brahman*.

Process of Negation and Assertion

Brahman, the supreme Reality pervades the macrocosm and microcosm. *Brahman* is right within you. To locate *Brahman* you need to go introvert. Seek your supreme Self through the process of negation and assertion. Negate your material bodies. Assert your real Self. Your present state is one of identification with the gross, subtle and causal bodies. You have restricted your life to the experiences of these bodies. And suffer from a self-imposed limitation. You need to liberate yourself from your terrestrial entanglement. Your focus of interest must move from the material equipments to your essential Self. Negate the conditioning bodies. Assert your unconditioned Self. Suggest to yourself powerfully that you are not the gross, subtle and causal bodies. That you are the immaculate Self.

The ignorance-of-Self is the cause of creation of the world. The variety show that appears before you is a mere passing phenomenon. It is transient, perishable in contrast to the eternal, imperishable *Brahman*. As you focus your attention upon the body, your physical personality arises. You relate to the gross objects of your senses. Just so, focussing upon the mind your psychological personality shows up. You then relate to feeling and emotion. And when your focus is upon the intellect, your intellectual personality predominates. You identify more with thought and idea. You must rise above the limitations of the body, mind and intellect and attune yourself to the underlying Self that enlivens them all. Concentrate, meditate upon your real Self. The show of object, emotion and thought folds back. You become established in the Self. You merge with the Self, *Atman*, *Brahman*.

Do away with your infatuation to this phenomenal world. Shift your concentration upon the Self, the supreme God. You have cast away a treasure and picked up trash. God resides in you. Realise your Self. You will then realise there exists nothing other than God. That is the stern reality. Prophet Mohammed declares: *Laa ilaha illallah There exists nothing but God.* So do Christ, Krishna and the rest of that galaxy. Vedanta roars with this truth. You innocently put more faith in the outward phenomenon than the Reality that supports it. You make the world more real than God. You have hypnotised yourself to believe in the reality of the world. Your involvement in the world has caused only suffering and sorrow. You must now direct your energy and strength to the Self within. Get to the Eternities, the supreme God. Feel That. Live That. Get lost in God as a cube of sugar in water. You will attain spiritual Enlightenment. Absolute peace and bliss.

The metaphor of butter permeating milk explains the immanent nature of *Brahman*. *Brahman* exists everywhere. Permeates every part of the world. Yet remains incognisable. As butter in milk. Butter exists in milk though not seen directly. The process of extracting butter from milk is strikingly similar to drawing the knowledge of *Brahman* from the world.

Mix a bit of yoghurt with lukewarm milk. Leave the mixture overnight. Next morning the milk turns into yoghurt. Milk is thin, fluid. Yoghurt is thick, firm. Churn the yoghurt with a cross ladle. Butter separates. Apply the same process to yourself. The mind is ever in a fluid state. It runs in all directions. Give yourself a little Vedantic knowledge. Allow yourself some time to react with the philosophy. The mind stabilises. Turns mature. Churn the mind by negating the outer phenomena and asserting the inner Self. Thus reflecting and meditating upon the Self you gain the Knowledge-of-Self.

Idea of Trinity

Brahman is transcendental. While human experiences are confined to the terrestrial realm. Your body, mind and intellect cannot reach the Transcendental. You are not able to conceive *Brahman*. It is not possible to describe *Brahman*. Even in the terrestrial realm you find it difficult to express subtle themes. Physical experiences are relatively easy to communicate to another. If you have seen the Taj Mahal or the Eiffel Tower you are able to express its beauty and majesty. You are able to put it in words. To describe it. But when you wish to communicate feeling and emotion of the mind you find it rather difficult to do so. Sometimes you do not find words to express them. You need a Matthew Arnold to do that. How magnificently he has captured the vivid emotions of a father and son in his poem *Sohrab and Rustum*. When it comes to thought and idea, the intellect finds it extremely difficult to communicate. Language becomes virtually inadequate. That explains why signs and symbols are used to convey scientific and mathematical ideas. The subtler the theme the greater the difficulty in expression.

Brahman, being subtler than the subtlest, defies all expression. Language breaks down completely. It is impossible to capture *Brahman* in words. However, Enlightened sages have employed ingenious methods to express the Inexplicable. One of their attempts is the idea of trinity. They described God in three facets. As *kshara* perishable, *akshara* imperishable and *uttama purusha* Supreme Being in the *Bhagavad Gita*. As son, holy ghost and Father respectively in the *Bible*.

The sages adopted the fundamental principle of education in their explanation of the supreme God. Which means proceeding from the known to the unknown. What is best known to humanity is the world. Thus they pointed to the world and said that is God. People then attributed the qualities of the world to God. Understood the perishable, changing world to be God. To remove this misconception they clarified that God is not the gross, perishable world but the imperishable, changeless substratum which supports it. Leading to the conclusion that God is confined to the parameters of the world.

Hence they introduced the third concept of God as the Supreme Being extending beyond the perishable and the imperishable.

The three-word explanation has been carefully introduced by starting from what is best known to you. You perceive the world before you. All your experience is confined therein. You have no idea of *Brahman*. You are in the position of a weary traveller who sees a mirage in a desert. And has no clue of what a desert is. He sees water. Not the hot sand beneath. Standing in the midst of a vast desert he asks what a desert is like. You point out the mirage that he sees and tell him that is it. He misunderstands the desert to be just water. You correct him. That the water is just an illusion. Projected upon the desert. The desert is that which supports the water. The water is a phenomenon that passes away. While the hot sand beneath is the actual desert that stays there. The mirage-water is the perishable while the sand below is the imperishable aspect of the desert. And now he misconstrues the entire desert to be confined to the area of the mirage. You correct him again. You further elucidate. That the desert lies as a vast expanse of sand even beyond the perishable mirage and the imperishable sand beneath it. Desert is all around. So does *Brahman* pervade the perishable and the imperishable facets of the terrestrial world and beyond into the Transcendental.

Three Schools of Thought

There are three schools of thought which explain the relation between a human being and God. They are known as *Dvaita* Dualism, *Advaita* Monism and *Vishishta Advaita* Qualified-monism.

The school of Dualism states that you are separate from God. You are a finite being. God is infinite. That you can never become one with God. Madhvacharya is the chief exponent of the dualistic theory. The school of Monism lays down the absolute oneness of God. That there can be no division or demarcation in the Absolute. The finite has no separate status in the Infinite. You cannot be separate from God. You are God. That is the philosophy enunciated by Adi Shankaracharya. The school of Qualified-monism considers you as an aspect of God. God is whole and you are a part of the whole. You will remain a part and can never merge with God. Ramanujacharya propounded this theory. The three schools seem to be contrasting, contradicting one another. Ironically, all three exponents have derived their philosophies from the same textbooks of Vedanta. Each tried to prove his point using the authority of these ancient texts. There is no use relying on authorities. You must make use of the views of these great masters and arrive at your own conclusion.

It is interesting to study Hanuman's view on the relation between a human and God. Hanuman is acclaimed as the greatest devotee, *bhakta* of Lord Rama. His life symbolised the ultimate in devotion to God. He gave the impression that the immortal God was far removed from his mortal self. That a human is separate from God. And yet when asked how he was related to God he answered thus:

Dehabhavena daso'smi
Jeevabhavena tvadamshakah
Atmabhavena tvamevaham.

Translation

When I consider my body, I am your servant. When I consider my mind, I am part of you. But when I consider my Self, you and I are one.

Even the proverbial *bhakta* has declared that he and God are one. On attaining spiritual Enlightenment you become one with the supreme Reality. You merge with God.

Different schools of philosophy. Different versions of Truth. Different knowledges of God. Have all turned into stone walls obstructing the vision of the Reality. Ironically, they are meant to aid your vision. Hence you must carefully reflect upon, understand the truths embedded in them. Convert the opaque stones into transparent lenses to gain the vision of the Reality. Attain spiritual Enlightenment.

CHAPTER XXI

THAT THOU ART

The Four Aphorisms

The *Vedas* have been distinguished as the foremost spiritual texts from time immemorial. They contain the perennial philosophy of Vedanta. Which has been indoctrinated in ancient India through four aphorisms known as *mahavakyas*. *Mahavakyas* literally means great statements, supreme declarations. They appear one in each of the four *Vedas* as follows:

Pragnanam Brahma: Brahman is Consciousness

Tat tvam asi: That thou art

Ayam Atma Brahma: This Self is *Brahman*

Aham Brahma asmi: I am *Brahman*

The first aphorism *Pragnanam Brahma, Brahman is Consciousness* appears in *Aitareya Upanishad* in the *Rig Veda*. This aphorism makes a general declaration that *Brahman*, the supreme Reality is Consciousness. The one homogenous Consciousness that pervades everywhere. That which functions in the macrocosm and the microcosm. The common substratum of the world and the individual. If the Consciousness pervading the world is likened to total-space, then the Consciousness in an individual would be the space-in-a-pot. But the space-in-a-pot cannot be segregated from total-space. The material of the pot cannot divide space. Space may be referred to as pot-space, room-space, open-space etc. All these spaces are one and the same. Space as such is homogenous, indivisible. Called differently for convenient reference. Likewise Consciousness is referred to differently. Depending on Its heterogeneous embodiments. Though It remains ever homogenous. The first aphorism pronounces Its homogeneity. It is known as *lakshana vakya* which means statement-of-definition.

The second aphorism *Tat tvam asi, That thou art* appears in *Chandogya Upanishad* in the *Sama Veda*. It declares you are pure Consciousness. *Tat, That* refers to the Consciousness, the supreme Reality, *Brahman. Tvam, thou* to the innermost Self, *Atman*, the Core of your personality. *Asi, art* establishes the oneness of the all-pervading Consciousness and your Self. *Brahman* and *Atman* are one and the same. The Consciousness is like the ocean. An individual like a wave. The water in the wave and the ocean is the same. Beings would be waves with distinct individualities. The Consciousness in every being is the same all-pervading Consciousness. Your Self is the infinite Reality. That thou art. This aphorism is in the form of an advice to a spiritual seeker. Hence it is known as *upadesha vakya*, statement-of-advice.

The third aphorism *Ayam Atma Brahma, This Self is Brahman* is in *Mandukya Upanishad* in the *Atharvana Veda. Ayam* means *this. Atma* is your supreme Self within. The aphorism states that the *Atman*, Self in you is *Brahman* pervading everywhere. If *Brahman* is likened to a conflagration, then an individual would be a spark arising from it. Conflagration is fire. So is spark. Both are the element fire. Spark is conflagration. So are you the supreme Consciousness. Your Self, *Atman* is *Brahman*. Remember this truth at all times. Repeat it to yourself. Entertain this thought until you realise your Self to be *Brahman*. Hence this aphorism is known as *abhyasa vakya*, statement-of-practice.

The last aphorism *Aham Brahma asmi, I am Brahman* appears in *Brihadaranyaka Upanishad* in the *Yajur Veda*. *Aham* means *I*. *Asmi* means *am*. And *Brahman* is God. So the aphorism means *I am God*. It is the ultimate pronouncement of a Self-realised person. Prior to Self-realisation you use the first person singular pronoun *I* to mean the waker, dreamer or deep-sleeper. You believe yourself to be the waker as long as you remain in the waking state of consciousness. And declare: I am the person-in-the-waking-state. When you enter the dream state of consciousness you assume the personality of the dreamer. You declare: I am the person-in-the-dream. And in deep-sleep: I am the person-in-sleep. Ironically, you use *I* in all the three states though you assume three distinct personalities. In truth, the *I* that you pronounce is your real Self. In the three states your Self is conditioned by your gross, subtle and causal bodies respectively. And the conditioned Self expresses as the waker, dreamer and deep-sleeper. The philosophy of Vedanta helps you to get over the conditioning. Apply this knowledge in your life. Transcend the limitation imposed by your material bodies. Expose your supreme Self. Reveal the nascent *I*. That pure, unconditioned, native *I* is God. My real Self is God. That is the ultimate experience of Self-realisation. Hence known as *anubhava vakya*, statement-of-experience.

The *Bhagavad Gita* expounds the aphorism *That thou art*. Its eighteen chapters can be divided into three sets of six chapters each. The first set relates to *thou*. The middle set deals with *That*. The last set with *art*. So the profound philosophy of the *Gita* expounds the aphorism. Such is the power and grandeur of the aphorisms.

The aphorisms pronounce that there is but one supreme Reality. That Reality you are. Realise That. The world is a mere passing phenomenon. A variety show. With no pith or substance. Yet you are lost in this empty show. The ignorance of your Self has caused it all. No more of that ignorance. Regain the Knowledge of your Self. Establish yourself in your supreme Being. Merge with the Reality. Gain the ultimate experience: I am God.

I am God

The entire humanity uses the pronoun *I* to indicate one's individual personality. To mean either the waker, dreamer or deep-sleeper. But never to mean the real Self, *Atman.* Everyone is hypnotised to believe oneself to be a finite, limited being. In such a hypnotic state it becomes extremely difficult to drive home the idea that you are not what you believe yourself to be. That you are the supreme Self. That you are God. You reject the thought as absurd. Something impossible. But the truth remains you are God. You must realise the truth. Discover your Self.

The affirmation, I am God, is not the same as affirming, I am Indian, I am bachelor, I am tall etc. These statements are fundamentally different from declaring yourself to be God. The words Indian, bachelor, tall qualify the subject I. *Indian* is one thing and I is quite another. So are the other qualifications, *bachelor* and *tall*, distinct from I. They are properties, attributes belonging to I. But the affirmation, I am God, conveys something different. The word God does not qualify I. God is not a property, attribute describing I. The statement, I am God, is not the same as, I am Indian. The statement means I and God are one.

Examine the analogy of the rope and snake. A boy mistakes the rope for a snake. He is caught up in an illusion. He states the snake is six feet long, four inches thick, black in colour. You declare the snake that he sees is just a rope. The statement of the boy is fundamentally different from yours.

The boy's statement that the snake is six feet, four inches and black is similar to the statement, I am Indian, I am bachelor, I am tall. The length, breadth and colour are properties of the snake. But the word *rope* is not so. Rope is not a property of the snake. The rope is not separate from snake. Snake is rope. They are one, the same. So too, when you declare, I am God, it means I and God are one, the same. God is not an attribute, property. You are God. I am God, *Brahman*, the supreme Reality.

What a hypnosis has overthrown the human mind! Every single individual in the world believes himself to be anything other than the Reality. People consider themselves to be man or woman, good or bad, brilliant or dull etc. None would even entertain the thought that one is God. And yet the stern reality remains that everyone is God. You are that eternal Being *Brahman*, not this assemblage of matter you have assumed yourself to be. Vedanta roars this truth. That you are God. Bids you pronounce this audaciously: I am God *Aham Brahma asmi*. But the people of the world are timid, hesitant to admit the truth. They dread the thought of losing their individuality. And dismiss the very idea of a human as God. They would rather cling to the world and suffer. Strange, but true. You denounce your intrinsic sovereignty and court slavery. Vedanta tirelessly appeals to your good sense to renounce your false life. Do not shy away from the truth of life. Hesitate no more. Get hold of the Reality. Take charge of the Kingdom within you. Be your sovereign Self. The King of kings. The supreme Lord. You have then gained all that is to be gained in life.

In the *Old Testament*, Moses is said to have fallen into this state of slavery. Walking in Mount Sinai, he encountered a serpent. And trembled at the sight of it. Just then he heard a voice say, 'Hold that serpent.' It was said to be the voice of

God. Moses hesitated. The voice insisted he get hold of it. He plunged and held the serpent. Instantly the serpent turned into a staff. And the staff worked miracles. Moses touched the rock with the staff and fresh water gushed forth from it. When the Israelites were fleeing for safety the Red Sea stood in their way. He again used the staff. No sooner his staff touched the sea than the waters parted and dry land appeared before them. The Israelites passed into safety.

Similarly, the inner voice bids you drop your ego and regain your supreme Self. But you are terrified at the thought of discarding your individuality, your personal identity. Mortified to leave the comforts of the known and plunge into the unknown. You would rather indulge in the pleasure of your senses than trade on the treasure of the Self. Your inherent ignorance is the cause of your trepidation. You must get over this ignorance and gain the Knowledge-of-Self. Embolden yourself to overcome the ego. Plunge into the Self fearlessly. Smother your selfishness. Assert your Divinity. Your supreme Self unfolds Itself. You become the supreme Lord.

You gain some idea of what you really are, how God operates, by studying an amazing similarity between God and petrol. God, the supreme Self functions in beings in the same way as petrol in motor vehicles. Here are three points of comparison which bring them remarkably close:

1. Petrol is the prime mover in all cars. But petrol does not move. It does not have a desire to go anywhere. Nor a desire to avoid going. Yet no car moves without petrol. Similarly the Self, *Atman* is the activating principle in all beings. But the Self does not act. It has no desire to act. Nor a desire to avoid action. Yet no action is possible without the Self.

2. The performance level of a small car is poor. In a medium car it is mediocre. In a big car, powerful. The performances of the three types are distinct, wide apart. Yet the petrol used in them is the same. So it is with the different personalities. The Self, *Atman* in an illiterate, uncivilised person is the same that is in an intelligent, civilised person and that in an exceptional, enlightened Sage. Their calibre and conduct are distinctly different. Yet the one *Atman* functions through them all.

3. A car goes off an embankment and crashes. The inmates of the car are hospitalised. While another car takes its passengers home safely. But the petrol in both the cars is the same. Petrol cannot be labelled as safe or unsafe. Yet if the first car had run out of petrol a few metres away, it would not have met with the accident. Nevertheless, petrol cannot be held responsible for the accident. Nor take credit for the safe arrival of the other car. So is it with the *Atman*. In a terrorist It manifests as atrocious acts of destruction. While in a sage It manifests as divine deeds of benevolence. The *Atman* remains neutral. Responsible neither for vice nor virtue that emanates from It.

Not realising these truths of life, diverse activities are attributed to the Self, to *Atman*, to God. You hold God responsible for everything that happens in the world. You blame God when something goes wrong. And praise God when all goes well. You must reflect carefully over this equation between God and petrol. Get out of this colossal misconception. Understand God as merely the substratum of all activities. And not hold God responsible for the variety of activities in the world.

People consider it sacrilegious to believe a human to be God. And prefer to humble themselves to the status of bondage and limitation. They are lost in ignorance. Remain blind to truth. It is false to believe yourself to be a mortal living a constricted, restricted life. You commit sin when you do not proclaim your immortal Self. When you deny your Self Its divinity. Therefore, gather up all your courage and conviction and face the stark Reality. Renounce the false world. Pronounce your real Self. Cry out to one and all: I am God *Aham Brahma asmi*.

A man met with an accident. His new limousine was smashed. The same evening he returned to his house and threw a party. His friends were revelling. No one knew the cause for his celebration. As the party was going on a few were curious and enquired. The man told them what had happened. Perplexed at his reply they asked, "Your new car is smashed and you are rejoicing?" He nodded, "You get me wrong. No doubt my car is destroyed but I am saved. Only my vehicle is gone, but here am I hale and healthy!"

Try to get the message from this simple narrative. Examine where people focus all their attention. Everyone is glued to one's body, mind and intellect. None turns towards the Self within. All you care for is your material equipments. You have no interest in the Self. You save the vehicle at the cost of your person. This is preposterous. You lose your imperishable Self and hang on to the perishable matter layers. What a blunder you commit in this choice. And yet you are blissfully unaware of it. Much less concerned. It is a wonder that you have lost sight of your inherent divinity. Forgotten your immortal Self. It is a strange oblivion. Pull yourself out of this slumber. Awake. Arise. Assert your real Self. Be your Self. You are God already.

Finite is Infinite

The finite presents itself as infinite. It may sound paradoxical, absurd. But on a careful scrutiny you find it to be true.

You see infinite expression in the finite. Examine the mineral, vegetable, animal and human kingdoms. Analyse their nature. You will arrive at the above conclusion.

The mineral kingdom is made up of matter. And matter is constituted of atoms. An atom is so minute, yet packed with enormous power. The nuclear explosion speaks eloquent of that. Just imagine all the power contained in the countless atoms in matter. It seems infinite.

In the vegetable kingdom also there is infinite expression. A single seed can generate an endless chain of trees and seeds. Sow a seed in the earth. It grows into a tree. A tree produces numerous seeds. These seeds in turn can produce countless trees and seeds. The chain goes on endlessly. Just imagine all these emerging from one seed. A seed packed with infinite potential, infinite power. You perceive the infinite concealed in the finite.

So it is with the animal world. The wise see the infinite portrayed in the finite. A cat produces a litter of kittens. The kittens grow up into cats. These cats again produce many more litters of kittens. Thus the progeny goes on endlessly. Innumerable cats emanating from a single cat.

The same principle holds good for the human species too. A single human being can generate an endless progeny. You may be finite but you display infinite potency and power. You would accept this infinite capacity in a human with respect to the past and future. But not so with regard to the present. At present you consider yourself to be a finite being with limited power and strength. This is not so. Even with respect to your present status you seem to possess immense capacity, inexhaustible potency, infinite power.

Think carefully. Analyse your day's activities. List them out. You woke up, had breakfast, drove to office, attended to your business, returned home, had a workout at the gym, showered and now, reading this book. Is that all? You answer, "Yes, that is all, perhaps a few odd things I may have missed out. No more." Now follow closely. You have actually done much, much more. But not aware of it. You have been executing countless activities which you do not mention. For instance, your eyes have been seeing objects. Each time you see an object, you subject the cells in your eyes to a series of subtle actions before the sight is registered.

M. Mitchell Waldrop writes in *Science 85*:

"Consider the capabilities involved in strolling down the road. Leaving aside such things as balance and co-ordination, you still have to see where you are going, which means you somehow have to make sense out of the ever-changing swirl of motion and colour and light and shadow. To accomplish this, you have at your command roughly 100 million receptor cells — the rods and cones — in the retina of each eye. The retina also contains four other layers of nerve cells; all together the system probably makes the equivalent of ten thousand million calculations a second before the image information even gets to the optic nerve. And once the visual data reaches the brain, the cerebral cortex has more than a dozen separate vision centres in which to process it. In fact, it has been estimated that vision in one form or another involves some 60 per cent of the cortex. Of course, you remain blissfully unaware of all this. You simply glance across the street and say, 'Oh, there's Sally.' "

All these activities emanate from you. You are responsible for them. Besides your eyes seeing, the other sense organs are also busy with their respective activities. They are again innumerable, countless. These activities are all yours. You have produced them. Furthermore, your mind entertains numberless feelings, emotions. You produce each one of them. So also your intellect conceives endless thoughts. You produce them all. Besides these, you are responsible for respiration and perspiration, eating and evacuating, digestion and distribution of food. Etcetera. Countless cells in your body, hair on your skin, blood in your arteries and veins are all functioning through you. At this very moment you are producing infinite actions. Remember this through your life. Realise this truth. What you consider as finite is actually infinite in nature. You must recognise your innate nature. Discover the truth in yourself. You are not a finite, limited, constricted being as you believe yourself to be. You are infinite. You are God Almighty. That is the truth.

Hold that view at any cost. Do not compromise on truth. Assert your Self: I am all. I am everything. The microcosm and the macrocosm are in Me. I am Infinite. God.

Characteristics of Self-development

God-realisation is the ultimate goal of human evolution. Those earnest in reaching it wish to know their present state. But find it difficult to evaluate their spiritual status. They are unaware of their position in the path of evolution. Few understand what exactly are the traits and characteristics of self-development. Worse still, people have their own standards of judgement. Thus many Enlightened sages have passed into history unknown, unsung. Ironically, people attribute greatness where it is least due. Confer divine qualities upon spiritual charlatans indiscriminately. Deify them as *gurus* and follow them blindly. Such following helps neither the disciple nor the *guru*. Do not fall a prey to such irrational practices. You cannot afford to commit such blunders. Try to understand clearly what constitutes the elements of spirituality. What marks the progress in the spiritual path. What are the chief characteristics of self-development. The true attributes of a spiritually advanced person. With this study and analysis you would be able to assess the strength of spirituality in yourself as well as others. A few traits and characteristics of spiritual evolution are listed below for your guidance.

Self-sufficiency

As a person evolves spiritually he develops self-sufficiency. Becomes independent of the world around him. He stands out a master of all he encounters in the world. Whereas a spiritually retárded person remains a slave of his body and its perceptions, his mind and its emotions, intellect and its thoughts. A self-developed person revels within his own Self. His peace and happiness is not dependent upon anything other than his Self. He does not crave for sense-objects or emotions, thoughts or ideas. He remains ever free, unaffected by the manifold pairs of opposites that constitute the world. Be it pleasure or pain, joy or sorrow, honour or dishonour. Only human beings have the spiritual potential to enjoy such independence. All other creatures are entirely dependent upon the world for their peace and pleasure.

You gain self-sufficiency by focussing your attention on the Self. The more you attune to the Self the less dependent you are on the objects and beings of the world. And by finding your union with the Self within, you gain absolute peace and bliss. Nothing in the world can augment that supreme state of fulfilment. You become totally self-sufficient. Truly spiritual.

You may wonder: How can one remain unaffected by the world? Become free from the persecutions of the body, mind and intellect? Keep a balanced mind amidst trials and tribulations? The answer lies in spiritual discipline. Through spiritual discipline you gradually detach yourself from the material equipments and their activities by attaching to the Self within. Until you become established in the Self. Thereafter the world cannot disturb you.

Take the example of a coconut. When a coconut is raw the kernel sticks to the shell. The bondage is firm. You break the shell, the kernel also breaks. But not so when the coconut dries up. When a coconut is completely dry the kernel separates clear from the shell. Becomes free. It shakes inside like a rattle. Now when the shell of the dry coconut is broken, the kernel does not break. It remains as it is. Unhurt, unaffected. The same is true of your Self. As long as you are attached to your body-mind-intellect you are affected when they are affected. But when you detach yourself from them you remain equanimous regardless of any affliction they go through. You gain your independence, liberation.

Universal love

The love that people claim to have for their near and dear ones is far from true love. Actually it is preferential attachment. Uneven love. You love your child more than any other. How is it that your love is concentrated on your child alone? Think. Your child caters to your personal demands more than others. Satisfies your physical, emotional and intellectual needs. Fulfils your self-centred, selfish interests. Thus the love you claim for your child is all but directed to your own wellbeing. You are merely loving yourself when you say you love your dear ones. True love is even, same to one and all. Love in its purest form has to be universal, not concentrated in one. Universal love is an essential trait of self-development.

Jesus Christ attained that supreme state. His love was unabated in the worst circumstance. When Christ was crucified he maintained the same feeling. As he was nailed on the cross, his last words were dripping with love: *Father, forgive them, they know not what they do.*

Objectivity

An essential quality of the spiritually evolved is objectivity. Objectivity means maintaining an impersonal, detached attitude in life. Not being involved in the affairs of the world. Some become involved in amassing wealth, seeking power, name and fame. Others are lost in feelings and emotions, thoughts and ideas. Ironically, the worst form of attachment, involvement is found among the religious. Those are the ones extremely attached to their creed. Who turn into religious fanatics, extremists, even terrorists.

Those who are detached, not lost in their own field of activity are said to be objective. They become a witness, *sakshi* to all happenings in the world. Watch the procession of perception, emotion and thought go by. Thus must you attune to the real *Sakshi*, the Self within. Treat your body, mind and intellect as your possessions. Something other than you. The world can only affect these equipments but not the Self. Resign to the Self. And look at the world from the balcony of the Self. That is objectivity.

Cheerfulness

Another trait of the spiritually developed person is cheerfulness. Which he may not necessarily manifest at all times. A spiritually evolved person is replete with cheer and joy though he may express it discreetly. However, he maintains that feeling all through life. On the contrary those who lack self-development, not spiritually evolved are morose, gloomy, depressed. They suffer from mental sickness. Such people should not contaminate the society with their melancholy. They need to be quarantined to prevent their mental disease from spreading.

Lord Krishna is a personification of mirth, of fun and frolic. Though his life posed continual trial and tribulation, opposition and challenge. He was a picture of cheerfulness effervescing with laughter.

Dynamism

As you evolve to higher heights of perfection, you shed your *tamas*, lethargy, indolence. You become bright, active, dynamic. Those who lack spiritual development are self-centred, selfish. They suffer from mental agitation which causes fatigue, loss of energy. The spiritually evolved are relatively selfless. Their minds are calm and composed. That generates power and energy within them. Thus the evolved have in different periods of history shown great dynamism in their fields of activity. They have poured out enormous physical, mental and intellectual energies into the world for the welfare of the people.

Selflessness

This trait stands out above all. It is the very backbone of character and conduct of the spiritually evolved. The acid test of spirituality is one's selflessness. The lowest category of human beings is immersed in gross selfishness. They dissipate their lives in mere indulgence in physical senses, emotional attachments and personal views and ideas. As a person advances spiritually his ego and egocentric desires, his selfish and self-centred nature diminishes. And when he attains the highest spiritual Enlightenment he becomes totally selfless. Selflessness paves the way to spiritual progress.

The above qualities are not exhaustive. They serve as guidelines to assess one's spiritual status. Study them closely. Use them to determine the passage to your spiritual evolution. The direction set thus should help you unveil your Self. Reach the goal of Self-realisation.

Know thy Self

The aphorisms declare the staggering truth that thou art God. Godhood is your essential Being at all times. Never have you fallen from that state of Divinity. If that be so, you are God before you attain Self-realisation. So are you God after Self-realisation. What then determines the marked difference before and after realisation? What change does spiritual Enlightenment bring about in a person? Is there a change at all? A careful scrutiny will reveal one significant change above all. That is your *awareness* of Godhood and all that goes with it. Though Godhood has been your perennial Being you remain *unaware* of your divine state before you attain Enlightenment. Whereas after Enlightenment you become fully *aware* of your Divinity. That is the difference.

There once lived a royal couple. They had a baby boy. In their state there was a terrible deluge. Half the state was washed away by the floods. The baby prince was thoughtfully placed in a floating cradle. The king and queen were drowned. It was a dreadful blow to the people of the state. The waters receded gradually. The ministers of the state took stock of the situation. They found the bodies of the king and queen. But no trace of the prince. A peculiar birthmark on the baby's left shoulder was the only clue they were left with. They ordered a statewide search for the missing prince as he was the heir to the throne. The search went on for years while a regent took charge of the administration of the state.

In that very state a beggar was known for long to beg in the marketplace. The shopkeepers knew him. Some obliged. Some spurned him. Some were indifferent towards him. At the end of the day he collected enough money to make a living. He continued thus for over sixteen years. One morning the authorities of the state got hold of the beggar. They drove him to the palace. The regent and the ministers examined him carefully. Only to find the peculiar birthmark of the lost prince on his left shoulder. All were amazed at the discovery. They declared the beggar was the missing prince. And crowned him king. The entire state rejoiced.

The youth took time to realise the full implication of his sudden fortune. It was a year before he settled down and established himself as the lawful king of the state. Having done so, one day he disguised himself with his old beggar clothes and went into the market begging for alms. The shopkeepers were surprised to see him back after a long lapse. He received the same treatment from them. Some obliged. Some spurned. Some were indifferent. He collected the same amount as before. And returned to his royal abode.

Carefully analyse the difference between the two experiences. His begging before and after he became the king. On both occasions he faced variations, fluctuations, alternations in the outer world. In the earlier state, before discovering himself to be the king he was affected by them. He anxiously looked forward for gains and was disappointed at losses. Whereas later, after discovering his true identity he remained totally unaffected, indifferent, disinterested in gain or loss. External happenings could not in the least affect him. He stood well above any worry or anxiety. Being totally fulfilled, independent, self-sufficient.

It is interesting to note the distinct change in his life. What exactly was the change in his personality? Was it brought about by the beggar becoming king? No, that cannot be the reason. For he was king before and after his discovery. King even when he was begging in the first instance. The only difference is that earlier he did not *know* that he was king while later he *knew* himself to be the king. It is knowledge of his kingship that made him a totally different person.

So it is with your life. The kingdom of heaven is within you. You are God. But you are not aware of your Godhood at present. You know not you are God. Consequently, the perennial alternations of life cause you suffering and sorrow. The variations and fluctuations of this world plague you. The moment you realise your Self, you know yourself to be God, none of these external changes and disturbances affect you. You remain peaceful and blissful, revelling in your own Self. That is the difference.

Thus must you discover the Eternities. Thine own Self. That thou art.